PRAISE FOR *SHOWTIME AT THE APOLLO*

★ "This graphic treatment adds a new dimension to a music book that was already hailed as a classic. Most graphic adaptations aim to reach new generations of readers with a work that is flashier but less substantial than the original. This collaboration between Fox (*In the Groove: The People Behind the Music*) and illustrator Smith represents a new experience for readers, one with an immediacy and vitality that text alone might never approach . . . an entertaining, lively narrative with profiles that match the spirit, drawings that seem as musical as the music described within the text. The renewal of spirit through this striking collaboration reflects the way the Apollo has renewed itself through the decades."

—*Kirkus Reviews*, starred review

"Chronicling the history of the Apollo has been Fox's passion project for almost 40 years . . . If you don't know the connection Aretha Franklin and Dr. Martin Luther King Jr. have to the Apollo—or even if you do—consider picking up a copy of this graphic novel."

—amNewYork

"A graphic novel that not only tells the story of how the Apollo Theater came to be but also provides a glimpse into Black culture in Harlem that provided the backdrop for such a culturally iconic space to emerge."

—becauseofthemwecan.com

"Music lovers and history buffs alike will delight in this updated classic, and Smith's stunning visuals will bring this important and exciting work to a whole new generation of readers."

—*Bookish*

"Brings Harlem's legendary theater to gorgeous life. It's a fizzy, entertaining, jubilant window into a space where so many artists became icons, overcoming hate and ignorance. It's an essential guide to one of New York City's greatest cultural institutions."

—*Entertainment Weekly*

"If you want a broad overview of African American music—and how the Apollo made so much of it possible—this is a great read."

—*GeekDad*

"Just plain wonderful . . . a brand-new, delicious graphic book . . . an engaging, rich tale of one of America's musical landmarks and the performers who made famous."

—*History News Network*

"*Showtime* not only adapts Fox's book, originally published in 1983, it expands upon it, bringing the story of the venue up to date, including events as recent as 2018, as it tells the complete story of one of the most iconic venues in the country."

—*Hollywood Reporter*

"An excellent example of graphic non-fiction. 4.5 out of 5 stars."

—ICv2

"Anyone interested in African American music and history and pop culture history will find this a captivating read."

—*Library Journal*

"Even those who are deeply familiar with the Apollo will find some delightful surprises in this evocative fusion of text and images."

—*New York City Jazz Record*

"Sit back, relax, and enjoy the cartoon drawings and dialogue on every page. They'll make you laugh or cry, sing or dance . . . An entertaining and captivating read for those interested in African American history, its culture, and pop music."

—*New York Journal of Books*

"The graphic novel *Showtime at the Apollo: The Epic Tale of Harlem's Legendary Theater* is like a sprawling Hollywood biopic . . . The book also shines a light on Harlem and black culture in America."

—*New York Times*

"Smith's art has a . . . mythmaking quality—all his depictions of the Apollo's performers are iconic. He draws these entertainers at their best possible moments, just as they'd like to see themselves . . . he captures numerous electrifying onstage scenes."

—**NPR**

"The reader cannot help but be swept away by Fox's reverence for all the characters he meets and features throughout this narrative. Smith's illustrations are equally loving and embrace the hope all these performers seemed to feel that the success they could attain on the stage of the Apollo would speak for everybody in the theater, in Harlem, and the world . . . This graphic version is a beautiful, heartfelt, and rich tribute to a musical form, a vital location, and a pure American vision of connecting with the audience in the theater and everywhere else. We can feel the Apollo's heartbeat on every page, and that sensation will make a true believer of even the most jaded reader."

—*PopMatters*

"Smith's exuberant lines ably transmit the book's dense energy, as though the narrative is at risk of breaking its bounds . . . a vibrant, exultant, and soulful history."

—*Publishers Weekly*

"If you love the Apollo, this book is for you! If you've never heard of it, this book is for you! Have you listened to any American music from the twentieth century? This book is for you! . . . A dynamic, fact-filled offering for teens curious about musical history."

—*School Library Journal*

"Scrupulously researched . . . As a graphic history, *Showtime at the Apollo* is a shimmering spectacle in itself."

—**Michael Tisserand,** *Chicago Tribune*

"This lively graphic novel traces the theater's place in rhythm and blues, jazz, and hip-hop history and its significance to New York City."

—*Variety*

SHOWTIME AT THE APOLLO

PRAISE FOR THE ORIGINAL BOOK

"Mr. Fox has recaptured [the Apollo's] spirit."
—*New York Times*

"The essential book, mandatory for the most casual student
as well as the most ardent fan."
—**David Hinckley, *Daily News***

"The definitive history of Harlem's (and black America's) essential theater."
—*New York*

"*Showtime at the Apollo* is not only a history of that wonderful theater, but also a
fascinating insider's view of the Harlem music scene."
—**John Hammond**, legendary producer and talent scout who discovered Billie
Holiday, Aretha Franklin, and Bob Dylan, among many others

"I could almost feel and taste the Apollo again."
—**Doc Pomus**, Rock and Roll Hall of Fame inductee and classic
songwriter for musicians such as Elvis Presley

"A wonderful book."
—**Tavis Smiley**, PBS talk show host

"Ted Fox made the Apollo come alive for me again."
—**Jerry Wexler**, cofounder of Atlantic Records

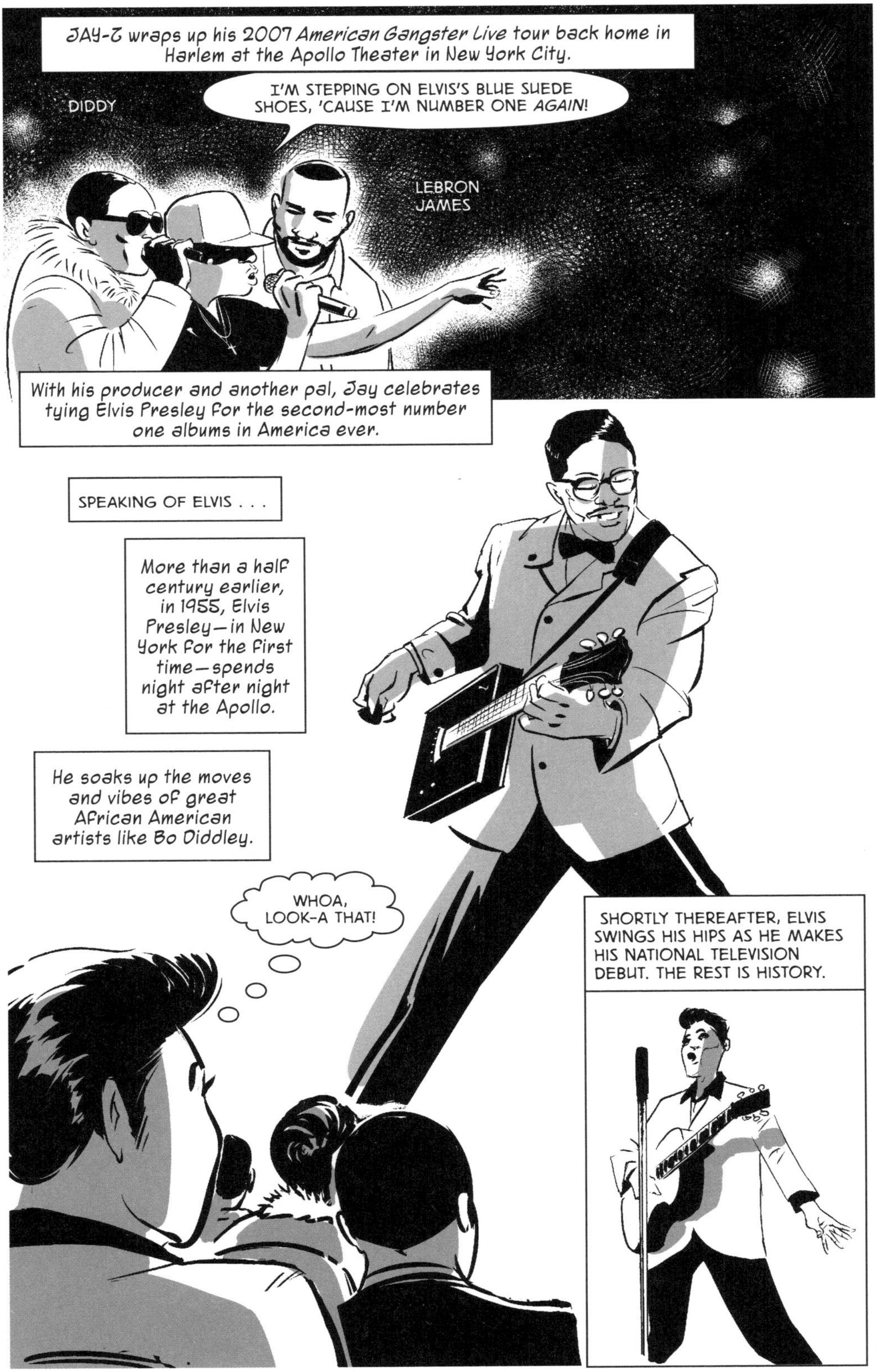

JAY-Z wraps up his 2007 *American Gangster Live* tour back home in Harlem at the Apollo Theater in New York City.
DIDDY
I'M STEPPING ON ELVIS'S BLUE SUEDE SHOES, 'CAUSE I'M NUMBER ONE *AGAIN*!
LEBRON JAMES
With his producer and another pal, Jay celebrates tying Elvis Presley for the second-most number one albums in America ever.
SPEAKING OF ELVIS . . .
More than a half century earlier, in 1955, Elvis Presley—in New York for the first time—spends night after night at the Apollo.
He soaks up the moves and vibes of great African American artists like Bo Diddley.
WHOA, LOOK-A THAT!
SHORTLY THEREAFTER, ELVIS SWINGS HIS HIPS AS HE MAKES HIS NATIONAL TELEVISION DEBUT. THE REST IS HISTORY.

CHRIS ROCK TAPES HIS HBO COMEDY SPECIAL *BIGGER AND BLACKER* AT THE APOLLO IN 1999.

PHARRELL WILLIAMS MAKES HIS APOLLO DEBUT IN JUNE 2014 AND JOINS THE THEATER'S BOARD OF DIRECTORS JUST FIVE MONTHS LATER!

APOLLO THEATER 03/09/12, A LIVE ALBUM BY BRUCE SPRINGSTEEN AND THE E STREET BAND, IS RELEASED IN 2014, AND IS THE FIRST ALBUM OFFICIALLY RELEASED THROUGH THE BRUCE SPRINGSTEEN ARCHIVES.

PAUL MCCARTNEY FINALLY GETS TO PLAY THE APOLLO ON DECEMBER 13, 2010, PERFORMING FOR A CELEBRITY-STUDDED AUDIENCE AT A LIVE SIRIUS XM RADIO BROADCAST.

I WANT TO TAKE A MOMENT . . . I JUST WANT TO JUST SOAK IN THE APOLLO . . .

THIS IS VERY SPECIAL FOR US BRITISH BOYS . . . THE HOLY GRAIL. I DREAMED OF PLAYING HERE FOR MANY A YEAR.

PAUL MCCARTNEY MAKES SURE TO TOUCH THE LEGENDARY TREE OF HOPE.

In fact, McCartney is checking off an item from his bucket list.

WHEN THE BEATLES FIRST FLY TO AMERICA IN FEBRUARY 1964, THEY PESTER NOTORIOUS PRODUCER PHIL SPECTOR TO TELL THEM ALL ABOUT THE APOLLO.

THE APOLLO IS THE FIRST PLACE WE WANT TO SEE WHEN WE GET TO AMERICA! *YEAH, YEAH, YEAH!*

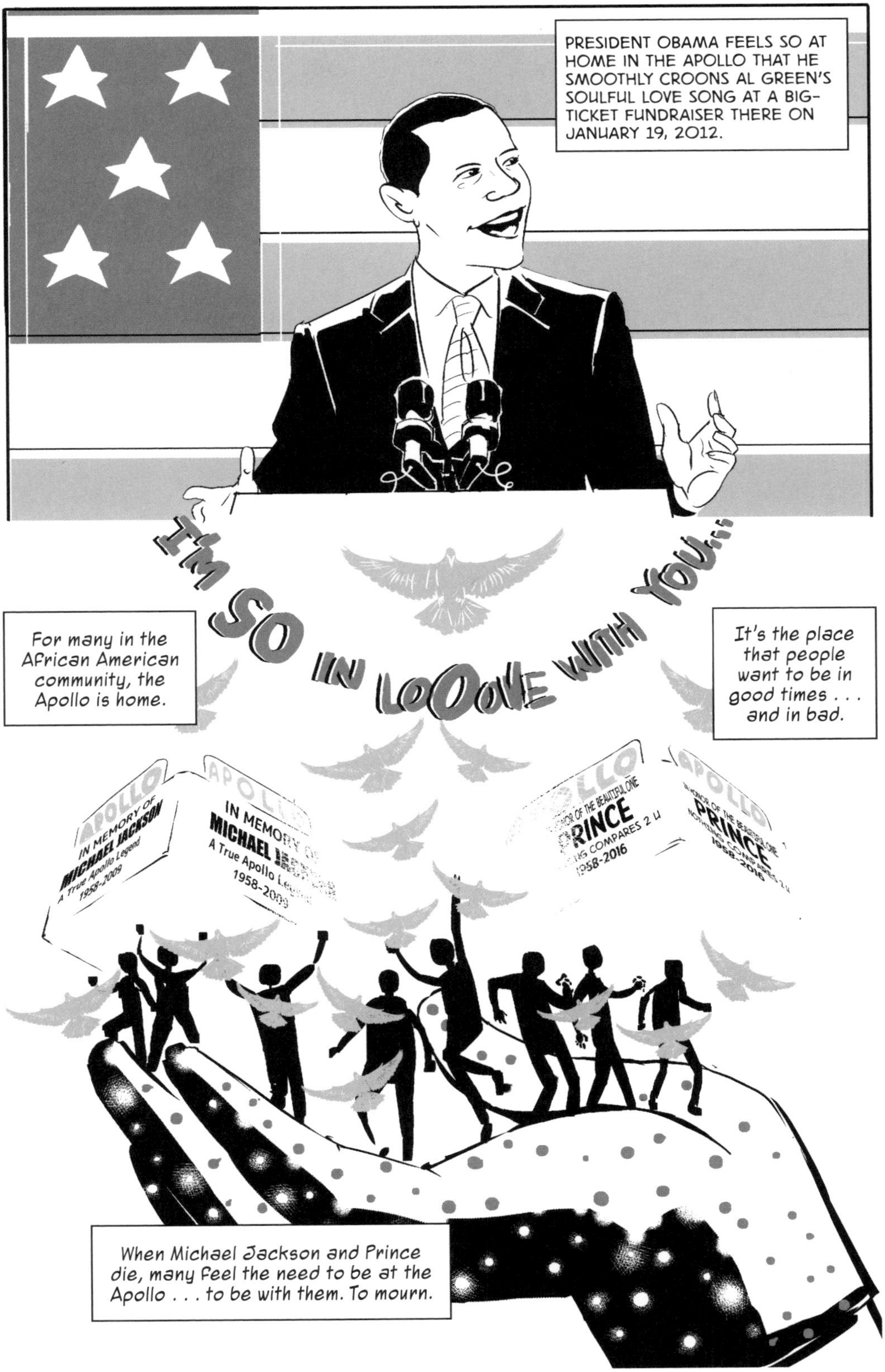
PRESIDENT OBAMA FEELS SO AT HOME IN THE APOLLO THAT HE SMOOTHLY CROONS AL GREEN'S SOULFUL LOVE SONG AT A BIG-TICKET FUNDRAISER THERE ON JANUARY 19, 2012.
I'M SO IN LOOOVE WITH YOU...
For many in the African American community, the Apollo is home.
It's the place that people want to be in good times . . . and in bad.
APOLLO IN MEMORY OF MICHAEL JACKSON A True Apollo Legend 1958-2009
APOLLO IN HONOR OF THE BEAUTIFUL ONE PRINCE NOTHING COMPARES 2 U 1958-2016
When Michael Jackson and Prince die, many feel the need to be at the Apollo . . . to be with them. To mourn.

AND, FOR THE GODFATHER OF SOUL . . .

REST IN PEACE APOLLO LEGEND
THE GODFATHER OF SOUL
JAMES BROWN
1933–2006

"SOUL POWER!"

JAMES BROWN'S TWENTY-FOUR-CARAT GOLD COFFIN COMING HOME TO THE APOLLO

"SAY IT LOUD! I'M BLACK AND I'M PROUD!"

THE REVEREND AL SHARPTON, ONCE JAMES BROWN'S ROAD MANAGER AND SPIRITUAL ADVISOR, STANDS BY THE CASKET OF HIS GREAT FRIEND.

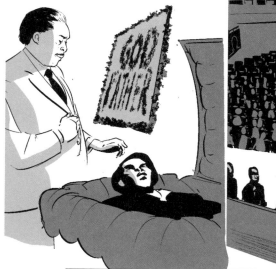

Brown's first funeral service is held at the Apollo on December 28, 2006, officiated by Reverend Sharpton.

BUT WHY HERE? WHY THE APOLLO?

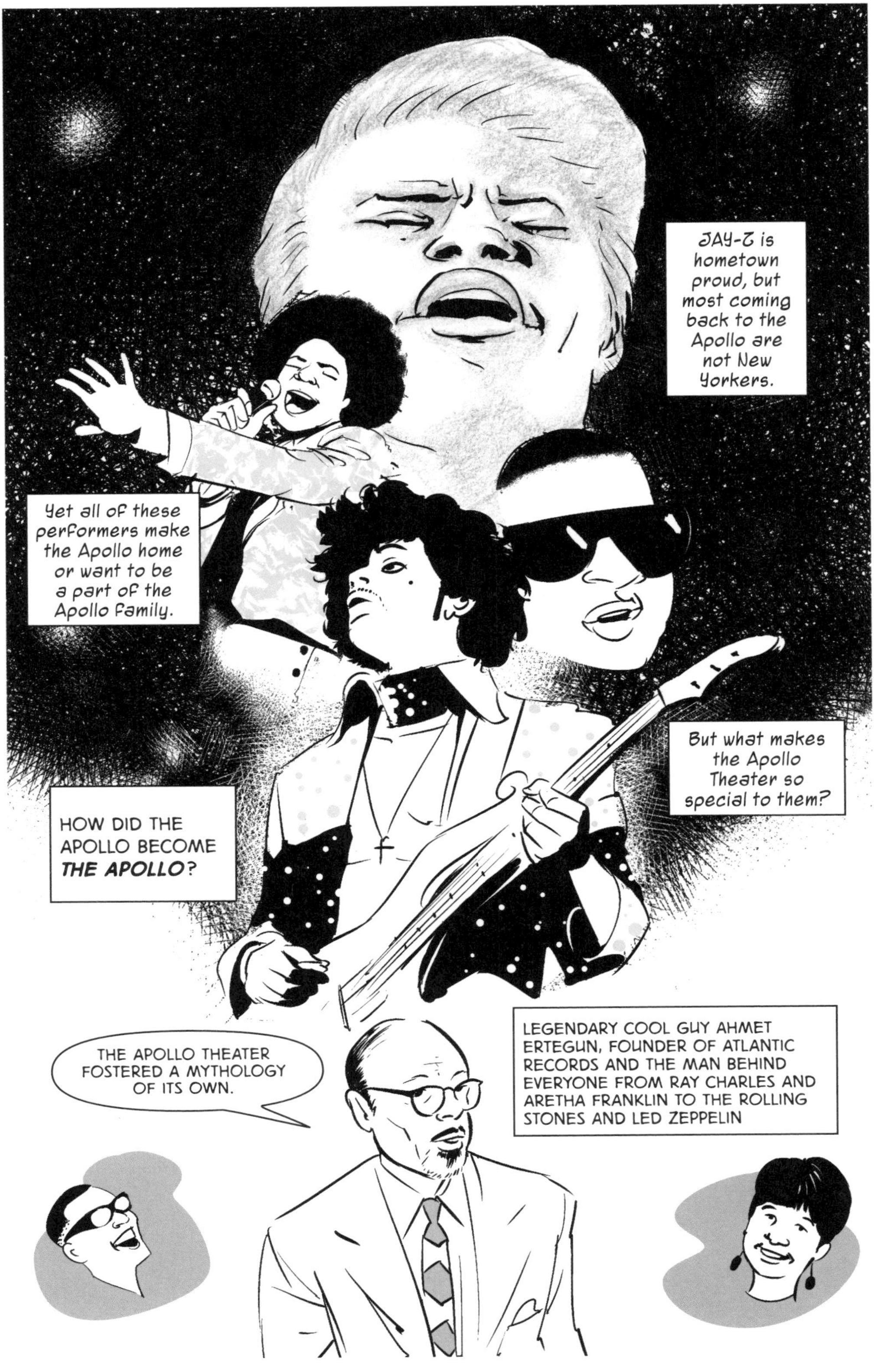
JAY-Z is hometown proud, but most coming back to the Apollo are not New Yorkers.
Yet all of these performers make the Apollo home or want to be a part of the Apollo family.
But what makes the Apollo Theater so special to them?
HOW DID THE APOLLO BECOME *THE APOLLO*?
LEGENDARY COOL GUY AHMET ERTEGUN, FOUNDER OF ATLANTIC RECORDS AND THE MAN BEHIND EVERYONE FROM RAY CHARLES AND ARETHA FRANKLIN TO THE ROLLING STONES AND LED ZEPPELIN
THE APOLLO THEATER FOSTERED A MYTHOLOGY OF ITS OWN.

It is an epic tale.

A story of struggle and triumph, pathos and glee, spanning generations and many changes in society, culture, and style.

A tale made by and told by characters both heroic and quite ordinary.

A story of creativity, expression, hard work, and fun, triumphing again and again in the face of adversity and injustice . . .

And, ironically, it is the story of how that spells doom for the little theater . . .

. . . only to bring it to a celebratory comeback and rebirth.

The truth of the Apollo's great history is the stuff of which myths are made.

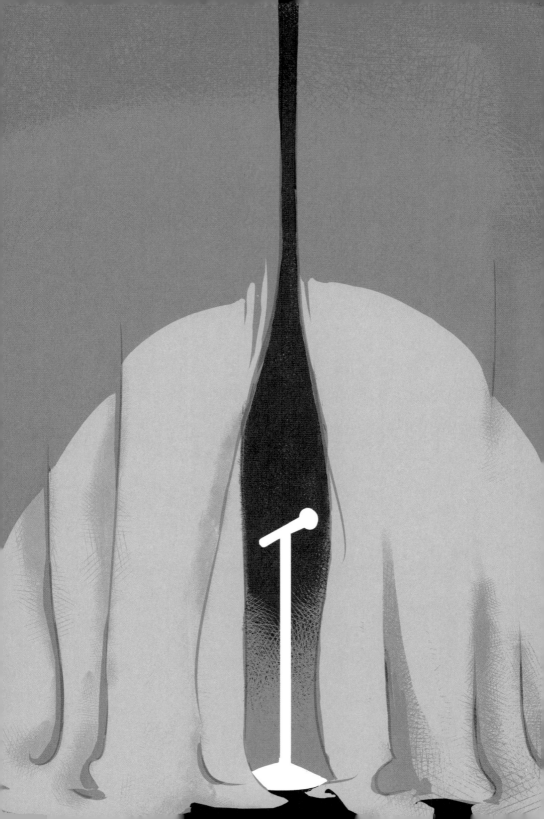

SHOWTIME AT

THE EPIC TALE OF HARLEM

BY TED FOX   ILLUSTR

THE APOLLO

S LEGENDARY THEATER

TED BY JAMES OTIS SMITH

Abrams ComicArts   New York

To the women and men who lived the Apollo story and made it happen. —T.F.
To my mother. Thanks for all the music. —J.O.S.

ACKNOWLEDGMENTS

This book would not exist without the recollections and insights of the many participants in the Apollo story I have interviewed over the years, detailed in A Note on Sources and Methods.

Thank you, Jonelle Procope, and everyone at the Apollo Theater Foundation for your dedication and vision.

I'd like to thank James Otis Smith for his prodigious efforts to beautifully depict this epic tale. Thank you for bringing to life the scenes and images that heretofore only lived in my mind.

My representatives, Joan Hilty and Pete Friedrich of Pageturner, worked relentlessly to make this book a reality: They schooled me about the world of graphic novels, made the deal happen, coached me in my efforts to create the manuscript, pitched in when work needed to be done, interfaced on every aspect of its development, and rode herd on the entire process from beginning to end. You are the best.

To Charlie Kochman, editorial director at Abrams ComicArts (a.k.a. The Hardest Working Man in Publishing), thank you for your understanding, enthusiasm, and passion, your unflagging hard work on every aspect of this project, your attention to detail, your great ideas for improving the book—and for always doing what you said you'd do. Also at Abrams, managing editor Amy Vreeland did a magnificent,

thorough job copyediting the manuscript, and art director Siobhán Gallagher's work yielded such a beautiful design. Thank you.

I give great thanks, and all my love, to my wife, Ann Derry. In addition to patiently serving as my consiglieri and counselor for all aspects of this project, she reviewed, edited, and talked me through every word and made this book immeasurably better in the process.

Thanks to my daughter, O. K. Fox, for hipping me to the world of graphic novels and comics. You are responsible for planting the seed that became this work. Thanks also, my dear, for introducing me to our mutual Purchase College alum Dean Haspiel at Zinefeast Vol. 1, which you founded at Purchase in 2013. In the world of comics and graphic novels, Dino is the man. He is the connection behind so much and between so many—and he still manages to create tremendous amounts of his own remarkable work when he isn't helping good people make good things happen. Thanks, Dino, for introducing me to Joan and Pete and James, and for being my guru whenever I have needed one.

—Ted Fox

Special thanks to Cav and Dino for getting things done.

—James Otis Smith

Editor: Charles Kochman
Book Production: Pageturner. Producer: Pete Friedrich.
    Art assist: Mike Cavallaro, Nick Bertozzi, Gabrielle Gomez, Victoria Lau, and Stephen Gullo. Color assist: Frank Reynoso, Victoria Lau, Sally Han
Designer: Siobhán Gallagher
Managing Editor: Amy Vreeland
Production Manager: Erin Vanderveer

Library of Congress Cataloging-in-Publication Data:
Names: Fox, Ted, 1954- author. | Smith, James Otis, illustrated.
Title: Showtime at the Apollo : Harlem's legendary theater / written by Ted Fox ; illustrated by James Otis Smith.
Description: New York : Abrams ComicArts, 2018.
Identifiers: LCCN 2017053733 | ISBN 9781419731389 (hardcover with jacket)
Subjects: LCSH: Fox, Ted, 1954- Showtime at the Apollo--Adaptations--Comic books, strips, etc. | Apollo Theater (New York, N.Y. : 125th Street)--Comic books, strips, etc. | African American theater--New York (State)--New York--History--20th century--Comic books, strips, etc. |African American entertainers--Comic books, strips, etc. | Music-halls (Variety-theaters, cabarets, etc.)--New York (State)--New York--Comic books, strips, etc. | New York (N.Y.)--Buildings, structures, etc.--Comic books, strips, etc. | Harlem (New York, N.Y.)--History--Comic books, strips, etc. | Graphic novels. Classification: LCC PN2277.N52 A686 2018 | DDC 792.09747/1--dc23

Hardcover ISBN 978-1-4197-3138-9
Paperback ISBN 978-1-4197-3925-5

Copyright © 2019 Ted Fox
Text by Ted Fox; illustrated by James Otis Smith

Adapted from *Showtime at the Apollo: The Story of Harlem's World Famous Theater* by Ted Fox, published by Holt, Rinehart, and Winston in 1983; Da Capo Press in 1993; and Mill Road Enterprises in 2003.

Printed and bound in USA
10 9 8 7 6 5 4 3 2 1

Abrams ComicArts books are available at special discounts when purchased in quantity for premiums and promotions as well as fundraising or educational use. Special editions can also be created to specification. For details, contact specialsales@ abramsbooks.com or the address below.

Abrams ComicArts® is a registered trademark of Harry N. Abrams, Inc.

ABRAMS The Art of Books
195 Broadway, New York, NY 10007
abramsbooks.com

The Apollo Theater is located at 253 West 125th Street, New York, NY, 10027
For tickets and to learn more about the Apollo, its upcoming events, broadcasts, livestreams, podcasts, and more, visit apollotheater.org

CONTENTS

PREFACE

People all over the world know the Apollo Theater. It's a legend. A mythical place. Busloads of visitors from around the world descend on the theater in New York City's Harlem, perhaps to take a tour or to experience for themselves the wild Wednesday Amateur Night shows they have seen on television. Apollo lore piques their curiosity, yet the story of how and why the theater became this fabled showplace is a tale that remains to be discovered.

Some of the Apollo's great African American artists, who were the bedrock of so much of the vital music and entertainment that we enjoy today, are unknown to new generations. Those men and women were the greatest stars in the black community at a time when it was difficult or impossible to "cross over" to white audiences. Any contemporary superstar would acknowledge the influence of these performers and hail them as the pioneers of the "urban" sound and look that dominates today's popular culture.

This ultimate cultural triumph did not come easily. It took decades. There was great fun, excitement, and joy along the way. But it was a struggle, too—and the Apollo Theater was a leader. That story—that epic tale—is essential to understanding our popular culture. Yet I believe it is a remarkably undertold and underacknowledged story. The Apollo has been in my life since I began to conceive what would become my book, *Showtime at the Apollo: The Story of Harlem's World Famous Theater*, originally published in 1983. That book remains the only full-scale history of Harlem's legendary showplace, and I'm honored that it has been called the definitive book on the Apollo. Now, in this graphic novel, through focused storytelling and James Otis Smith's amazing artwork, we can bring the tale to life in a whole new way.

As the Apollo marks its 85th anniversary in 2019, it is thriving—bursting with music, theater, and dance. It looks marvelous—an appropriate state for this iconic American cultural institution—thanks to substantial investments in renovations and upgrades. It is both a triumph and a challenge for the Apollo as it figures out how to keep its doors open in a fast-gentrifying neighborhood, while serving what is still the heart and soul of New York's African American community.

Entertainers—both black and white—now routinely sell out glittering arenas that seat tens of thousands and feature the latest in technology. Concert tickets cost hundreds of dollars. Spectacle is as important as substance in these rigorously choreographed stage shows. But behind much of today's extravaganza is the grit, imagination, creativity, innovation, and hard-earned soulfulness that the funky little theater on 125th Street gave the world. And the top stars and celebrities who still long to come back to the Apollo—from JAY-Z to Bruce Springsteen to President Obama to Paul McCartney—know it.

Working the Apollo, as readers will see, could be terribly difficult back in the day. An Apollo engagement meant doing thirty-one shows a week in its classic era, and some called the theater "the workhouse" or "the penitentiary." The atmosphere was sometimes threatening. Dressing room hustles and rip-offs were common. The physical condition of the struggling theater was often atrocious. By today's standards, no one was getting rich. In the earliest days, you could purchase a ticket for as little as a dime—and you could stay all day. Even in the mid-1970s, tickets topped out at six bucks.

Yet performers always looked forward to playing the Apollo—to them it was home.

It was home, too, for the people of Harlem, where a night out at the Apollo was something special. The Apollo was an indispensable part of the community. The theater's mainly African American audience sat at the center of the greatest city in the world, in the middle of the most important black neighborhood in the country, right on Harlem's main street, in the top black theater of all time. There they were at ease and invincible—even when it may have been difficult for them to feel that way in the wider world.

As the civil rights movement began to alter the nation's consciousness in the 1950s and '60s, other areas of opportunity became available to African American performers. The racist, segregated system the Apollo was forced to work within for so many years—and actively fought against—began to collapse, at least in part because of the Apollo's tenacity and its inspiring creative innovations. The eager and far-reaching acceptance of black culture as a cornerstone of the world's popular culture was the beginning of something brand-new then, if not now. There was triumph in that, but tragedy, too, capped by a stunning rebirth for the little theater that had done so much to make that happen.

This is that story.

Ted Fox

New York City

March 2018

A Quest

Today, the Apollo is celebrated and honored. But that wasn't always so.

YOUR AUTHOR, AGE TWENTY-FIVE, BACK IN THE DAY—MARCH 1980.

IT IS A BLEAK TIME IN NEW YORK CITY, BUT THE BEGINNING OF A QUEST FOR ME.

NEGLECTED BY THE CITY FOR YEARS, HARLEM IS STILL STRUGGLING TO RECOVER FROM THE HORRIBLE RIOTS AFTER THE BLACKOUT OF JULY 1977.

Exit 125 Street

THE CITY IS BROKE. CRIME IS RAMPANT. DRUGS ARE A SCOURGE.

HARLEM IS STRUGGLING.

THE APOLLO HAD BEEN SHUTTERED BY ITS OWNER, **BOBBY SCHIFFMAN**, IN 1976, AND SAT EMPTY AND NEGLECTED FOR YEARS.

BOBBY'S FAMILY HAD RUN THE APOLLO SINCE 1935, A YEAR AFTER ITS OPENING.

APOLLO PARLIAMENT FUNKADELIC

THIS IS THE LATEST SPUTTERING ATTEMPT TO REVIVE THE DETERIORATING VENUE. THE THEATER SEEMS ON ITS LAST LEGS.

I KNOW THAT GUY.

BOBBY KNOWS EVERYBODY.

BOBBY GOLFS WITH **MARVIN GAYE**

BOBBY HUNTS WITH **REDD FOXX**

BOBBY HANGS OUT WITH **GLADYS KNIGHT**

BOBBY SCHIFFMAN IS A RIOT— A FABULOUS RACONTEUR WHO LOVES TELLING STORIES OF HIS TIME AT THE APOLLO. AND I LOVE HEARING HIS STORIES.

HE HOOKS ME.

BOBBY, I WANT TO WRITE A BOOK ABOUT THE APOLLO.

HMM, THIS LITTLE PISHER?

Still, he gives me his blessing and agrees to sit for extensive interviews.

He has one caveat:

WRITE ABOUT THE WAY THE APOLLO REALLY WAS, THE **GOOD** AND THE **BAD**.

Little of it seemed to have any value at the time.

SOUL!

BOBBY AND HIS FAMILY KEPT SOME FILES AND OTHER MATERIALS, BUT WHEN THE APOLLO CLOSED IN 1976, PILES OF HISTORICAL PHOTOS, POSTERS, HANDBILLS, AND OTHER EPHEMERA WERE TOSSED OUT.

No one thought this material would matter.

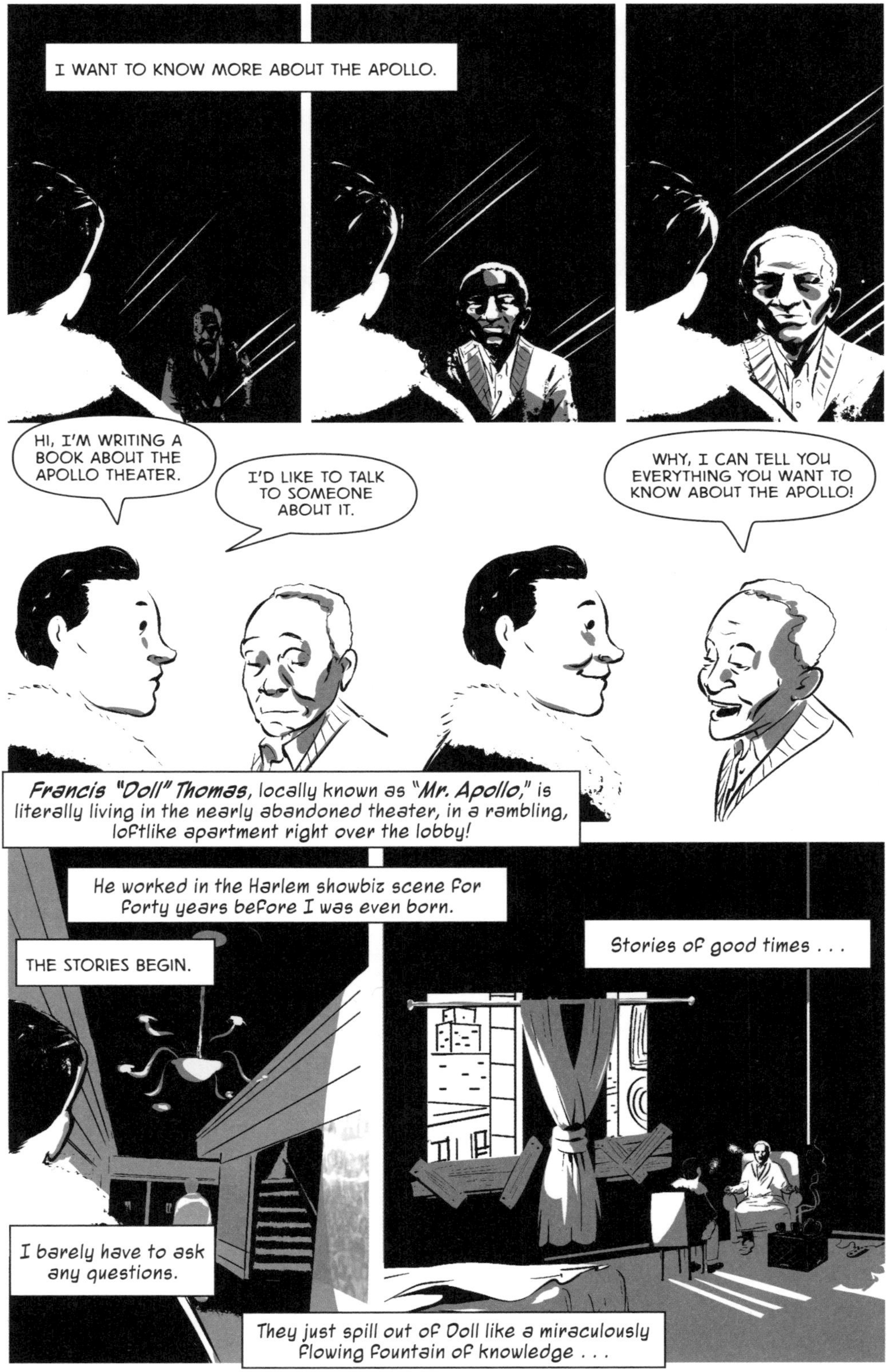
I WANT TO KNOW MORE ABOUT THE APOLLO.
HI, I'M WRITING A BOOK ABOUT THE APOLLO THEATER.
I'D LIKE TO TALK TO SOMEONE ABOUT IT.
WHY, I CAN TELL YOU EVERYTHING YOU WANT TO KNOW ABOUT THE APOLLO!
Francis "Doll" Thomas, locally known as "*Mr. Apollo*," is literally living in the nearly abandoned theater, in a rambling, loftlike apartment right over the lobby!
He worked in the Harlem showbiz scene for forty years before I was even born.
THE STORIES BEGIN.
Stories of good times . . .
I barely have to ask any questions.
They just spill out of Doll like a miraculously flowing fountain of knowledge . . .

DOLL THOMAS

JOSEPHINE BAKER HAD A PRIVATE DRESSING ROOM BUILT RIGHT OFF THE STAGE.

AFTER EACH NUMBER, ONE MAID WOULD HELP HER OFF WITH ONE COSTUME, AND THE OTHER WOULD HAVE THE NEXT COSTUME READY.

SHE'D STEP OUT OF THAT AND INTO THIS, AND SHE WOULD DO IT IN EIGHT BARS, ON THE SAME RHYTHM!

AND BAD TIMES . . .

COLORED GANGSTERS TRIED TO MOVE INTO THE APOLLO.

IT COST THE APOLLO ANYWHERE FROM $1,000 TO $5,000 *A WEEK* TO STAY OPEN.

YOU HAD TO PAY THAT MUCH GRAFT OR YOU'D HAVE A VERY UNHAPPY THEATER.

This was long before Brecher teams up with Bobby's father, the legendary *Frank Schiffman* . . .

Doll goes to work as a silent film projectionist for theatrical landlord *Leo Brecher* in 1914.

. . . and more than twenty years before they take over the Apollo.

4

WHOA!

I start tracking down well-known artists who played the Apollo.

I can get five "contacts" for free if I sign up for a trial offer at an outfit called Celebrity Service.

Doll has truly seen it all.

That's how I learn *Dionne Warwick* has an apartment in the *Waldorf Towers* in New York City.

MAY I HAVE DIONNE WARWICK, PLEASE?

In those more trusting days, the switchboard puts me right through to her.

She picks up herself!

WHAAAT?!

WHEN I TELL HER I'M WRITING A BOOK ON THE APOLLO, SHE SCREAMS SO LOUD I HAVE TO HOLD THE PHONE AWAY FROM MY EAR!

THAT VERY AFTERNOON I SPEND THREE HOURS WITH DIONNE IN HER SUITE AS SHE TALKS AND TALKS AND TALKS ABOUT WHAT IT MEANS TO PERFORM AT THE APOLLO AND BE A PART OF ITS FAMILY . . .

I'VE BEEN WAITING MY WHOLE LIFE FOR SOMEONE TO TELL THAT STORY!

WHAT ARE YOU DOING RIGHT NOW?

5

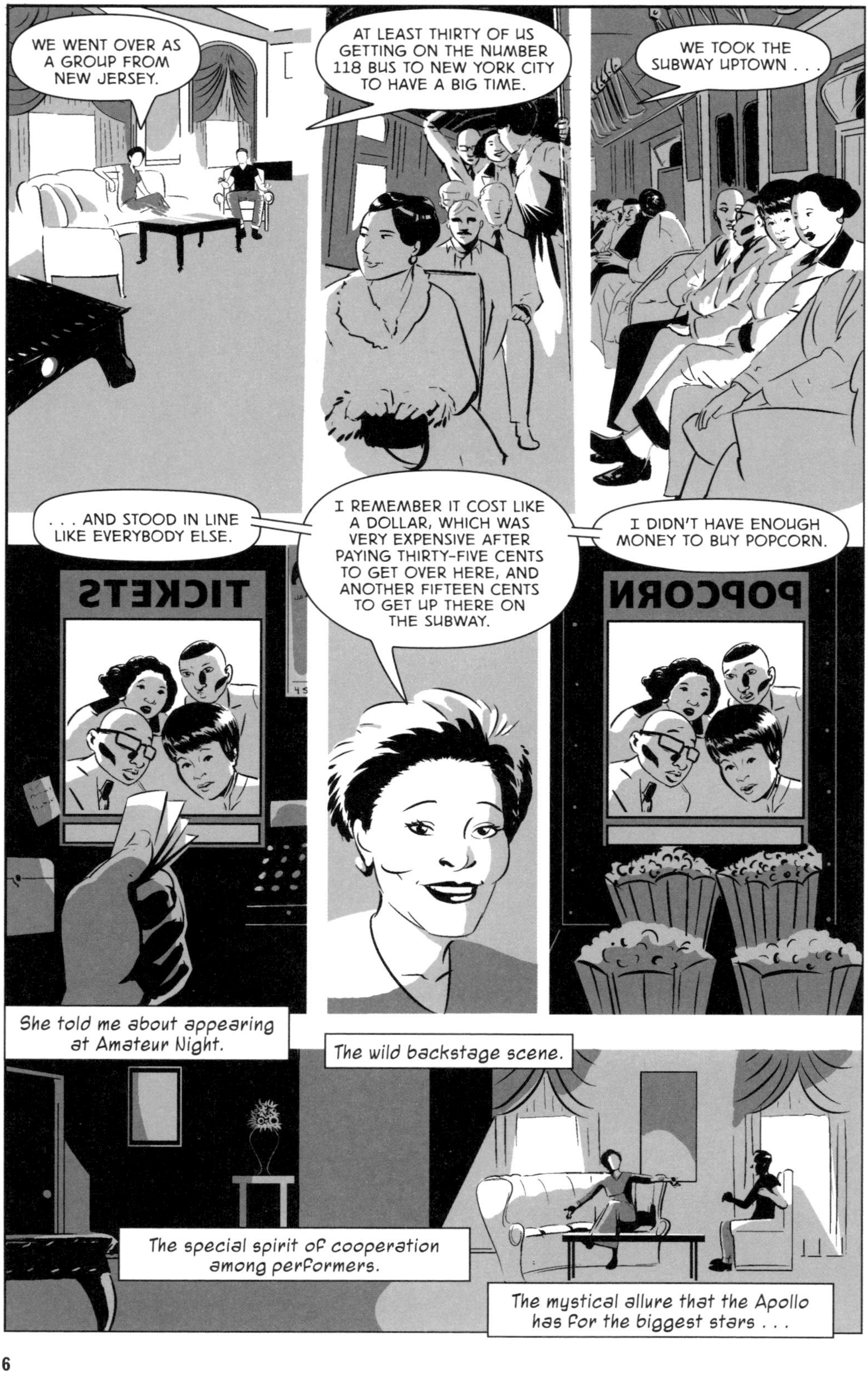
WE WENT OVER AS A GROUP FROM NEW JERSEY.
AT LEAST THIRTY OF US GETTING ON THE NUMBER 118 BUS TO NEW YORK CITY TO HAVE A BIG TIME.
WE TOOK THE SUBWAY UPTOWN . . .
. . . AND STOOD IN LINE LIKE EVERYBODY ELSE.
I REMEMBER IT COST LIKE A DOLLAR, WHICH WAS VERY EXPENSIVE AFTER PAYING THIRTY-FIVE CENTS TO GET OVER HERE, AND ANOTHER FIFTEEN CENTS TO GET UP THERE ON THE SUBWAY.
I DIDN'T HAVE ENOUGH MONEY TO BUY POPCORN.
TICKETS
POPCORN
She told me about appearing at Amateur Night.
The wild backstage scene.
The special spirit of cooperation among performers.
The mystical allure that the Apollo has for the biggest stars . . .

I COME OUT OF THE SCEPTER RECORDS OFFICE ON THE CORNER OF 54TH AND BROADWAY.

THERE'S A GUY WITH A T-SHIRT AND A PAIR OF JEANS AND A LEATHER JACKET AND SUPER-BLUE EYES.

IT'S *TOM JONES*.

WHERE ARE YOU GOING?

I'M GOING TO THE APOLLO.

CAN I—I—I— GO WITH YOU?!

OF COURSE!

THAT NIGHT, TOM JONES SANG AT THE APOLLO.

I THINK THAT WAS THE BEGINNING OF HIS CAREER.

HAVE YOU TALKED TO *SAMMY* YET?

I KNOW EXACTLY WHO SHE IS TALKING ABOUT.

HE KILLED THE AUDIENCE. IT WAS WONDERFUL.

HE SAID IN HIS ENTIRE LIFE, HE'D NEVER FELT ANYTHING LIKE THAT BEFORE.

UM, SAMMY DAVIS JR.?

I haven't talked to any other entertainers yet, and *Sammy Davis Jr.* is one of the biggest stars in the world at that time. But I don't even know if I can do this book yet. I have no deal. No agent. I haven't written a word.

NO. NO, I SURE HAVEN'T TALKED TO SAMMY YET.

WHY, HE'S AT THE *PLAZA*. I'M GOING TO CALL HIM RIGHT NOW!

WHAAAT?!

SAMMY, IT'S DIONNE. I'VE GOT THIS YOUNG GUY HERE, AND HE'S WRITING A BOOK ABOUT THE APOLLO THEATER . . .

THE VERY NEXT DAY IN **HIS** SUITE AT THE PLAZA HOTEL . . .

FOR HOURS, SAMMY DAVIS JR. REGALES ME WITH STORIES OF PLAYING THE APOLLO IN THE '40S WITH HIS FATHER AND UNCLE IN THE **WILL MASTIN TRIO** . . .

. . . TELLS ME HOW MUCH PRIDE HE FELT WALKING TO WORK FROM HIS FAMILY'S NEARBY APARTMENT . . .

. . . HOW DIFFERENT IT WAS PLAYING A TOUGH CROWD AT A BIG-TIME GANGSTER-RUN JOINT LIKE THE **COPACABANA** VERSUS THE APOLLO'S LEGENDARY **"WORLD'S TOUGHEST AUDIENCE . . ."**

YOU DIDN'T GO INTO THE COPA LIGHTWEIGHT— THEY'D BREAK YOUR LEGS.

BUT AT THE APOLLO, THEY'D BREAK YOUR **HEART**.

Sammy even shows me dance steps, sings, and kills me with impressions of Hollywood greats.

HAVE YOU TALKED TO **LIONEL HAMPTON** YET?

8

And so it goes . . .

One person leads to another. One story leads to another.

I begin to understand what the Apollo is all about by talking to the people who were there . . .

. . . And by digging around, researching, and reconstructing its history.

My book, *Showtime at the Apollo: The Story of Harlem's World Famous Theater,* originally published in 1983, starts to take shape.

A forgotten old man.

One of the world's great chanteuses.

A Hollywood showbiz legend.

And a wet-behind-the-ears white kid with few bona fides.

All that matters is that the tale is told. That the history they lived—a history that means so much to them—is passed on and preserved.

THE WORLD FAMOUS APOLLO THEATER

"The good and the bad."

CHAPTER 1

The Apollo: Home

THE APOLLO WILL ALWAYS BE SOMETHING SPECIAL FOR US. WE GOT OUR TRAINING THERE . . .

YOU'D HEAR THE *REUBEN PHILLIPS BAND* HIT THE APOLLO THEME SONG, AND YOU KNEW THE SHOW WAS BEGINNING . . .

"I MAY BE WRONG (BUT I THINK YOU'RE WONDERFUL) . . ."

IT WAS THE MOST BEAUTIFUL FEELING IN THE WORLD.

THE SHIRELLES' BEVERLY LEE

Nearly everyone who is a part of the Apollo describes it using that same word:

THE APOLLO WAS THE NUMBER ONE THEATER ON THE MAP.

IN THE APOLLO, IT WAS LIKE YOU WERE HOME!

HOME!

Souuul Man!!

DAVE PRATER OF SAM & DAVE

Home to a family of love and rivalry—but one bound together by shared experiences, hopes, and ambitions.

FOR GENERATIONS OF AFRICAN AMERICANS, THE APOLLO THEATER IS A SPECIAL PLACE TO COME OF AGE EMOTIONALLY, PROFESSIONALLY, SOCIALLY, AND EVEN POLITICALLY.

IF YOU PLAYED THE APOLLO AND THEY SAID, "YEAH, THAT'S GOOD," THEN THAT WAS IT.

THAT WAS *THE* STAMP OF APPROVAL.

R&B PIONEER *JOHNNY OTIS*

APOLLO

JOHNNY OTIS

THE POSTGRADUATE COURSE.

WE SERVE WHITES only

It is also a refuge from the indignities and difficulties of working—of being—black in Jim Crow America.

THE APOLLO WAS THE APEX OF BLACK ENTERTAINMENT.

In the theater, one can be at ease and just be oneself among the Apollo family and within one's community.

IF YOU'RE A BLACK ENTERTAINER IN CHARLOTTE OR MISSISSIPPI, YOU HAVE GREAT CONSTRAINTS PUT UPON YOU . . .

. . . BUT COMING TO HARLEM AND THE APOLLO WAS AN EXPRESSION OF THE BLACK SPIRIT IN AMERICA. IT WAS A HAVEN.

THE APOLLO THEATER STOOD FOR THE GREATEST—THE CASTLE THAT YOU REACH WHEN YOU FINALLY MAKE IT.

AHMET ERTEGUN

APOLLO
AMATEUR NIGHT

11

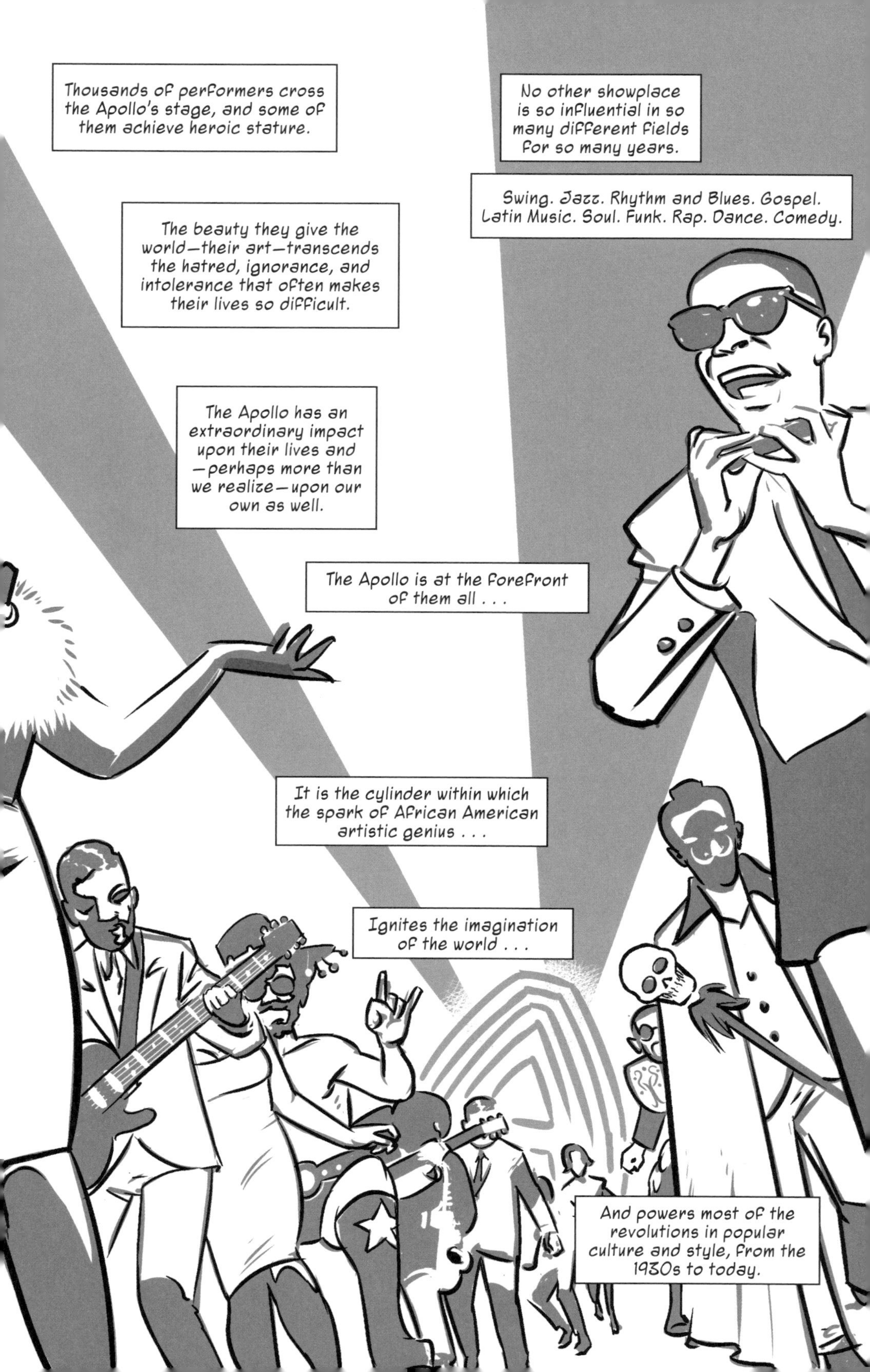
Thousands of performers cross the Apollo's stage, and some of them achieve heroic stature.
No other showplace is so influential in so many different fields for so many years.
Swing. Jazz. Rhythm and Blues. Gospel. Latin Music. Soul. Funk. Rap. Dance. Comedy.
The beauty they give the world—their art—transcends the hatred, ignorance, and intolerance that often makes their lives so difficult.
The Apollo has an extraordinary impact upon their lives and —perhaps more than we realize—upon our own as well.
The Apollo is at the forefront of them all . . .
It is the cylinder within which the spark of African American artistic genius . . .
Ignites the imagination of the world . . .
And powers most of the revolutions in popular culture and style, from the 1930s to today.

THIS **HOME** HAS THIRTEEN DRESSING ROOMS ON FOUR FLOORS.

Within their tacky, cold, painted cement walls beats the heart of the Apollo Theater.

HERE **LOUIS ARMSTRONG** ENTERTAINS GUESTS AND WELL-WISHERS IN HIS UNDERWEAR.

JAMES BROWN HOLDS COURT.

ELLA FITZGERALD SETS OUT HER USUAL SPREAD.

ADVICE IS GIVEN AND LESSONS LEARNED. DEALS ARE MADE. SONGS, DANCE STEPS, AND COMEDY BITS ARE CREATED.

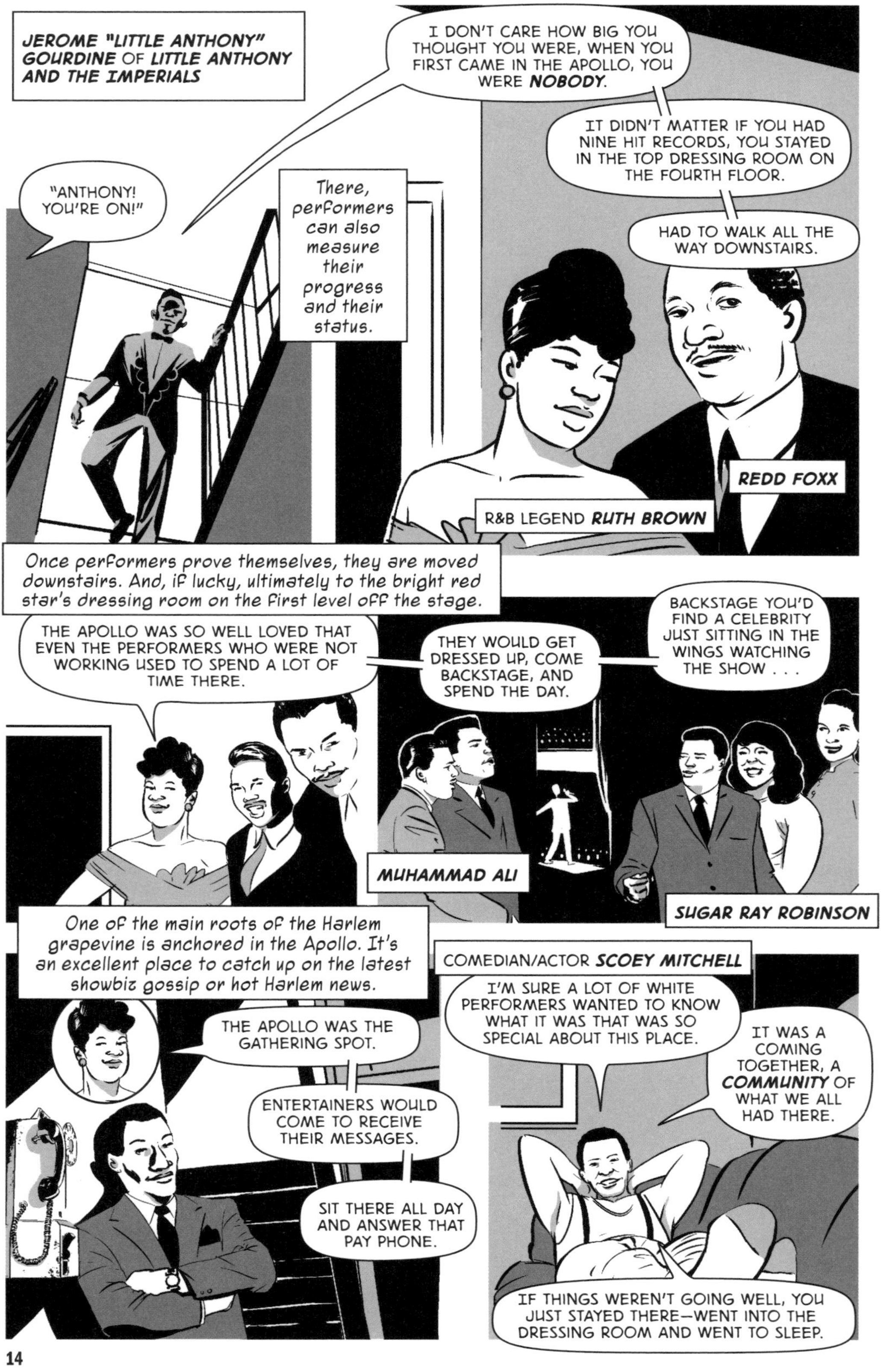
JEROME "LITTLE ANTHONY" GOURDINE OF LITTLE ANTHONY AND THE IMPERIALS
I DON'T CARE HOW BIG YOU THOUGHT YOU WERE, WHEN YOU FIRST CAME IN THE APOLLO, YOU WERE NOBODY.
IT DIDN'T MATTER IF YOU HAD NINE HIT RECORDS, YOU STAYED IN THE TOP DRESSING ROOM ON THE FOURTH FLOOR.
"ANTHONY! YOU'RE ON!"
There, performers can also measure their progress and their status.
HAD TO WALK ALL THE WAY DOWNSTAIRS.
REDD FOXX
R&B LEGEND RUTH BROWN
Once performers prove themselves, they are moved downstairs. And, if lucky, ultimately to the bright red star's dressing room on the first level off the stage.
THE APOLLO WAS SO WELL LOVED THAT EVEN THE PERFORMERS WHO WERE NOT WORKING USED TO SPEND A LOT OF TIME THERE.
THEY WOULD GET DRESSED UP, COME BACKSTAGE, AND SPEND THE DAY.
BACKSTAGE YOU'D FIND A CELEBRITY JUST SITTING IN THE WINGS WATCHING THE SHOW . . .
MUHAMMAD ALI
SUGAR RAY ROBINSON
One of the main roots of the Harlem grapevine is anchored in the Apollo. It's an excellent place to catch up on the latest showbiz gossip or hot Harlem news.
THE APOLLO WAS THE GATHERING SPOT.
ENTERTAINERS WOULD COME TO RECEIVE THEIR MESSAGES.
SIT THERE ALL DAY AND ANSWER THAT PAY PHONE.
COMEDIAN/ACTOR SCOEY MITCHELL
I'M SURE A LOT OF WHITE PERFORMERS WANTED TO KNOW WHAT IT WAS THAT WAS SO SPECIAL ABOUT THIS PLACE.
IT WAS A COMING TOGETHER, A COMMUNITY OF WHAT WE ALL HAD THERE.
IF THINGS WEREN'T GOING WELL, YOU JUST STAYED THERE—WENT INTO THE DRESSING ROOM AND WENT TO SLEEP.

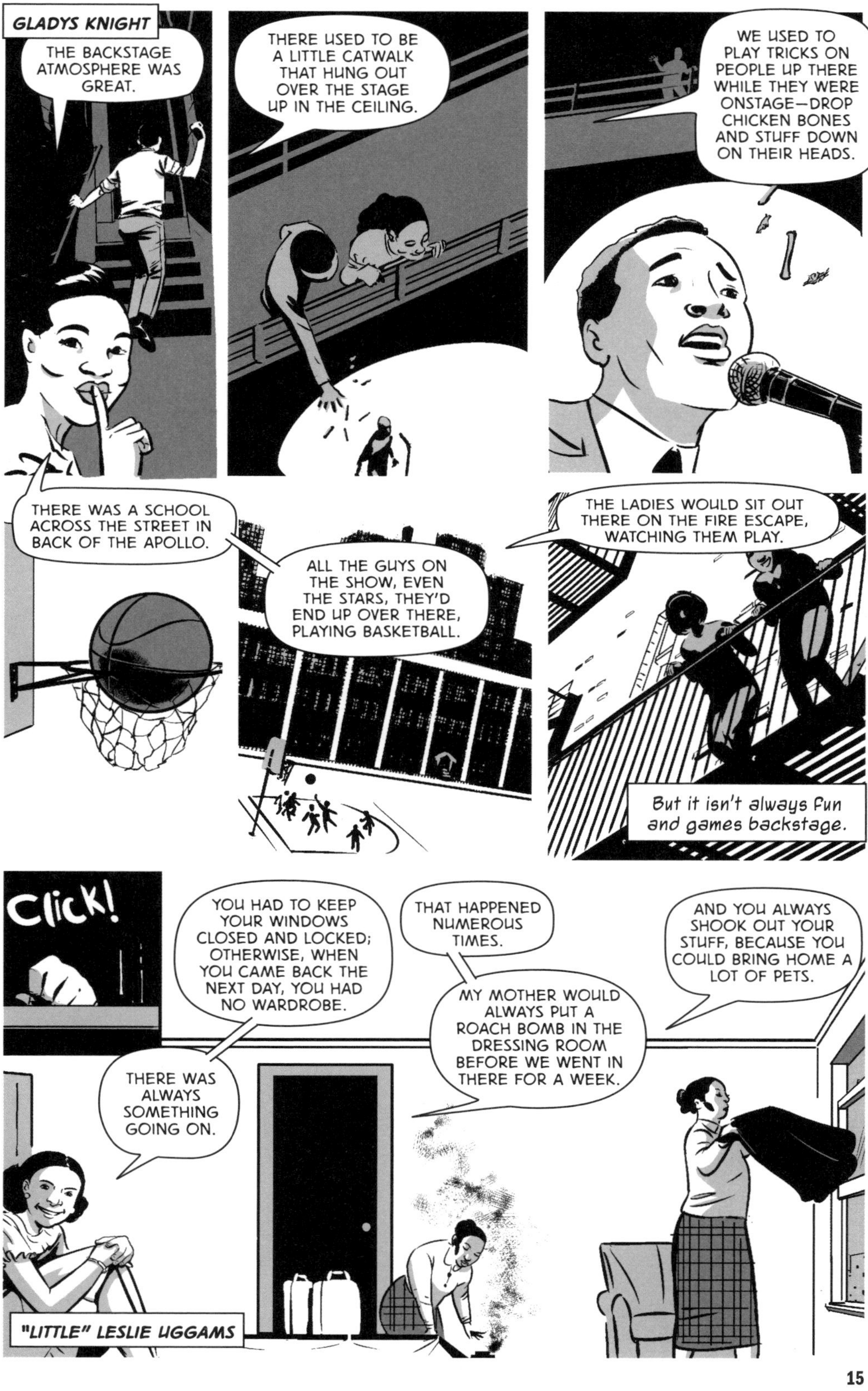
GLADYS KNIGHT
THE BACKSTAGE ATMOSPHERE WAS GREAT.
THERE USED TO BE A LITTLE CATWALK THAT HUNG OUT OVER THE STAGE UP IN THE CEILING.
WE USED TO PLAY TRICKS ON PEOPLE UP THERE WHILE THEY WERE ONSTAGE—DROP CHICKEN BONES AND STUFF DOWN ON THEIR HEADS.
THERE WAS A SCHOOL ACROSS THE STREET IN BACK OF THE APOLLO.
ALL THE GUYS ON THE SHOW, EVEN THE STARS, THEY'D END UP OVER THERE, PLAYING BASKETBALL.
THE LADIES WOULD SIT OUT THERE ON THE FIRE ESCAPE, WATCHING THEM PLAY.
But it isn't always fun and games backstage.
Click!
"LITTLE" LESLIE UGGAMS
THERE WAS ALWAYS SOMETHING GOING ON.
YOU HAD TO KEEP YOUR WINDOWS CLOSED AND LOCKED; OTHERWISE, WHEN YOU CAME BACK THE NEXT DAY, YOU HAD NO WARDROBE.
THAT HAPPENED NUMEROUS TIMES.
MY MOTHER WOULD ALWAYS PUT A ROACH BOMB IN THE DRESSING ROOM BEFORE WE WENT IN THERE FOR A WEEK.
AND YOU ALWAYS SHOOK OUT YOUR STUFF, BECAUSE YOU COULD BRING HOME A LOT OF PETS.

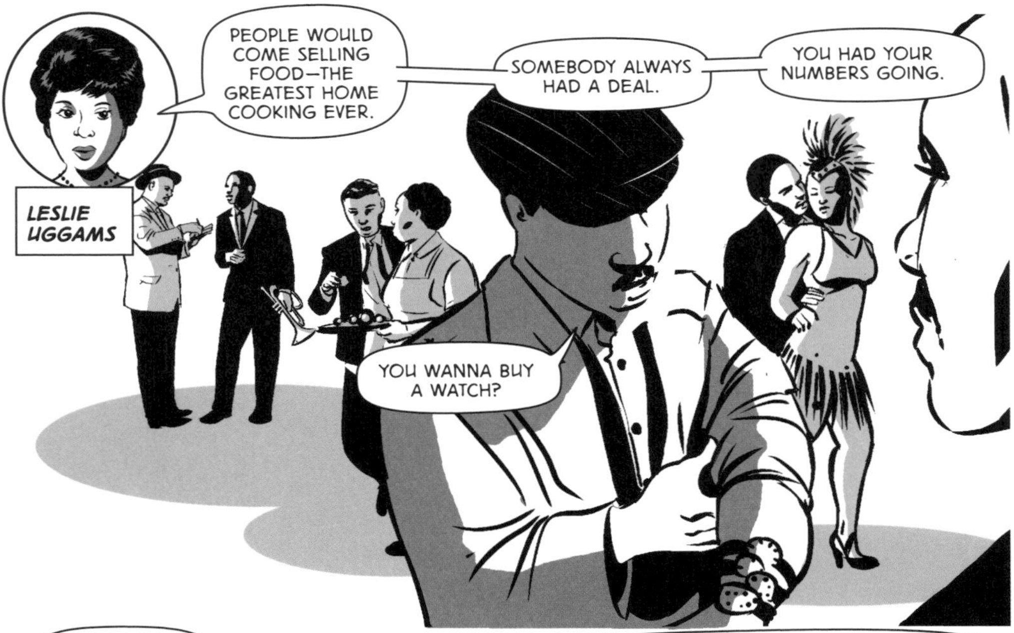

LESLIE UGGAMS
PEOPLE WOULD COME SELLING FOOD—THE GREATEST HOME COOKING EVER.
SOMEBODY ALWAYS HAD A DEAL.
YOU HAD YOUR NUMBERS GOING.
YOU WANNA BUY A WATCH?

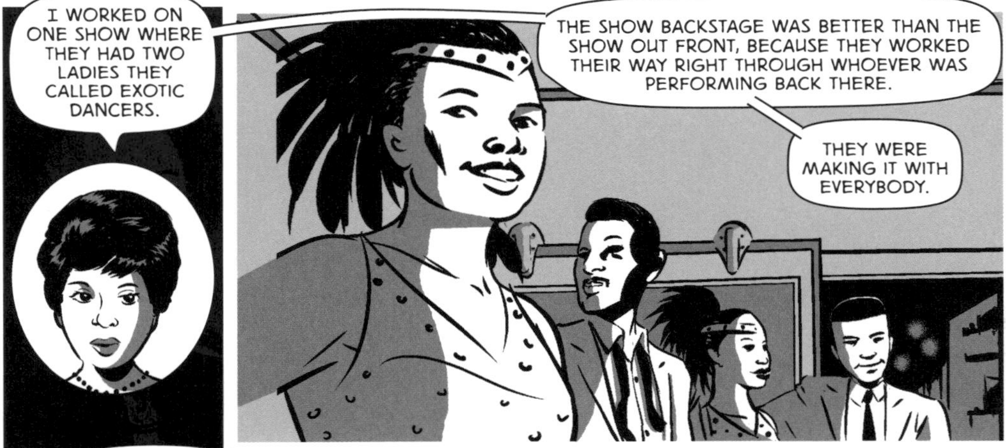

I WORKED ON ONE SHOW WHERE THEY HAD TWO LADIES THEY CALLED EXOTIC DANCERS.
THE SHOW BACKSTAGE WAS BETTER THAN THE SHOW OUT FRONT, BECAUSE THEY WORKED THEIR WAY RIGHT THROUGH WHOEVER WAS PERFORMING BACK THERE.
THEY WERE MAKING IT WITH EVERYBODY.

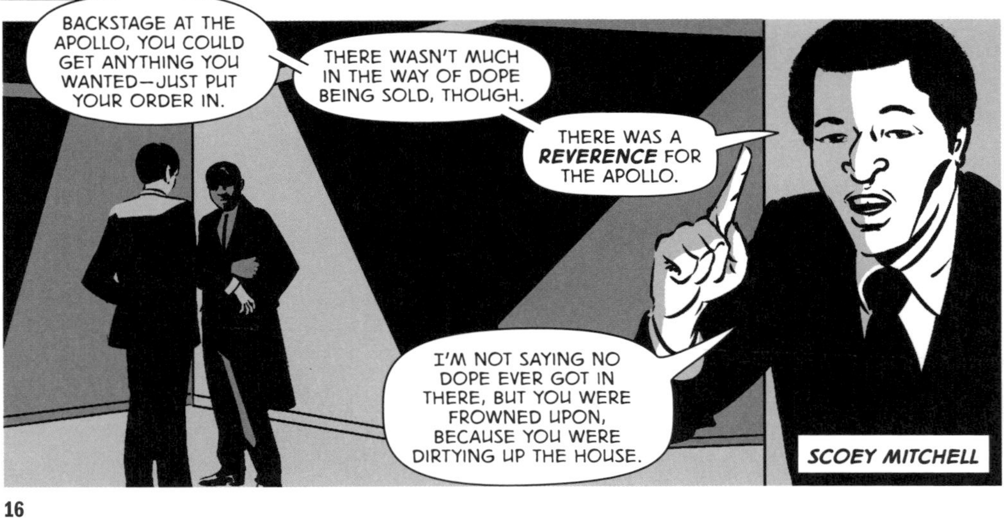

BACKSTAGE AT THE APOLLO, YOU COULD GET ANYTHING YOU WANTED—JUST PUT YOUR ORDER IN.
THERE WASN'T MUCH IN THE WAY OF DOPE BEING SOLD, THOUGH.
THERE WAS A ***REVERENCE*** FOR THE APOLLO.
I'M NOT SAYING NO DOPE EVER GOT IN THERE, BUT YOU WERE FROWNED UPON, BECAUSE YOU WERE DIRTYING UP THE HOUSE.
SCOEY MITCHELL

YOUNG **DIONNE WARWICK** WAS VERY SHELTERED.

I'VE GOT SOME REALLY **GREAT STUFF** HERE.

ONE TIME THIS GUY CAME UP TO MY ROOM WITH A BROWN PAPER BAG.

IN MY MIND I THOUGHT HE MEANT DIAMONDS, EMERALDS, RUBIES.

OH, THIS IS TOBACCO!

I HAD NO IDEA IT WAS MARIJUANA!

THE MAN RAN DOWN THE STEPS AND STOPPED AT EVERY DRESSING ROOM AND TOLD THEM WHAT HAPPENED ON THE THIRD FLOOR!

DIONNE WARWICK

CRAPS

PAPA NEEDS A NEW PAIR OF SHOES!

One of the primary attractions and diversions backstage is the around-the-clock gambling scene . . . although the management discourages it.

LITTLE JOKER!

BID WHIST

POKER

CALL! WHAT YOU GOT?

DAMN, BUSTED MY FLUSH!

THERE WERE ALWAYS POKER GAMES IN EVERYBODY'S DRESSING ROOM, OR BID WHIST . . .

YOU COULD **HEAR** THE GAMES WHEN YOU WENT IN, AND IF YOU LOST YOUR MONEY IN THE TONK GAME, YOU COULD GO UP AND PLAY BID WHIST FOR NOTHING.

SAMMY DAVIS JR.

TONK

IF YOU WANTED TO PLAY TONK, YOU WENT DOWN TO THE REHEARSAL HALL IN THE BASEMENT . . .

The main game is tonk, a fast-paced, big-betting, rummy-style card game normally played for two to five dollars a hand, but sometimes much more.

I'VE SEEN SOME GUYS LIKE REDD FOXX DAMN NEAR MISS THE SHOW, 'CAUSE THEY DIDN'T WANT TO LEAVE THE TABLE.

THEY'D COME OUT ON THE STAGE WITH HALF THEIR COSTUMES ON.

FIVE MINUTES, REDD . . .

I'LL BE RIGHT THERE!

COMEDIAN **REDD FOXX**

SANDMAN SIMS, DANCER, AMATEUR NIGHT EXECUTIONER, APOLLO FIXTURE

REDD, YOU'RE ON!

BE RIGHT THERE!

Rehearsal Hall

BEING BLIND DOESN'T STOP *RAY CHARLES* FROM PLAYING TONK, ASSISTED BY HIS VALET.

RAY CHARLES USED TO PLAY. HE HAD A GUY SITTING BY HIS SHOULDER TELLING HIM WHAT HE'S GOT, AND WHAT THE OTHERS PLAYED.

HE DOESN'T LIKE TO LOSE.

COMEDIAN **WILLIE LEWIS**

DAMN CHEATER! SHOW ME WHERE HE'S AT! POINT ME AT HIM!

THE STAGEHANDS CONTROL ACCESS TO THE DRESSING ROOMS, AS WELL AS THE LIGHTS, SOUND, AND SCENERY.

SMART ENTERTAINERS KEEP THE STAGEHANDS HAPPY.

ESPECIALLY IMPORTANT IS A GRUFF CHARACTER NAMED **WILLIAM SPAYNE**.

I REMEMBER THE FIRST TIME I SAW THAT MEAN OLD SPAYNE. HE GAVE ME THE DIRTIEST LOOK IN THE WORLD.

OTHERWISE, ONE'S ACT CAN DEVELOP MYSTERIOUS **TECHNICAL DIFFICULTIES** OR THE ACT'S GUESTS MIGHT BE KEPT **COOLING THEIR HEELS** IN THE BASEMENT WAITING ROOM.

COME HERE, ANTNEE. NOW HERE'S THE RULES.

LIKE A DRILL SERGEANT, SPAYNE WAS THE **LAW**.

SPAYNE COULD TELL YOU EVERYTHING ABOUT EVERYBODY.

THINGS ABOUT THE PERSONAL LIVES OF SOME OF THE PEOPLE. PHILANDERINGS THAT WERE GOING ON. THE GOOD PEOPLE AND THE BAD.

HE WAS A **NEWSPAPER**!

LITTLE ANTHONY

THE APOLLO WAS A REAL FAMILY FEELING.

EVERYBODY WORKED FOR THE GOOD OF THE SHOW. EVERYONE WENT OUT AND DID THEIR BEST.

RUTH BROWN IS THE "QUEEN OF R&B" IN THE 1950S.

Thanks to her string of hits such as "(Mama) He Treats Your Daughter Mean," her label, Atlantic Records, is dubbed "The House That Ruth Built."

I DIDN'T KNOW ANYTHING ABOUT SHOW BUSINESS WHEN I WENT IN TO THE APOLLO.

BUT THE REST OF THE ENTERTAINERS WOULD BE IN THE WINGS OR OUT IN THE AUDIENCE, AND THEY'D TELL YOU WHAT YOU WERE DOING **WRONG**, OR WHAT YOU **SHOULD DO**.

SEE, THE ENTERTAINERS **MADE** THE ACTS.

THIS IS HOW THE THEATER WAS BUILT—ON **SELF-HELP**. WE DIDN'T HAVE NO **CRITICS**.

Even though the work is difficult and the conditions often atrocious—some call the theater "the workhouse" or "the penitentiary" —performers always look forward to returning to the Apollo. To coming home.

DIONNE WARWICK

ARTISTS DIDN'T LOOK FORWARD TO THE FIVE SHOWS A DAY OR THE FILTHY DRESSING ROOMS.

BUT THEY DID LOOK FORWARD TO THE FEELING VERY MUCH.

THE THEATER WAS TERRIBLE: DRAFTY, DIRTY, SMELLY—*AWFUL*. AND WE *LOVED* EVERY MINUTE OF IT!

One of the keys to the Apollo's success is its *adaptability* and *nimbleness*.

A typical Apollo bill opens on Friday morning, with the entire retinue staying for a week—sometimes doing five shows a day, up to *thirty-one* shows a week.

JAMES BROWN AT APOLLO

LOUIS JORDAN

LITTLE WILLIE JOHN

SARAH VAUGHN

During any season, the Apollo offers all types of shows for all types of audiences, interspersed.

JACKIE WILSON

DINAH WASHINGTON

JOE LOUIS

ONE WEEK YOU GO AFTER THE SARAH VAUGHAN FANS. ONE WEEK YOU GO AFTER THE JACKIE WILSON FANS. THE NEXT WEEK THE DINAH WASHINGTON FANS. THEN THE SPORTS FANS WITH JOE LOUIS. THEN THE CHURCH PEOPLE.

YOU TRY TO NURTURE EVERY MARKET.

YOU COULDN'T TAP THE SAME PEOPLE EVERY WEEK; YOU WOULD DRAIN THEM DRY.

BOBBY SCHIFFMAN

WE USED TO SCHEDULE SOME OF OUR SHOWS TIMED WITH THE PAYOFF OF THE CITY EMPLOYEES EVERY OTHER WEEK.

AND THE WELFARE CHECKS WERE VERY IMPORTANT: IF THEY CAME OUT THE FIRST AND THIRD WEEKS OF THE MONTH, THAT'S WHEN WE WOULD SCHEDULE THE SHOWS THAT THE MORE ELDERLY PEOPLE WOULD BE INTERESTED IN.

IF YOU WERE SELLING FIVE TICKETS TO SOMEBODY FOR SIX DOLLARS APIECE IN A NORMAL THEATER, A GUY WOULD COME UP AND DROP A TWENTY-DOLLAR BILL AND A TEN TO BUY THEM.

WHEN I FIRST STARTED AT THE APOLLO, WE WERE CHARGING SEVENTY CENTS. THE HIGHEST PRICE I EVER CHARGED WAS SIX DOLLARS. I TRIED SEVEN FOR REDD FOXX ONCE, AND THEY STAYED AWAY IN DROVES.

REDD FOXX TONIGHT

WE KNEW THAT YOUNG PEOPLE WILL FIND THE MONEY ANYTIME.

IN THE APOLLO, THEY WOULD DROP SOMETHING LIKE A TEN-DOLLAR BILL, SIX DOLLARS IN QUARTERS, TEN DOLLARS IN DIMES. PEOPLE WERE *SCRATCHING* TO GET ENOUGH MONEY.

WE WERE IN BUSINESS NO MATTER WHAT. WE ALWAYS DID A SHOW— SOME OF THEM GREAT, SOME OF THEM FAIR, SOME OF THEM LOUSY— BUT WE DID A SHOW EVERY WEEK.

THE APOLLO CREATES ITS OWN STAGE SETS AND CHANGES THEM EVERY WEEK.

WE WERE *OUTRAGEOUS* PROMOTERS, AND WE USED TO DO EVERYTHING WE COULD TO MAKE THE STAGE SHOW AS GLAMOROUS AND AS ELEVATED AS WE POSSIBLY COULD.

The main reason for the Apollo's success is a firm belief in the old adage: "The show must go on!" Good old-fashioned showbiz *tenacity*.

PEOPLE WOULD COME TO THE APOLLO TO ESCAPE FROM REALITY—FANTASIZE THAT THEY WERE PART OF THE ELEGANT LIVING THEY WERE SEEING PORTRAYED.

THE $600 MOHAIR SUITS, THE FANCY SHOES, THE FANCY CARS, AND THE BEAUTIFUL WOMEN— THIS WAS THE GLAMOUR OF SHOW BUSINESS.

WE WOULD SPEND *HOURS* PLANNING HOW TO GLAMORIZE THE STAGE.

To ensure that the show goes on and keeps going on in the future, the Apollo nurtures new talents—some discovered on its legendary Amateur Night—who later become the stars who keep the theater packed, generation after generation.

I USED TO DO SEVEN OR EIGHT ACTS ON EVERY SHOW.

THE THREE OR FOUR ACTS AT THE TOP OF THE SHOW WERE THE ONES THAT SOLD THE TICKETS.

THOSE AT THE BOTTOM WERE THE ONES WE WERE GIVING THE OPPORTUNITY TO DISPLAY THEIR WARES.

JAMES BROWN WAS ONCE THE OPENING ACT FOR LITTLE WILLIE JOHN.

REDD FOXX USED TO PLAY THE THEATER ALL THE TIME FOR $300, $400, $500.

AL GREEN WAS ONCE AN OPENING ACT.

GLADYS KNIGHT WOULD ALWAYS BE AN OPENING ACT BECAUSE SHE WAS SO ANIMATED.

THE SPINNERS WERE A LOCAL ACT, AND EVERY TIME WE NEEDED AN OPENING ACT AND COULDN'T THINK OF SOMEONE TO PUT IN THERE, WE'D GO BUY THE SPINNERS.

THE **SCHIFFMANS**: PATRIARCH **FRANK**, SONS **BOBBY** AND **JACK**. THE THEATER IS RUN BY A WHITE JEWISH FAMILY, BUT THEY ARE ALWAYS UP ON THE LATEST IN BLACK ENTERTAINMENT.

ALL BOBBY SCHIFFMAN HAD TO DO WAS STICK HIS HEAD OUT THE DOOR, AND THERE WERE THREE RECORD SHOPS ON 125TH STREET BLARING THE NEW HIT RECORDS.

As something new comes along, the Apollo seizes it and brings it into the theater.

The ability to do this, while retaining its old clientele, for nearly fifty years, is an unmatched achievement in show business.

BOBBY WOULD ALSO CHECK WITH THE RECORD COMPANIES TO SEE WHO WAS HOT AND WHO WAS COMING UP.

AHMET ERTEGUN

TAKE THE LEGEND OF THE **ORIOLES**:

The myth says that, out of nowhere, they storm the Apollo with a new look and sound, levelling everything before them, and **rhythm and blues** is born.

In fact, the **Orioles** had been shaking things up in Baltimore for at least a year before they make it at the Apollo.

R&B REVOLUTIONARIES ARE ACTIVE IN OTHER CITIES AND VENUES, LIKE BANDLEADER **JOHNNY OTIS** IN THE BARREL HOUSE IN LOS ANGELES . . .

AND **FATS DOMINO** IN THE HIDEAWAY BAR IN NEW ORLEANS . . .

Yet the theater is not a fomenter of cultural revolutions; rather, it is a legitimizer—the Apollo is the **Establishment**.

JOHNNY OTIS
THE ORIOLES
FATS DOMINO

The Apollo often leads the way in finding and presenting the latest thing.

As revolutionaries, artists "fight" in various places around the country. But they all know the ultimate battle is conquering the Apollo.

23

FRANK SCHIFFMAN IS THE APOLLO'S FATHER FIGURE.

HE IS ALSO A CONTROVERSIAL FIGURE IN HARLEM.

He is, as we will see, a vicious competitor who tries to eliminate anyone invading his turf.

He is loved and hated, hailed as a *progressive genius*, and denigrated as a *lucky opportunist*.

FRANK SCHIFFMAN WAS MARVELOUS.

HE HAD TO SHOW A PROFIT, BUT AT THE SAME TIME HE WAS MAKING THESE ELABORATE SHOWS AVAILABLE FOR A REASONABLE PRICE.

HE HAD AN AWARENESS OF COMMUNITY PROBLEMS.

HAROLD "STUMPY" CROMER OF THE COMEDY DUO **STUMP AND STUMPY**

FRANK SCHIFFMAN WITH NEW YORK MAYOR **FIORELLO LA GUARDIA**

LEONARD REED, LEGENDARY SHOW PRODUCER, DANCER, COMEDIAN, MC—AND APOLLO MANAGER

HE WAS THE SMARTEST THEATER OPERATOR I EVER KNEW.

FRANK SCHIFFMAN KNEW BLACK SHOW BUSINESS. HE WAS A **GENIUS**.

EVERYBODY USED TO TALK ABOUT HIM: "CHEAP SON OF A BITCH. HE WON'T DO THIS AND HE WON'T DO THAT." I WOULD SAY, "THE MAN'S NOT CHEAP, HE'S A BUSINESSMAN."

IN TWO YEARS, I LEARNED MORE ABOUT SHOW BUSINESS FROM FRANK SCHIFFMAN THAN I LEARNED IN TWENTY YEARS OF KNOCKING AROUND THEATERS.

HOWEVER, **JOHN BUBBLES**—ONE OF THE GREATEST DANCERS OF HIS TIME, AND HALF THE DUO OF **BUCK AND BUBBLES**—IS SKEPTICAL OF SCHIFFMAN.

HE WAS JUST LUCKY TO GET A THEATER AND HAVE NEGRO ENTERTAINMENT. WHAT DID HE KNOW?

ESTRELLITA BROOKS-MORSE, WHO FORMED THE POPULAR COMEDY TEAM OF **APUS AND ESTRELLITA** WITH HER HUSBAND **APUS BROOKS**, REMEMBERS A MAN WHO WAS KIND BUT FIRM . . .

SOME PEOPLE SAY HE WAS A LITTLE ROUGH, BUT HE WAS "POP" TO ME. HE GAVE MANY PERFORMERS BREAKS.

HE'D ALWAYS GIVE YOU A DRAW ON YOUR PAY, HE'D NEVER SAY NO. ON OPENING DAY, THEY'D KEEP BUGGING HIM : "POP, CAN I HAVE A DRAW?"

ONLY THING HE KNEW WAS HOW TO GET PEOPLE AS CHEAP AS HE COULD, AND WORK THEM AS LONG AS HE COULD. HE **MISUSED** THE PEOPLE.

JOHN HAMMOND, WHO PRODUCED AND POPULARIZED BILLIE HOLIDAY, COUNT BASIE, BOB DYLAN, AND BRUCE SPRINGSTEEN, WAS A GOOD FRIEND OF FRANK'S AND CALLED HIM "A GENUINE SHOW BUSINESS PHENOMENON." BUT STILL SAYS:

Many credit Frank Schiffman with maintaining the Apollo's consistently high standard of performance.

FRANK HAD NO ARTISTIC TASTE WHATEVER. HE LOOKED AT A SINGER IN TERMS OF WOULD SHE DRAW OR WOULDN'T SHE. COULD HE MAKE A DECENT PROFIT OFF HER.

WHATEVER HIS TRUE MOTIVES, MOST KNOW POP SCHIFFMAN AS A KEY FACTOR IN THE DEVELOPMENT OF THE APOLLO'S SHOWS.

He has strong ideas about the way the acts should present themselves.

THE MORNING BEFORE THE WEEKLY SHOW WOULD START, POP WOULD STAND IN BACK, LEANING UP AGAINST THE WALL IN THE REHEARSAL HALL.

HE WOULD LOOK AT THE SHOW, AND WHATEVER HE DIDN'T LIKE, HE'D TAKE OUT.

WHEN YOU DID A JOKE, FRANK SCHIFFMAN COULD TELL YOU . . .

LOOK, DO IT THIS WAY.

IT'S NOT GOING TO GO OVER. BUT IF YOU TURN IT AROUND AND DO IT THIS WAY, IT'S GOING TO CLICK.

HE WAS RIGHT.

IN THE LATE '40S AND EARLY '50S, FRANK AND HIS ELDER SON, JACK, ROPE OFF A SECTION IN THE CENTER ORCHESTRA AND COMMUNICATE VIA WALKIE-TALKIE WITH THE STAGEHANDS AND LIGHT OPERATORS.

Frank keeps meticulous notes, sometimes using a little penlight to write in the darkened theater, and later types up file cards of every performer and every performance.

Unless a miraculous change takes place Billie's value to us is lost. She has lost her public favor. She seems unable to remain away from stimulants.

Gave a good show. Very cooperative in finale. Sang fairly well. No misbehavior. Salary received is top value for her.

10/15/49
5/25/50 $500.00
7-26-51 $500.00

12/5/52 $2000.00

Behaved well. Gave adequate but not exciting performance. Was over-paid.

Terrible! She was sick, but she was also under the influence of stimulants. Only a miracle can restore her worthwhile playing her again.

BOBBY AND JACK SCHIFFMAN DONATE SOME WONDERFUL MATERIAL TO THE SMITHSONIAN INSTITUTION IN 1996, INCLUDING MANY OF THE INDIVIDUAL ARTIST'S FILE CARDS.

SANDMAN SIMS REMEMBERS A MAN WHOSE OCCASIONAL DISPLAYS OF AFFECTION COULD BE THE KISS OF DEATH.

SCHIFFMAN WAS A VERY EDUCATED MAN, AND VERY QUIET. YOU HARDLY HEARD HIM, AND WHEN HE WAS AROUND, YOU WOULD NEVER KNOW HE WAS THERE.

IF YOU DID A BAD ACT, HE WOULD NEVER EMBARRASS YOU. HE WOULD ALWAYS COME AND PUT HIS ARMS AROUND YOU.

HE'D COME OVER JUST SO SOFT AND NICE AND YOU'D SEE HIM DO THAT HUGGIN', AND YOU KNEW THAT ACT WAS **THROUGH**.

HE'D SAY . . .

OH, MR. SIMS, YOUR ACT DIDN'T GO OVER TOO WELL. YOU BETTER GO BACK AND TRY AGAIN. YOU'RE NOT ON THE NEXT SHOW. I'M SORRY.

There was a saying backstage at the Apollo: "Don't send out your laundry until after the first show."

He'd either laugh— or fire them.

When Schiffman comes backstage after the show, he's greeted with . . .

HEY, MR. SCHIFFMAN. SHOULD WE SEND OUT OUR LAUNDRY?

BOBBY'S OLDER BROTHER, JACK, HELPS HIS FATHER RUN THE THEATER IN THE LATE '40S AND EARLY '50S.

But he soon moves on, eventually settling in Florida where he becomes involved in citrus management. He passes away there in 2009 at age eighty-seven.

MY BROTHER HAD BEEN ON THE JOB FOUR OR FIVE YEARS, AND I USED TO LISTEN WITH MY MOUTH OPEN TO THE MANNER IN WHICH HE AND MY DAD DEALT WITH SOME OF THE PERFORMERS.

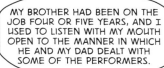

BOBBY WAS ONE OF THE PEOPLE. HE HAD A GOOD RAPPORT WITH **EVERYBODY**.

HE COULD DEAL WITH THIS PERSON WHO'S STRUNG OUT ON DRUGS—HE STILL GOT THEM TO THE SHOW— OR DEAL WITH THIS PERSON WITH A DRINKING PROBLEM.

LEARNING THE ROPES FROM BOYHOOD, BOBBY SPENDS A GREAT DEAL OF TIME IN HIS FAMILY'S THEATER.

I WORKED WITH A HALF DAY OFF EVERY OTHER WEEK. FROM TEN IN THE MORNING TILL MIDNIGHT. THIRTY-FIVE DOLLARS A WEEK.

BOBBY BECOMES ACTIVE IN RUNNING THE APOLLO IN THE EARLY '50S. IN 1961, HE PERSUADES HIS FATHER TO LET HIM TAKE OVER.

HEY, DAD, I THINK IT'S TIME WE CHANGED CHAIRS. YOU BE MY ASSISTANT. LET ME RUN THE THEATER.

I'VE BEEN WAITING FOR YOU TO TELL ME THAT. I'LL BE GLAD TO DO IT.

AFTER BOBBY TAKES OVER, FRANK GOES INTO SEMIRETIREMENT. BUT HE CONTINUES TO KEEP AN EYE ON THINGS UNTIL HIS DEATH IN 1974 AT AGE EIGHTY.

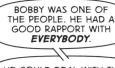

LESLIE UGGAMS

APOLLO MANAGEMENT IS LIKE **FAMILY**, WELL KNOWN TO MANY.

I FELT WE WERE IMPORTANT, BUT THE REASON THE APOLLO SUCCEEDED WAS THE **PEOPLE OF THE COMMUNITY**, THE JOE ON THE STREET WHO CAME IN AND PLUNKED DOWN HIS MONEY.

IT WAS THE COMMUNITY OF HARLEM THAT MADE THE APOLLO FLOURISH.

BABIES IN THE APOLLO? WHY NOT? AND IT'S CHEAPER THAN A SITTER!

THE APOLLO IS A VITAL PART OF HARLEM'S MAIN DRAG, 125TH STREET.

A HOT SHOW AT THE APOLLO MEANS MONEY IN THE BANK FOR EVERYONE ON 125TH STREET.

Ka-ching!

THE SCHIFFMANS CONSCIOUSLY TRY TO MAKE THE APOLLO A PART OF THE HARLEM COMMUNITY—AND KEEP THEM VESTED IN THE THEATER'S FATE.

THE COMMUNITY DOES FEEL BAD WHEN THE APOLLO HAS TROUBLES. BUT MORE OFTEN THAN NOT, THEY HAVE REASON TO FEEL GOOD.

I WANT THEM TO FEEL BAD WHEN A PERFORMER GIVES US THE SHAFT.

I WANT THEM TO FEEL BAD WHEN THE ROOF LEAKS.

I WANT THEM TO FEEL BAD WHEN WE CAN'T GET A FIRST-RUN FILM . . .

BOBBY SCHIFFMAN

FOR YEARS, THE THEATER IS BILLED AS "HARLEM'S HIGH SPOT"—AND THAT IT IS.

CHAPTER 2

Harlem Before the Apollo

The story of the Apollo Theater begins much earlier than its opening in *1934*—years before 125th Street becomes the *Main Street* of America's greatest African American community.

BETWEEN THE END OF WORLD WAR I AND THE BEGINNING OF THE GREAT DEPRESSION, GROUNDBREAKING AFRICAN AMERICANS LEAD A FLOWERING OF CREATIVITY KNOWN AS THE *HARLEM RENAISSANCE*.

Harlem becomes fashionable to the city's white socialites and intelligentsia.

The white world takes note.

They can imagine no more exciting an evening than a raucous crawl through Harlem's swankiest clubs.

NO SMART NEW YORK PARTY IS CONSIDERED COMPLETE WITHOUT A SMATTERING OF HARLEM RENAISSANCE INTELLECTUALS.

COUNTEE CULLEN

LANGSTON HUGHES

ZORA NEALE HURSTON

LEGENDARY SPOTS SUCH AS THE COTTON CLUB FEATURE THE GREATEST AFRICAN AMERICAN ARTISTS OF THE DAY, LIKE *DUKE ELLINGTON*.

OR *FATS WALLER* AT *CONNIE'S INN*.

CLUBS THAT, ALONG WITH *SMALLS PARADISE* AND *BARRON WILKINS' EXCLUSIVE CLUB*, MAKE UP HARLEM'S *BIG FOUR*.

SMALLS PARADISE

BARRON WI XCLUSIVE

But while African American artists draw crowds of rich white "swells" to the top clubs, black customers are usually **barred** from entering these legendary nightspots.

AT THE COTTON CLUB, **W. C. HANDY**, THE "FATHER OF THE BLUES," IS TURNED AWAY BY THE CLUB'S GANGSTER MANAGER, **GEORGE "BIG FRENCHY" DE MANGE**, WHILE WHITE REVELERS INSIDE SOAK UP THE MUSIC HE HELPED TO INVENT.

I DON'T CARE WHO YOU ARE.

LENA HORNE BEGINS HER CAREER AT THE COTTON CLUB AS A SIXTEEN-YEAR-OLD CHORINE.

LENA HORNE

THE SHOWS HAD A PRIMITIVE, NAKED QUALITY THAT WAS SUPPOSED TO MAKE A "CIVILIZED" AUDIENCE LOSE ITS INHIBITIONS.

DUKE ELLINGTON, KENTUCKY CLUB HOUSE BAND, 1923–28; COTTON CLUB, 1928–31.

FLETCHER HENDERSON, ROSELAND BALLROOM HOUSE BAND, 1924–31.

CAB CALLOWAY, COTTON CLUB HOUSE BAND, 1931–34.

The best black orchestras are booked for lengthy engagements at some of the top spots in the heart of Harlem and down on **Broadway**.

Even where black people aren't overtly **kept** out, they're often **priced** out.

THE JAZZ AGE

Stride piano players such as *James P. Johnson*, *Willie "The Lion" Smith*, and their protégé, *Fats Waller*, are at the height of their popularity and influence in the early '20s.

The music is modern, sophisticated, and wild—nearly everything Prohibition-era hedonists desire.

THEY TAKE THE BASIC RAGTIME TUNES POPULAR SINCE THE TURN OF THE CENTURY . . .

THE FINAL INGREDIENT—SENSUALITY—IS PROVIDED BY CLASSIC FEMALE BLUES SINGERS SUCH AS **MAMIE SMITH** AND **BESSIE SMITH**.

. . . SEPARATE THE RAGTIME BEAT WITH A STEADY LEFT HAND . . .

. . . AND JAZZ UP THE MELODY WITH THE DEXTEROUS DIGITS OF THE RIGHT HAND.

MAMIE SMITH'S HISTORIC 1920 RECORDING, "*CRAZY BLUES*," IS SELLING EIGHT THOUSAND RECORDS A WEEK.

CRAZY BLUES

ER JAZZ HOUNDS

It was called the first recording of an "actual blues performance by a Negro artist with Negro accompaniment."

JAZZ IS INVENTED BY BLACKS IN NEW ORLEANS. YET A WHITE GROUP FROM THAT TOWN, THE **ORIGINAL DIXIELAND JAZZ BAND**, MAKES THE FIRST JAZZ RECORDING IN 1917.

The band's New York debut generates national headlines and helps popularize jazz.

BANDLEADER *PAUL WHITEMAN* IS CROWNED THE *"KING OF JAZZ"* BY CAPITALIZING ON THE MUSIC OF BLACK JAZZ INNOVATORS.

In Harlem, this leads to a strange dichotomy: The music that Harlemites hear on their radios is often a white dilution of black jazz.

BUDDY BOLDEN

JOSEPH "KING" OLIVER

FREDDIE KEPPARD

Harlem's black music buffs buy and play their own records—and find plenty of ways to "dig" their own music among their own people.

FOR MOST OF HARLEM, THE PLACE TO REALLY LET LOOSE IS AT A *RENT PARTY* IN SOMEONE'S APARTMENT, WITH THE LIGHTS DOWN LOW, THE SOUL FOOD PILED HIGH, AND THE MUSIC BLARING.

The rent party tradition begins in the South, with church socials designed to raise money. In Harlem, the concept is refined—a quarter or a buck at a time.

WILLIE "THE LION" SMITH REMEMBERS THEM IN HIS MEMOIR, *MUSIC ON MY MIND*.

AN ENTIRE FAMILY WOULD WORK FOR DAYS PREPARING.

THERE'D BE PILES OF HOG MAWS, PICKLED PIGS' TAILS, PIGS' FEET, SOUTHERN-FRIED CHICKEN, MASHED POTATOES, CHITTERLINGS, POTATO SALAD, CORN BREAD, RED BEANS AND RICE, CRAB SOUP, AND SOMETIMES THEY'D EVEN COME UP WITH A CHINESE DINNER WITH PILES OF CHOP SUEY . . .

THEY WOULD CROWD A HUNDRED OR MORE PEOPLE INTO A SEVEN-ROOM RAILROAD FLAT, AND THE WALLS WOULD BULGE.

SOME OF THE PARTIES SPREAD TO THE HALLS AND ALL OVER THE BUILDING.

GALLONS OF GIN, BEER, WINE, WHISKEY, EGGNOG, AND BRANDY WERE AVAILABLE TO WASH DOWN ALL THOSE VITTLES . . .

WHEN THERE WASN'T A CRAP GAME, OR POKER, GOING IN THE BACK BEDROOM, THEY'D USE IT FOR A PLACE TO REST UP, OR SLEEP OFF, OR MAKE LOVE.

THE RENT PARTY WAS THE PLACE TO PICK UP ON ALL THE LATEST JOKES, JIVE, AND UPTOWN NEWS.

IT GOT TO BE A BIG BUSINESS. THEY WOULD ADVERTISE A HOUSE-RENT PARTY FOR A MONTH IN ADVANCE . . . THEY EVEN BUILT UP MAILING LISTS.

AFTER A RENT PARTY, HARLEMITES MIGHT END UP AT ONE OF THE JOINTS ON *"JUNGLE ALLEY"*—THE PRIME LOCALE FOR CLUBS PATRONIZED BY BLACKS, BUT ALSO FREQUENTED BY "SLUMMING" WHITES.

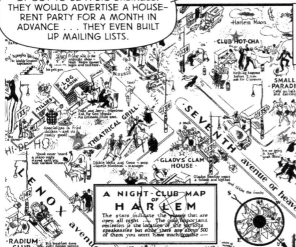

At spots such as *Pod's and Jerry's*, or *Mexico's*, the real action doesn't start until the early hours of the morning and goes until well after sunrise.

AFTER THEIR GIGS AT THE BIG CLUBS WRAP UP, JAZZ GREATS MEET THERE IN FURIOUS *"CUTTING CONTESTS,"* PITTING THEM AGAINST YOUNG HOPEFULS TESTING THEIR CHOPS.

I'MA TAKE ON HAWK!

BEN WEBSTER, DON BYAS, AND *COLEMAN HAWKINS*

Jungle Alley and the Big Four nightclubs are in what is then black Harlem—many blocks north of 125th Street.

125TH STREET IN 1927. *DOLL THOMAS* LIVES AND WORKS IN HARLEM THEN.

THERE WERE NO BLACKS ON 125TH STREET. EVEN IN 1927, THE NEIGHBORHOOD WAS STRICTLY WHITE.

IF BLACK FOLKS WANTED TO GO INTO THE THEATER THAT'S NOW THE APOLLO, THEY ENTERED FROM 126TH STREET. HAD TO GO UP THE BACK STAIRS TO THE BALCONY.

THEY JUST WOULDN'T SELL US AN ORCHESTRA SEAT. THEY WERE EITHER "SOLD OUT" OR THEY'D FLATLY REFUSE.

ON 125TH STREET, *FRANK'S LUNCHROOM*—WE COULDN'T GET SERVED IN THERE.

ACROSS THE STREET WAS *CHILD'S*. WE COULDN'T GET SERVED IN THERE.

NEXT DOOR WAS *LOFT'S CANDY SHOP*. COULDN'T GET SERVED IN THERE.

RIGHT DOWN THE STREET WAS *FABIAN'S SEAFOOD SHOP*. COULDN'T GET SERVED IN THERE EITHER.

ALL THE BARS AND EVERYTHING ELSE WAS THE SAME WAY.

MANHATTAN'S BLACK MIGRATION

The history of African Americans in New York begins at the opposite end of the island of Manhattan from Harlem.

In *Lower Manhattan*, the first Africans are brought as slaves by the Dutch in 1626, and later settle in the rough *Five Points* neighborhood.

Over more than 300 years, African Americans gradually migrate uptown.

By the middle of the nineteenth century, *Greenwich Village* is known as *Little Africa*.

Around the turn of the twentieth century, African Americans are forced out of Manhattan's West Side.

HARLEM

CENTRAL PARK

LOWER MANHATTAN

Uptown speculators build too many apartments in anticipation of the Lenox Avenue elevated subway in 1904. They turn to African Americans to fill in.

By 1914, Harlem is the fashionable place for blacks who can't afford Brooklyn.

In 1919, there is a relatively isolated black section of Harlem from 130th Street to 143rd Street and from about Seventh Avenue to Madison Avenue.

By 1930, a major part of present-day Harlem—including 125th Street—is black.

ON 125TH STREET, IN 1914, THE FUTURE APOLLO THEATER OPENS AS **HURTIG & SEAMON'S MUSIC HALL**.

HURTIG & SEAMON'S MUSIC HALL
BACKSTAGE PASS
Issued to—

THE BLACK THEATRICAL SCENE IN HARLEM IS COMING UNDER THE CONTROL OF TWO MEN—ALTHOUGH THEY WON'T TAKE OVER THE APOLLO UNTIL 1935.

A *vaudeville* house and *burlesque* joint, it presents mainly white shows to white audiences.

FRANK SCHIFFMAN AND *LEO BRECHER*

UP HERE, MR. BRECHER OWNED THE **ODEON** ON 145TH STREET AND THE **ODEON ANNEX** . . . PRIMARILY MOVIE THEATERS. HE OWNED THE **ROOSEVELT** AT 145TH AND FIFTH, THE **DOUGLAS** AT 142ND AND LENOX . . . AND OF COURSE THE **LAFAYETTE** AT 132ND AND SEVENTH.

THEY OWNED ALL THE THEATERS IN HARLEM.

I WENT TO WORK FOR MR. LEO BRECHER IN 1914, LONG BEFORE HE TIED UP WITH MR. SCHIFFMAN.

HE WAS VERY NICE, VERY SHREWD, AND VERY SMART.

LEO BRECHER

BRECHER WAS THE LANDLORD FOR THE COTTON CLUB, WHICH WAS IN THE UPSTAIRS LOBBY OVER THE **DOUGLAS THEATER**.

DOLL THOMAS

IN THOSE DAYS, THE FILM PROJECTIONIST WENT DOWNTOWN AND GOT THE FILM **BEFORE** THE SHOW, AND TOOK THE FILM BACK **AFTER** THE SHOW.

The Austrian immigrant is the *money man*.

IF YOU HAD BOOKED A FILM THAT A RIVAL MOVIE HOUSE EXHIBITOR WANTED, HE HAD A GANG WAITING TO TAKE THE FILM AWAY FROM YOU.

THEY'D REMOVE THE FILM FROM THE BOX AND ROLL IT UP AND DOWN THE STREET!

SO MR. SCHIFFMAN CREATED A FILM DELIVERY SERVICE—THE FIRST ONE IN NEW YORK CITY—AND MET MR. BRECHER.

THEY FORMED ONE OF THE MOST AIRTIGHT AND SUCCESSFUL THEATER COMBINATIONS THAT THERE WAS, ESPECIALLY IN BLACK SHOW BUSINESS.

FILM DELIVERY

Brecher is content to remain a silent partner until his death in 1980 at the age of ninety.

Frank Schiffman is a former schoolteacher who grew up on the Lower East Side, manages the theaters, and eventually becomes co-owner of the Apollo.

IN 1922, SCHIFFMAN AND BRECHER TAKE OVER THE **HARLEM OPERA HOUSE** ON 125TH STREET.

That's where the *Apollo* name first appears on 125th Street. A dozen years later, the name will be taken by its larger neighbor.

Just down the block from Hurtig & Seamon's, the Harlem Opera House features stage comedies and musicals featuring *Al Jolson* and the *Four Marx Brothers*.

A small competing theater over the lobby is variously known as **Hammerstein's Music Hall**, **Minsky's Burlesque** . . . and, finally, the **Apollo** Burlesque.

SCHIFFMAN AND BRECHER'S POWER UPTOWN BECOMES INDOMITABLE IN 1925 WHEN THEY ASSUME CONTROL OF THE GRANDDADDY OF ALL BLACK THEATERS, THE LAFAYETTE, ON SEVENTH AVENUE AND 132ND.

AND THEY WOULDN'T ALLOW ANY COMPETITION.

"*DARKTOWN FOLLIES*" AT THE LAFAYETTE, 1913

They inherit a theater with more than a decade's tradition as the "*Cradle of Stars*."

Although until they take over, African Americans are admitted to the Lafayette only grudgingly—relegated to the balcony.

ACCORDING TO HARLEM RENAISSANCE WRITER *JAMES WELDON JOHNSON*:

The "Darktown Follies" drew space, headlines, and cartoons in the New York papers; and consequently it became the vogue to go to Harlem to see it . . .

The beginning of the nightly migration to Harlem in search of entertainment began.

The Lafayette quickly becomes *the* theater in Harlem to see top black stars. A Lafayette debut is as important as an Apollo debut will soon become.

ETHEL WATERS, ONE OF THE GREATEST SINGERS AND ACTRESSES OF HER DAY, SPEAKS ABOUT HER 1918 LAFAYETTE DEBUT IN HER AUTOBIOGRAPHY.

I WAS ASKED TO APPEAR AT ONE OF THE SPECIAL SUNDAY-NIGHT SHOWS AT THE LAFAYETTE THEATER, THE **UPTOWN PALACE**. THOSE SUNDAY SHOWS WERE EVENTS.

HARLEM'S DICTYS GOT THEIR FIRST GANDER AT MY WORK THAT EVENING. THEY KNEW PERFORMERS, AND THEY DECIDED THAT I HAD A FUTURE BIGGER THAN MY PRESENT OR MY PAST.

Ethel Waters later becomes an Apollo favorite, too.

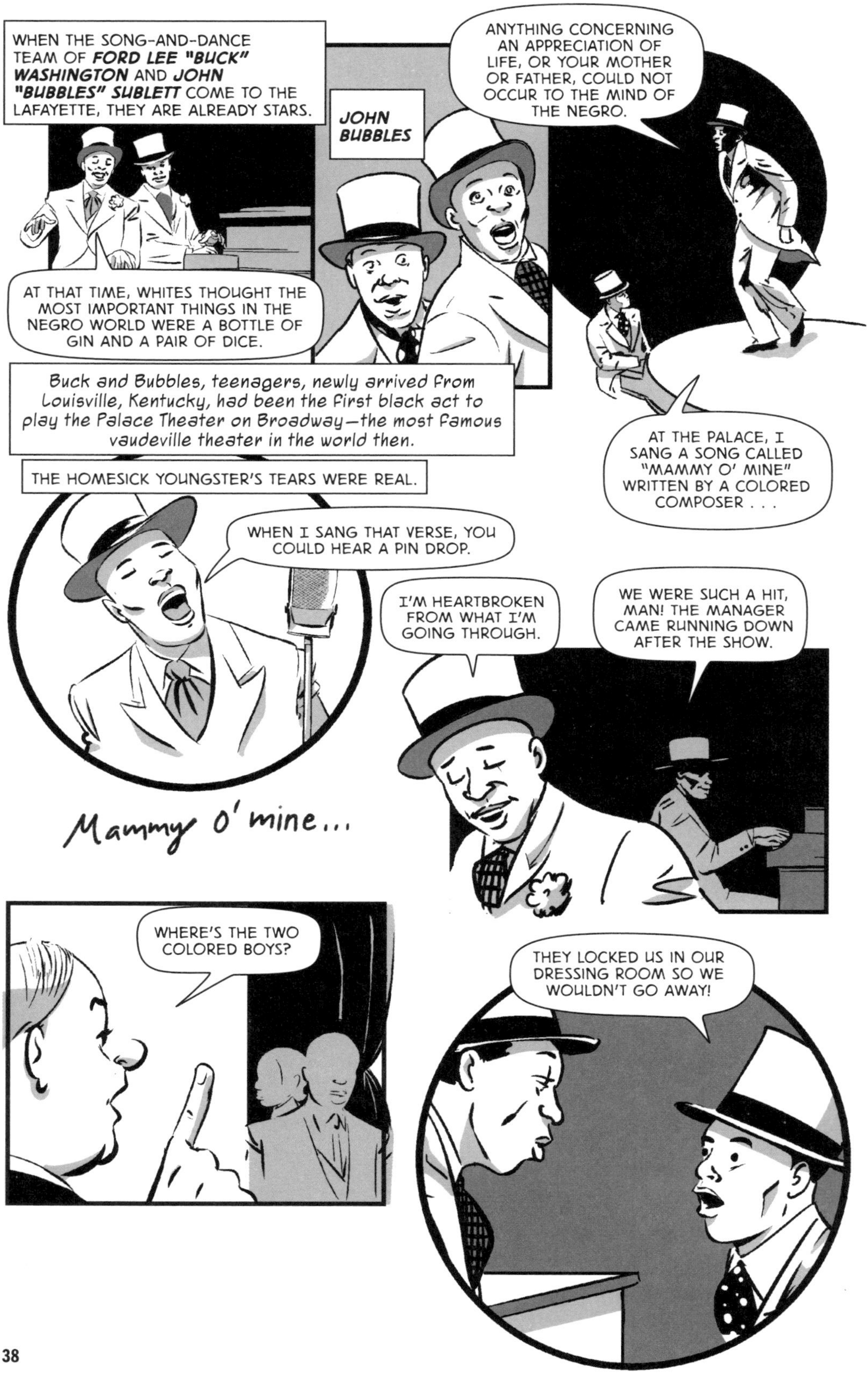

WHEN THE SONG-AND-DANCE TEAM OF FORD LEE "BUCK" WASHINGTON AND JOHN "BUBBLES" SUBLETT COME TO THE LAFAYETTE, THEY ARE ALREADY STARS.
JOHN BUBBLES
ANYTHING CONCERNING AN APPRECIATION OF LIFE, OR YOUR MOTHER OR FATHER, COULD NOT OCCUR TO THE MIND OF THE NEGRO.
AT THAT TIME, WHITES THOUGHT THE MOST IMPORTANT THINGS IN THE NEGRO WORLD WERE A BOTTLE OF GIN AND A PAIR OF DICE.
Buck and Bubbles, teenagers, newly arrived from Louisville, Kentucky, had been the first black act to play the Palace Theater on Broadway—the most famous vaudeville theater in the world then.
AT THE PALACE, I SANG A SONG CALLED "MAMMY O' MINE" WRITTEN BY A COLORED COMPOSER . . .
THE HOMESICK YOUNGSTER'S TEARS WERE REAL.
WHEN I SANG THAT VERSE, YOU COULD HEAR A PIN DROP.
I'M HEARTBROKEN FROM WHAT I'M GOING THROUGH.
WE WERE SUCH A HIT, MAN! THE MANAGER CAME RUNNING DOWN AFTER THE SHOW.
Mammy O' mine...
WHERE'S THE TWO COLORED BOYS?
THEY LOCKED US IN OUR DRESSING ROOM SO WE WOULDN'T GO AWAY!

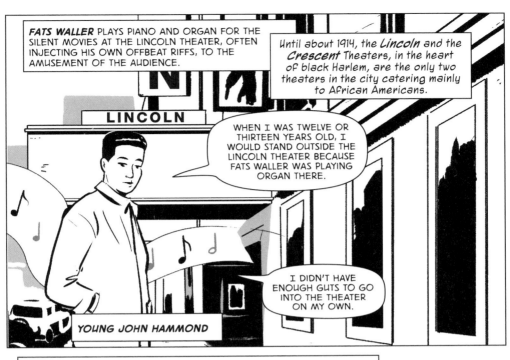

FATS WALLER PLAYS PIANO AND ORGAN FOR THE SILENT MOVIES AT THE LINCOLN THEATER, OFTEN INJECTING HIS OWN OFFBEAT RIFFS, TO THE AMUSEMENT OF THE AUDIENCE.

Until about 1914, the *Lincoln* and the *Crescent* Theaters, in the heart of black Harlem, are the only two theaters in the city catering mainly to African Americans.

WHEN I WAS TWELVE OR THIRTEEN YEARS OLD, I WOULD STAND OUTSIDE THE LINCOLN THEATER BECAUSE FATS WALLER WAS PLAYING ORGAN THERE.

I DIDN'T HAVE ENOUGH GUTS TO GO INTO THE THEATER ON MY OWN.

YOUNG JOHN HAMMOND

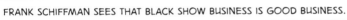

FRANK SCHIFFMAN SEES THAT BLACK SHOW BUSINESS IS GOOD BUSINESS.

THE NEW YORK AGE

In all New York, Harlem was the last to show signs of business falling off.

He wants *in* on this action in his new neighborhood.

AT THE HEIGHT OF THE DEPRESSION, A CONFERENCE OF MOVIE EXHIBITORS TELLS HARLEM NEWSPAPER THE *NEW YORK AGE* . . .

THE NEW YORK AGE

Harlemites will not allow hard times to make hermits and recluses out of them, but will scrape up enough to take in their amusements.

From his headquarters at the Lafayette, Schiffman devotes himself to the development of black entertainment— and the elimination of his competitors.

SCHIFFMAN WAS **IMPOSSIBLE** TO COMPETE WITH.

HIS CONTRACTS WOULD SAY $1,000 A WEEK FOR A PLAYER—HE'D ACTUALLY PAY THEM $300, BUT AS LONG AS THEY COULD SHOW THAT PIECE OF PAPER AROUND TO HIS COMPETITOR—

THERE WAS A TAP DANCER NAMED EDDIE RECTOR, AND HE HAD ONE OF THESE PIECES OF PAPER THAT SAID $1,000.

EDDIE RECTOR IS THE SHOWBIZ PARTNER OF HARLEM LEGEND **RALPH COOPER**, WHO CREATES **AMATEUR NIGHT**.

SOMETIMES THE PLOY BACKFIRES.

HE HAD DRAWN PART OF IT, BUT WHEN HE CAME FOR THE REST, IT WASN'T THERE.

JOHN HAMMOND

USUALLY SCHIFFMAN COULD SWEET-TALK THESE PEOPLE.

BUT EDDIE CHASED SCHIFFMAN AROUND THE LAFAYETTE WITH A **GUN**!

BESSIE SMITH PLAYED THE LAFAYETTE JUST ONCE AFTER SHE PLAYED THE ALHAMBRA. SHE HAD TO COME **CRAWLING** BACK TO DO IT.

SCHIFFMAN HAD TO CALL THE **POLICE**.

IF YOU WANTED TO WORK BLACK THEATERS IN GENERAL, YOU HAD TO DEAL WITH SCHIFFMAN.

FRANK SCHIFFMAN HAD TO CLAW HIS WAY UP. SHOW BUSINESS WAS **ROUGH** IN THE OLD DAYS.

BESSIE SMITH

40

YES, THAT'S TRUE . . . I WORKED AT THE **ALHAMBRA THEATER**, DOWN SEVENTH AVENUE. A PERFORMER WOULD COME TO US AND SAY:

"IF YOU GIVE ME MORE THAN THIS, I'LL WORK FOR YOU."

IT WAS JUST SCHIFFMAN'S WAY OF HIKING THE COSTS TO HIS COMPETITORS.

HE HAD ALL KINDS OF TRCKS.

PERFORMERS WORKED FOR SCHIFFMAN AT THE LAFAYETTE OR THEY WORKED FOR **NOBODY**. WHATEVER HIS PRICE WAS, THAT WAS THE BEST THEY COULD GET, AND THEY HAD TO TAKE IT.

IF THEY WORKED AT THE ALHAMBRA, THEY COULDN'T WORK FOR SCHIFFMAN AGAIN.

DOLL THOMAS

BY THE END OF 1931, THE ALHAMBRA FOLDS. ONE DOWN, MORE TO GO.

RKO ALHAMBRA CLOSED

BY 1930, BURLESQUE THEATERS ARE IN TROUBLE. THEY ARE BECOMING PASSÉ AND INCREASINGLY THREATENED BY SEXY BROADWAY REVUES.

BARE LEGS— SHOCKINGLY, NO STOCKINGS!

BURLESQUE TAKES OFF ITS GLOVES AND ITS STOCKINGS AND FIGHTS BACK WITH BARE KNUCKLES AND KNEES AND MORE AND MORE BARE SKIN.

I PLAYED THE APOLLO WHEN IT WAS HURTIG & SEAMON'S, AS A CHILD STRIPPER. I WAS ABOUT FIFTEEN.

THE FIRST PART OF THE SHOW WOULD BE ALL WHITE.

BUT THE SECOND HALF WOULD BE A BLACK CHORUS LINE AND A BLACK COMEDIAN AND A BLACK SINGER—AND THEN THEY'D HAVE A BLACK STRIPPER.

ESTRELLITA BROOKS-MORSE

IT WASN'T VULGAR OR ANYTHING LIKE THAT. WE WERE WORKING TO BEAUTIFUL MUSIC, AND TAKING OFF PIECES BEAUTIFULLY. VERY *ARTISTIC*.

Mayor Demands Burlesque Ban

In 1933, newly elected Mayor *Fiorello La Guardia* begins a campaign against burlesque.

Hurtig & Seamon's is forced to go bankrupt.

SOON THE CITY FATHERS FEEL IT HAS GONE TOO FAR.

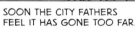

The little theater over the Harlem Opera House has to close, too.

In 1934, the landlord, *Sidney Cohen*, takes the Apollo name . . .

. . . and, with his manager, *Morris Sussman*, reopens the much larger Hurtig & Seamon's Burlesque as the new *125th Street Apollo Theatre*, featuring black entertainment for the newly black neighborhood.

An unusual ad appears in the Theatricals section of the New York Age.

THE APOLLO'S INAUGURAL SHOW, FRIDAY, JANUARY 26, 1934: "JAZZ A LA CARTE"

SCHIFFMAN FEELS OUT OF IT UPTOWN AT THE LAFAYETTE. 125TH STREET IS NOW HARLEM'S SHOW BUSINESS AND COMMERCIAL CENTER.

EVEN RALPH COOPER'S NEWLY LAUNCHED WEDNESDAY AMATEUR NIGHT AT THE LAFAYETTE, ALONG WITH A PRICE REDUCTION TO AS LITTLE AS A DIME, CAN'T STANCH THE FLOW OF CUSTOMERS DOWN TO 125TH STREET.

LAFAYETTE

HARLEM OPERA HOUSE

SCHIFFMAN HALTS SHOWS AT THE LAFAYETTE . . .

. . . AND MOVES TO THE HARLEM OPERA HOUSE, JUST DOWN THE STREET FROM THE APOLLO, ON JUNE 9, 1934.

The Apollo and the Harlem Opera House are now the *only* black theaters left in Harlem.

The show business battle for 125th Street is brutal, but it occurs in the midst of a true horror—Harlem's first major *riot*.

ON MARCH 19, 1935, THE WHITE STAFF AT THE STORE **S. H. KRESS & CO.**, DIRECTLY ACROSS FROM THE APOLLO, IS ACCUSED OF BEATING A YOUNG BLACK SHOPLIFTER.

RIOTING AND LOOTING DESTROYS WHITE-OWNED BUSINESSES ON THE STREET AND ELSEWHERE IN HARLEM, ALTHOUGH THE THEATERS ARE LEFT UNTOUCHED.

THREE ARE KILLED AND HUNDREDS WOUNDED.

AFTER ALREADY SUFFERING THROUGH THE TRIBULATIONS OF THE GREAT DEPRESSION, THE REMAINING HOPE AND OPTIMISM OF THE HARLEM RENAISSANCE LITERALLY AND FIGURATIVELY GO UP IN SMOKE.

The rioting is a one-day event. But the economic and social factors behind the rampage reset the cultural stage as white infatuation with Harlem wanes—and the battle for the hearts and minds of Harlemites intensifies on 125th Street.

AROUND THE TIME OF THE RIOT, **RALPH COOPER** TAKES HIS **WEDNESDAY AMATEUR NIGHT** TO **COHEN AND SUSSMAN'S APOLLO** AND BEGINS HIS INFLUENTIAL WMCA BROADCAST, **"AMATEUR NIGHT IN HARLEM."**

Schiffman fights back with his own *Tuesday Amateur Night,* broadcast on WNEW.

SIDNEY COHEN, HOWEVER, DOESN'T HAVE THE STOMACH, OR THE HEART, FOR THIS KIND OF BATTLE. SO HE TURNS TO AN OLD FAMILY FRIEND, **JOHN HAMMOND**, TO HELP HIM AT THE APOLLO.

I WOULD BOOK THE SHOWS, COHEN WOULD PUT UP THE CAPITAL, AND I WOULD HAVE A PERCENTAGE OF THE PROFITS.

I WAS ON MY WAY TO SIGN THE PAPERS.

I CALLED UP THE OFFICE ON 44TH STREET TO CONFIRM.

WE'RE TERRIBLY SORRY TO TELL YOU, BUT MR. COHEN HAS JUST HAD A HEART ATTACK. HE'S DEAD.

JUST LIKE **THAT**.

ON MAY 13, 1935, IT IS ANNOUNCED THAT THE APOLLO AND THE HARLEM OPERA HOUSE ARE MERGING.

EXCELLENT WORK, FRANK. YOU'VE BEEN A GOOD AND FAITHFUL MANAGER.

I'M GIVING YOU A HALF INTEREST IN THE APOLLO.

LEO BRECHER

But the *merger* is really a *takeover*.

The Harlem Opera House turns to *movies*.

And, Schiffman and Brecher move their operation to the Apollo.

FRANK SCHIFFMAN IS NOW CO-OWNER OF THE FINEST THEATER IN HARLEM—AND UNDISPUTED KING OF THE UPTOWN SCENE.

THE ONLY STAGE SHOW IN HARLEM

The Apollo changes its billing to *"The Only Stage Show in Harlem"* . . . and the legend begins.

45

CHAPTER 3

The 1930s: Swingin'

With a virtual monopoly on Harlem's main street, the Apollo attracts and features the finest entertainment.

Word spreads uptown and downtown that something exciting is happening on 125th Street.

The theater stands behind a gaudy neon sign on West 125th Street, between a haberdashery and a leather goods store.

The *New York World-Telegram* provides its curious readers with an "inside view" of the "Harlem Stompers" at the four-year-old Apollo in January 1937:

The sidewalk outside is a favored location for old men lugging sandwich signs and pitchmen unloading razor blades and patent medicines.

At a candy counter, you can buy chocolate bars and peanuts, but no gum. That is to protect the seats.

CHECK IT OUT! CHECK IT OUT, FOLKS!

TWO IN THE ORCHESTRA PLEASE.

THAT'LL BE ONE DOLLAR.

DADDY, I WANT SOME PEANUTS.

the 2. ... on.

You buy your ticket at a sidewalk booth— from fifteen-cent mornings to a fifty-cent top Wednesday and Saturday nights.

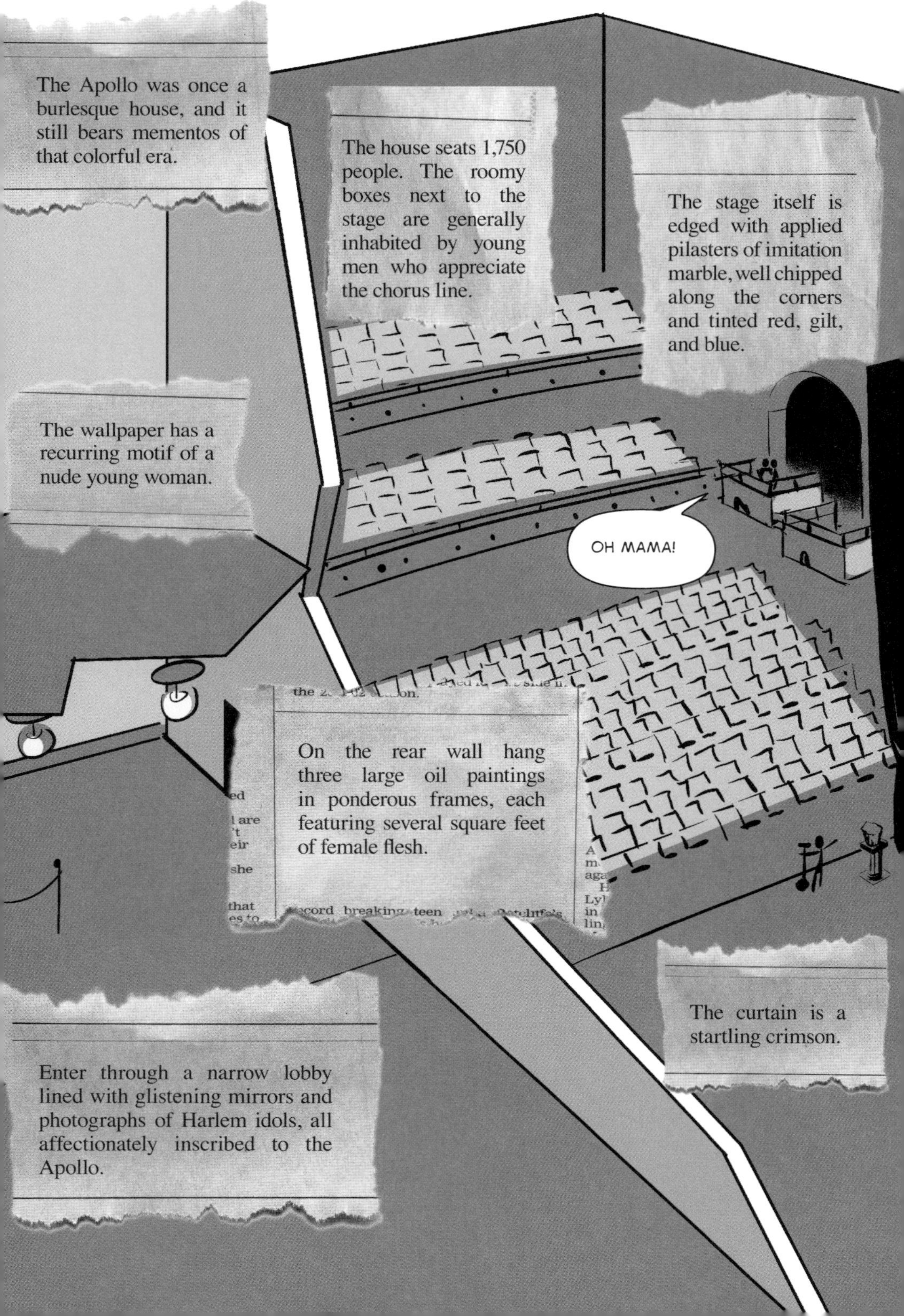

The Apollo was once a burlesque house, and it still bears mementos of that colorful era.
The house seats 1,750 people. The roomy boxes next to the stage are generally inhabited by young men who appreciate the chorus line.
The stage itself is edged with applied pilasters of imitation marble, well chipped along the corners and tinted red, gilt, and blue.
The wallpaper has a recurring motif of a nude young woman.
OH MAMA!
On the rear wall hang three large oil paintings in ponderous frames, each featuring several square feet of female flesh.
The curtain is a startling crimson.
Enter through a narrow lobby lined with glistening mirrors and photographs of Harlem idols, all affectionately inscribed to the Apollo.

THE APOLLO OPENS AT 10:00 AM.

OOH, I JUST LOVE THE NICHOLAS BROTHERS!

AIN'T NO SCHOOL FOR ME TODAY!

Night workers, housewives, and hooky-playing schoolchildren dig deep for their nickels and dimes, and enter a world where they are welcome to stay all day if they like.

IF YOU LIVED IN HARLEM DURING THE 1930S, YOU HAD TO MAKE IT TO THE APOLLO EACH AND EVERY FRIDAY TO CATCH THE NEW SHOW.

MANY *DO* STAY ALL DAY, CATCHING THREE, FOUR, OR FIVE SHOWS, TAKING CATNAPS BETWEEN PERFORMANCES.

ZZZZZZZZZZZZZ

SO I SEZ TO HIM, I SEZ . . .

PLAYWRIGHT LOFTEN "BUBBLING BROWN SUGAR" MITCHELL

STROLLED AROUND THE BLOCK UNTIL IT WAS SHOWTIME.

THEN YOU PAID FOR A SECOND BALCONY TICKET.

HEY, DADDY-O! HOW'S EVERY LITTLE THING?

JUMPIN', MAN!

YOU REACHED OVER AND FOUND SOME EXCUSE FOR SPEAKING TO A FINE BROWN CHICK WHO SAT IN FRONT OF YOU.

BEFORE THE APOLLO THEME SONG WAS THROUGH, YOU WERE SPIELING AND SINGING, TOO, "I THINK YOU'RE WONDERFUL."

48

THE SHOW STRUCTURE IS ALWAYS BASICALLY THE SAME: FIRST A SHORT FILM, PERHAPS A BETTY BOOP CARTOON.

NEXT, A NEWSREEL, FOLLOWED BY A FEATURE FILM.

UNIVERSAL NEWS

THEN A PAUSE. SILENCE.

AT LAST, THE MASTER OF CEREMONIES ANNOUNCES, TO THE RISING APPLAUSE AND SCREAMS FROM THE AUDIENCE: "LADIES AND GENTLEMEN, IT'S SHOWTIME AT THE APOLLO!"

BA-BA-BOOM! THE BAND BREAKS INTO THE APOLLO THEME SONG, "I MAY BE WRONG (BUT I THINK YOU'RE WONDERFUL)," AND THE SHOW IS ROLLING.

THE BAND DOES A NUMBER WITH THE CHORUS LINE PERFORMING IN FRONT OF THEM.

THEN THE MC BRINGS ON A "SIGHT ACT" SUCH AS A TAP DANCER, ACROBAT, OR ANIMAL ACT . . .

. . . FOLLOWED BY A SINGER, THE CHORUS AGAIN, A COMEDY ACT, AND FINALLY THE FEATURED ATTRACTION OR BAND IN THE FINALE.

THE SHOWS, OR REVUES, LOOSELY REVOLVE AROUND A THEME.

★Harlem Goes★
HOLLYWOOD

HILLBILLY REVUE

VOODOO DRUMS

Modern Rhythm♪♪

EBONY SHOWBOAT

HALF HOUR!

WHAT?! DAMN! ARE YOU KIDDIN' ME? THE *HALF'S* ALREADY IN?!

THERE IS A NEW REVUE EACH WEEK. THIRTY-ONE SHOWS A WEEK: FOUR A DAY, PLUS AN EXTRA SHOW ON WEDNESDAY, SATURDAY, AND SUNDAY.

MOST SHOWS RUN SIXTY TO NINETY MINUTES.

PERFORMERS OFTEN COMPLAIN THAT BY THE TIME THEY COME OFFSTAGE FROM ONE SHOW, THE BACKSTAGE BELL SIGNALING THIRTY MINUTES TO THE NEXT SHOW—THE HALF—HAS ALREADY RUNG.

MAKING THE SCENE AT THE APOLLO BECOMES THE ULTIMATE NIGHT ON THE TOWN . . .

. . . ESPECIALLY ON SATURDAY NIGHTS AND AT THE ANNUAL EASTER AND CHRISTMAS SHOWS, WHEN THE CROWDS REALLY "SHOW OUT."

The men appear in tight-belted, high-waisted coats, with freshly marcelled hair "conked" into beautifully rippling waves.

I HEAR COOP'S GOT SOME FINE SINGER WITH HIM.

YEAH, BILLIE SOMETHING, I THINK.

BABY, THAT NEW BARBER DID YOU RIGHT.

THANK YOU, DARLIN'. MMM, THAT PERFUME REALLY SENDS ME.

The women, fragrantly scented, gracefully glide through the lobby in tight slinky dresses, high heels, and veils.

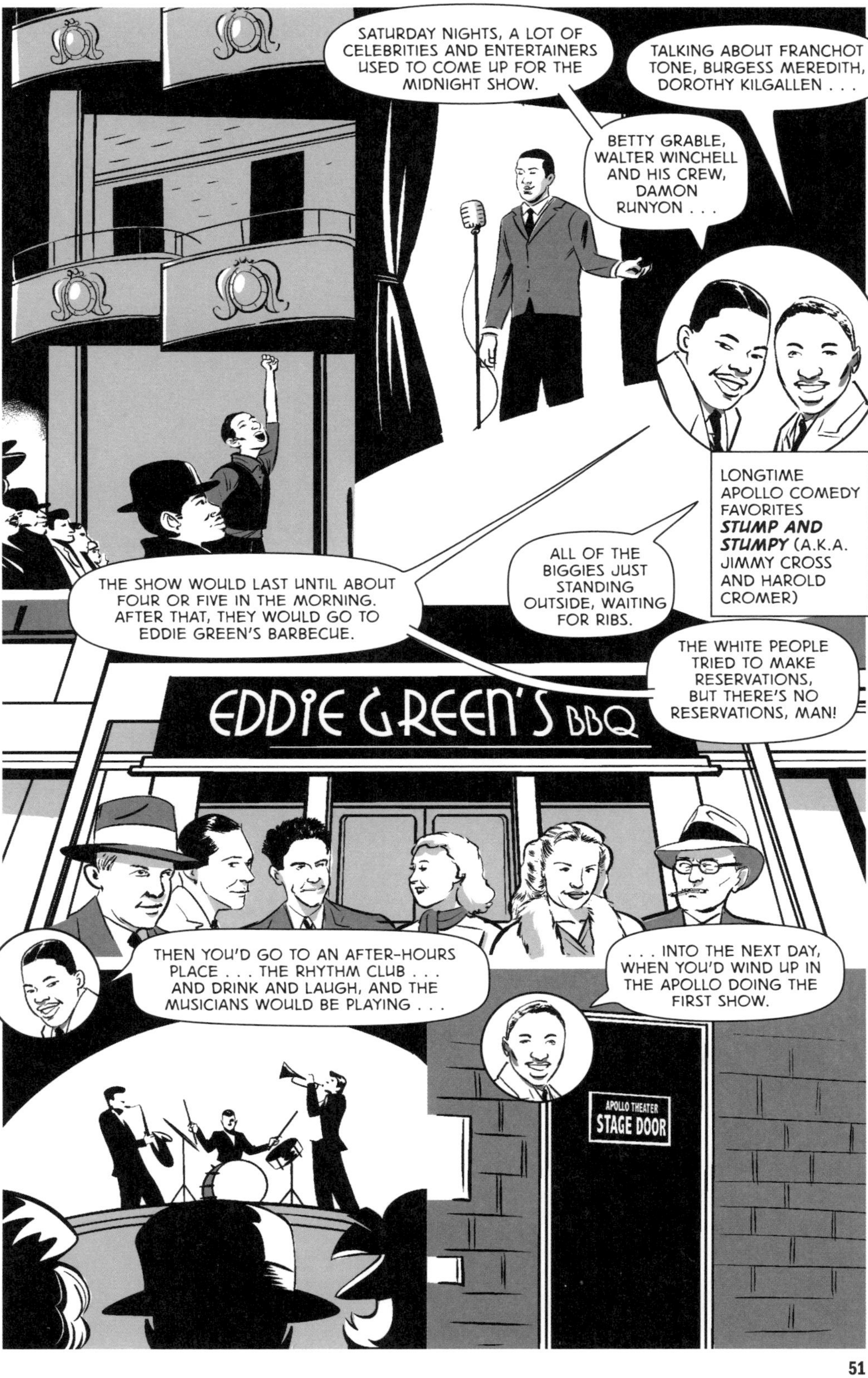
SATURDAY NIGHTS, A LOT OF CELEBRITIES AND ENTERTAINERS USED TO COME UP FOR THE MIDNIGHT SHOW.
TALKING ABOUT FRANCHOT TONE, BURGESS MEREDITH, DOROTHY KILGALLEN . . .
BETTY GRABLE, WALTER WINCHELL AND HIS CREW, DAMON RUNYON . . .
LONGTIME APOLLO COMEDY FAVORITES ***STUMP AND STUMPY*** (A.K.A. JIMMY CROSS AND HAROLD CROMER)
THE SHOW WOULD LAST UNTIL ABOUT FOUR OR FIVE IN THE MORNING. AFTER THAT, THEY WOULD GO TO EDDIE GREEN'S BARBECUE.
ALL OF THE BIGGIES JUST STANDING OUTSIDE, WAITING FOR RIBS.
THE WHITE PEOPLE TRIED TO MAKE RESERVATIONS, BUT THERE'S NO RESERVATIONS, MAN!
EDDIE GREEN'S BBQ
THEN YOU'D GO TO AN AFTER-HOURS PLACE . . . THE RHYTHM CLUB . . . AND DRINK AND LAUGH, AND THE MUSICIANS WOULD BE PLAYING . . .
. . . INTO THE NEXT DAY, WHEN YOU'D WIND UP IN THE APOLLO DOING THE FIRST SHOW.
APOLLO THEATER
STAGE DOOR

DOWNTOWN THEATERS SUCH AS THE PALACE, THE PARAMOUNT, AND THE ROXY ARE IN THE SAME CITY AS THE APOLLO, BUT THEY INHABIT DIFFERENT WORLDS.

Whites might come uptown for a night at the Apollo, but most of the black people who travel downtown are performers.

SOME PERFORMERS PLAY THE APOLLO AND ONE OF THE DOWNTOWN THEATERS SIMULTANEOUSLY, AN AWE-INSPIRING PRACTICE KNOWN AS *DOUBLING*.

Cab Calloway's piano player *Benny Payne* explains the routine in Calloway's autobiography.

STUMPY
(A.K.A. HAROLD CROMER)

WE WERE ALREADY PLAYING FIVE SHOWS A DAY AT THE APOLLO. FOR FOUR DAYS, WE PLAYED *EIGHT* SHOWS A DAY: TWO SHOWS AT THE APOLLO, THEN WE GOT TAXICABS DOWNTOWN TO THE PARAMOUNT . . .

. . . BACK UPTOWN JUST IN TIME FOR THE NEXT SHOW AT THE APOLLO, JUMPED IN CABS AGAIN TO GET DOWNTOWN FOR THE SECOND PARAMOUNT SHOW, CAME BACK UPTOWN, THEN DOWNTOWN AGAIN, THEN BACK UPTOWN FOR THE MIDNIGHT SHOW AT THE APOLLO.

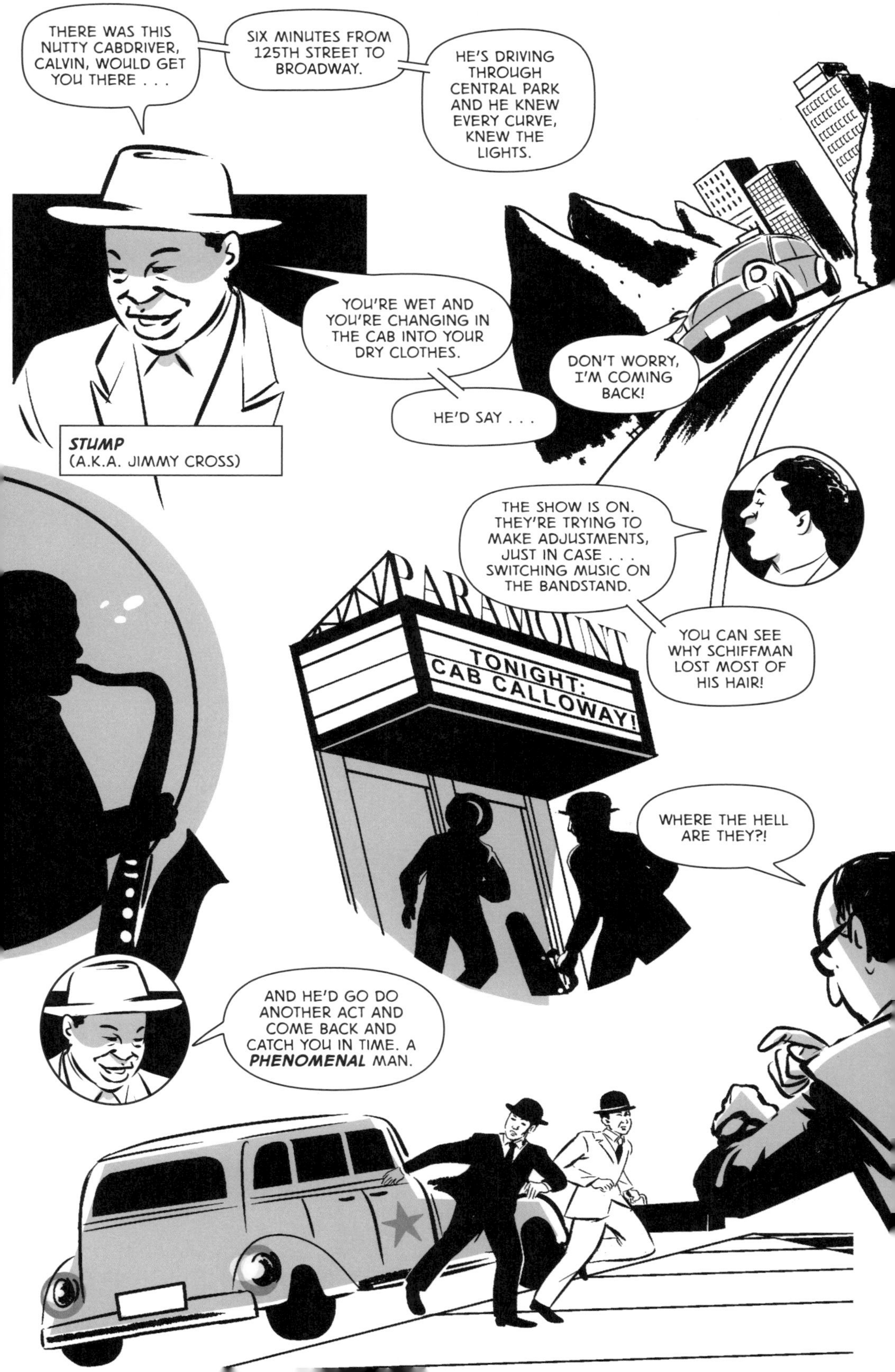
THERE WAS THIS NUTTY CABDRIVER, CALVIN, WOULD GET YOU THERE . . .
SIX MINUTES FROM 125TH STREET TO BROADWAY.
HE'S DRIVING THROUGH CENTRAL PARK AND HE KNEW EVERY CURVE, KNEW THE LIGHTS.
YOU'RE WET AND YOU'RE CHANGING IN THE CAB INTO YOUR DRY CLOTHES.
HE'D SAY . . .
DON'T WORRY, I'M COMING BACK!
STUMP (A.K.A. JIMMY CROSS)
THE SHOW IS ON. THEY'RE TRYING TO MAKE ADJUSTMENTS, JUST IN CASE . . . SWITCHING MUSIC ON THE BANDSTAND.
YOU CAN SEE WHY SCHIFFMAN LOST MOST OF HIS HAIR!
PARAMOUNT
TONIGHT: CAB CALLOWAY!
WHERE THE HELL ARE THEY?!
AND HE'D GO DO ANOTHER ACT AND COME BACK AND CATCH YOU IN TIME. A *PHENOMENAL* MAN.

THE WEEKLY REVUES ARE CREATED BY A HANDFUL OF AFRICAN AMERICAN PRODUCERS—**CHARLIE DAVIS**, **ADDISON CAREY**, **LEONARD HARPER**, **TEDDIE BLACKMAN**, AND **CLARENCE ROBINSON**—WHO WORK WITH THE ACTS.

While one revue unfolds on the Apollo's stage, the following week's show is created, rehearsed, and readied in the theater's basement rehearsal hall.

THE APOLLO CHORUS GIRLS ARE CONSIDERED THE **BEST** LINE IN NEW YORK.

THE PRODUCTION SCHEDULE IS PROBABLY TOUGHEST ON THE CHORUS GIRLS, SAYS FORMER HOOFER CAROL CARTER . . .

THESE POOR GIRLS WOULD DO A SHOW, THEN GO DOWNSTAIRS TO THE REHEARSAL HALL, LEARN THE NEW NUMBERS, GET FITTED FOR COSTUMES—WHICH WERE MADE IN THE APOLLO'S OWN TAILOR SHOP—AND, BY THE TIME THEY HAD FINISHED REHEARSAL, THEY ONLY HAD FIVE OR TEN MINUTES TO GO UPSTAIRS.

CAROL CARTER

THERE WAS A LITTLE EXIT IN THE REHEARSAL HALL SO YOU **WOULDN'T** HAVE TO GO OUT ON 125TH STREET—IN THE BACK, UP THE LITTLE STEPS AND THROUGH THE ALLEY, WHICH WOULD TAKE YOU TO 126TH STREET.

TAKE A LEFT TURN TOWARD EIGHTH AVENUE, RUN THROUGH THE STAGE DOOR . . .

. . . UPSTAIRS TO THE BIG DRESSING ROOM, AND GET INTO THEIR COSTUMES REAL FAST FOR THE NEXT SHOW!

THE MASTERS OF CEREMONY—ESPECIALLY **RALPH COOPER** AND **WILLIE BRYANT**—KEEP THE SHOWS MOVING AND LIVELY, PERFORMANCE AFTER PERFORMANCE, WEEK AFTER WEEK.

Some credit the Apollo with originating the modern-day concept of the master of ceremonies.

WILLIE BRYANT IS BELOVED BY ALL.

LEONARD REED, WHO, LIKE BRYANT, HAS A VERY LIGHT COMPLEXION, IS AN EARLY DANCE PARTNER OF BRYANT'S.

LEONARD REED

WILLIE WAS A GREAT SHOWMAN WHO COULD DO IT ALL. HE WAS ON THE BALL, BUT BITTER.

HE WAS PART NEGRO, AND DOWNTOWN THEY WOULDN'T LET HIM WORK. WILLIE WAS MADE TO STAY IN HARLEM. HE NEVER GOT THE CHANCE TO WORK IN PLACES THAT, SAY, BOB HOPE DID.

RALPH COOPER IS AN APOLLO ICON: SHOWMAN, BANDLEADER, HOOFER, COMEDIAN, MC, CREATOR OF AMATEUR NIGHT, AND MORE . . .

I WENT WHITE. WILLIE DIDN'T. I PLAYED ALL THE WHITE PLACES BY MYSELF . . .

WILLIE WAS A **GENIUS**. ONE OF THE GREATS IN SHOW BUSINESS THAT NEVER GOT ANYWHERE, BECAUSE OF HIS COLOR.

THE WHITE MAN ONLY LETS A FEW NEGROES THROUGH.

PLAYWRIGHT **LOFTEN MITCHELL** REMEMBERS RALPH COOPER IN THE *AMSTERDAM NEWS*—

THE GREATEST COMMENT ABOUT RALPH IS THAT HE USED TO WRITE OUT PASSES FOR US. WE KEPT THE PASSES FOR HIS AUTOGRAPH, THEN PAID OUR WAY INTO THE SHOW.

RALPH COOPER SERVED AS AN IDOL WHEN BLACK CHILDREN HAD PRECIOUS FEW.

AND IN THE DEPRESSION, THAT WAS REALLY **SOMETHING**!

RALPH COOPER AND FRANK SCHIFFMAN CALL A TRUCE.

All of Harlem assumes Schiffman resents Cooper for abandoning him back in 1934.

But Schiffman is far too smart to sacrifice a powerful attraction like Cooper out of personal pique.

Cooper, who is no fan of Schiffman, also knows they need each other.

RALPH COOPER BECOMES ONE OF HARLEM'S LEADING CELEBRITIES, THANKS TO THE SUCCESS OF AMATEUR NIGHT WHICH HE PIONEERS AT THE LAFAYETTE.

FOR MANY WHITES AROUND THE COUNTRY, THE APOLLO RADIO BROADCASTS ARE THEIR FIRST EXPOSURE TO THE NEW SOUNDS OF BLACK SWING MUSIC.

It don't mean a thing...

THROUGH COOPER'S WEDNESDAY "AMATEUR NIGHT IN HARLEM" RADIO SHOW, NOW BROADCAST LIVE FROM THE APOLLO OVER WMCA AND TWENTY-ONE OF ITS AFFILIATED STATIONS AROUND THE COUNTRY, THE APOLLO BECOMES NATIONALLY KNOWN.

Big bands have been the main force in music since the early '20s.

But a new musical form emerges by the time Duke Ellington hits in 1932 with the tune that gave the new sound a name.

WHITE BANDLEADERS ADOPT, REFINE, AND POPULARIZE THE **SWING** SOUND. BUT IT'S THE BLACK MUSICIANS IN THE SEMINAL BLACK ORCHESTRAS, WHO CREATE THE NEW MUSIC.

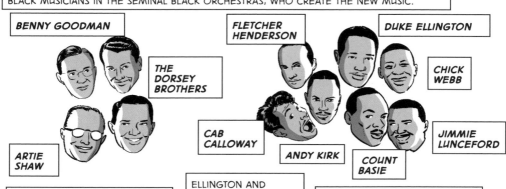

BENNY GOODMAN

THE DORSEY BROTHERS

ARTIE SHAW

FLETCHER HENDERSON

CAB CALLOWAY

ANDY KIRK

DUKE ELLINGTON

CHICK WEBB

JIMMIE LUNCEFORD

COUNT BASIE

DUKE ELLINGTON IS THE EPITOME OF URBAN SOPHISTICATION.

ELLINGTON AND COLLABORATOR BILLY STRAYHORN PRODUCE ETERNAL CLASSICS.

He, more than anyone else, has a right to be discouraged when the music became identified with white bandleaders. Yet he makes it work for him.

ELLINGTON HAS BEEN DEVELOPING AND HONING HIS SOUND FOR MANY YEARS BY THE TIME SWING BECOMES A NATIONAL PHENOMENON.

I MERELY TOOK THE ENERGY IT TAKES TO POUT, AND WROTE SOME BLUES.

WHILE DUKE ELLINGTON APPEALS TO HARLEMITES' SENSE OF STYLE, **COUNT BASIE** APPEALS TO THEIR SENSE OF EXCITEMENT.

HE BECOMES STRANDED ON TOUR IN KANSAS CITY IN THE EARLY '30S, AND SETTLES IN TO THE SCENE IN THE MIDWEST.

JOHN HAMMOND IS CAPTIVATED WHEN HE HEARS BASIE ON HIS CAR RADIO IN A LIVE BROADCAST FROM CHICAGO IN 1935.

Bill Basie is from New Jersey, and is greatly influenced by listening to Fats Waller play at Harlem's Lincoln Theater.

BASIE'S BAND EARNS A SIX-WEEK RUN AT THE ROSELAND BALLROOM DOWNTOWN IN NEW YORK.

But what really makes the band is their 1937 debut at the Apollo.

BASIE WAS SCARED BECAUSE HE REALIZED THAT UNLESS HE WENT OVER **BIG** AT THE APOLLO, IT WOULD TAKE HIM MUCH LONGER TO MAKE IT.

JOHN HAMMOND

AS SOON AS THEY PLAYED "I MAY BE WRONG," I KNEW BASIE WAS IN.

The Basie band become one of the most popular and influential outfits in jazz and continue as Apollo favorites for decades.

WHILE A LOCAL REVIEW IS KIND TO BASIE, THE REVIEWER RAVES ABOUT HIS FEATURED SINGER . . .

The sensation of the show is the statuesque and effervescent **Billie Holiday** . . . *the Apollo, the audience, and all the fixtures truly belong to her.*

ONE DAY, RALPH COOPER STOPS INTO A FAVORITE WATERING HOLE FOR A DRINK.

BY THE TIME THE APOLLO OPENS, BILLIE HAS BEEN SCUFFLING AROUND VARIOUS HARLEM DIVES FOR A FEW YEARS, AND MAKES A COUPLE OF LITTLE-NOTICED RECORDS.

COOPER LOVES BILLIE.

HE TOUTS HER TO FRANK SCHIFFMAN.

YOU NEVER HEARD SINGING SO SLOW, SO LAZY, WITH SUCH A DRAWL . . . IT AIN'T THE BLUES—I DON'T KNOW WHAT IT IS, BUT YOU GOT TO HEAR HER!

COOPER BUYS HER AN EVENING GOWN AND SLIPPERS.

HE PUTS HIS BAND THROUGH ITS PACES, FAMILIARIZING THEM WITH BILLIE'S ARRANGEMENTS.

THE APOLLO BOOKS HER FOR THE WEEK OF APRIL 19, 1935, ON A SHOW HEADLINED BY COOPER AND HIS ORCHESTRA.

In tiny type near the bottom of the bill, she is incorrectly listed as "Billie Halliday."

BILLIE IS NEARLY OVERCOME BY STAGE FRIGHT.

COMEDIAN PIGMEAT MARKHAM GENTLY NUDGES HER ON.

ONCE THE SPOTLIGHT HITS HER— LIKE MOONLIGHT—SHE REGAINS HER COMPOSURE.

What a little moonlight can do...

ENCORE!!

ENCORE!!

THEY WILL NOT LET HER GO WITHOUT AN ENCORE.

WOMEN ARE KEY TO THE SWING ERA, ALTHOUGH USUALLY AS FEATURED PERFORMERS IN THE BIG BANDS, NOT HEADLINERS.

Billie Holiday earns only seventy dollars a week with Count Basie, out of which she also has to maintain her wardrobe.

Life in the male world of the big bands is tough for women.

SOME, LIKE LENA HORNE, WHO LEAVES THE COTTON CLUB AND JOINS THE NOBLE SISSLE ORCHESTRA, HAVE MORE STAR POWER THAN THEIR BANDLEADERS.

NOBLE SISSLE

THE NONPAREIL IS **ELLA FITZGERALD**.

The story of her early days as a nervous amateur is frequently recounted— usually erroneously placing her at the Apollo's Amateur Night.

IN FACT, SHE IS DISCOVERED IN 1934 BY FRIENDS OF BANDLEADER **CHICK WEBB** AT AN AMATEUR-NIGHT PERFORMANCE AT SCHIFFMAN'S NEIGHBORING HARLEM OPERA HOUSE.

COMEDIAN **TIMMIE ROGERS** WAS THERE THAT NIGHT.

SHE DIDN'T KNOW THAT SHE COULD SING THAT WELL. SHE STARTED AS A **LINDY HOPPER** DANCING AT THE SAVOY BALLROOM.

SHE STOPPED THE SHOW COLD. THEY MADE HER TAKE AN ENCORE. SHE BROKE THE MOTHER *UP!*

The object of my affection...

ELLA IS INTRODUCED TO BANDLEADER CHICK WEBB, AND A CLASSIC PAIRING BEGINS.

WEBB IS A SUPERB DRUMMER WHOSE THUNDERING SOLOS ALSO ATTRACT A LARGE, SERIOUS JAZZ AUDIENCE.

Chick Webb has been thrilling the Lindy Hoppers at Harlem's *Savoy Ballroom* for years.

Chick is small and frail from an ongoing bout with tuberculosis, and he sits, hunchbacked, behind his massive drum set.

Chick's band with Ella Fitzgerald become Apollo favorites.

ELLA HELPS BRING CHICK NATIONAL PROMINENCE.

Ella, on the other hand, is large, gawky, and plain-looking.

Two beautiful ugly ducklings, they are blessed with abundant talent, and they are drawn together in a bond of love, respect, and support.

When Webb dies in 1939, she takes over the band and keeps it together for another three years.

FRANK SCHIFFMAN TELLS HIS SON JACK THAT THE MOST *MOVING* THING HE EVER HEARD WAS ELLA FITZGERALD SINGING "MY BUDDY" OVER WEBB'S CASKET.

My Buddy...

THE BIG BANDS ARE FEATURED ATTRACTIONS, BUT ALSO PLAY FOR ALL THE OTHER ACTS ON THE BILL.

ANDY KIRK'S CLOUDS OF JOY

BILL "BOJANGLES" ROBINSON

INSTEAD OF INJECTING YOURSELF, YOU'D SOFTEN DOWN, SO YOU COULD HEAR EVERY ONE OF THEIR STEPS.

I ENJOYED THE PERFORMERS THAT I BACKED UP.

WE ALWAYS HAD REGARD FOR THE ARTIST, WHATEVER HE WAS DOING.

WHEN WE DID *OUR* THING, THAT WAS WHEN WE'D FEATURE *OUR* MUSIC.

FOR THE FIRST FEW YEARS, ALL EXCEPT THE MIGHTIEST BIG BANDS PLAY IN THE *PIT*.

WHEN IT IS TIME FOR THE BAND'S SPECIALTY NUMBER, THE CURTAIN COMES DOWN, AND THE COMICS COME OUT TO COVER FOR THEM . . .

. . . AS THE BAND MEMBERS PICK UP THEIR INSTRUMENTS AND HEAD BACKSTAGE . . .

IN ANOTHER PRACTICE SOME CONDEMN AS DEGRADING, UNTIL THE LATE '40S MOST BLACK MALE COMICS WEAR EXAGGERATED BURNT-CORK "BLACKFACE" MAKEUP.

. . . TO THE FEATURED BANDSTAND ONSTAGE WHERE THEY PERFORM THEIR BIG NUMBER.

Many bandleaders find this degrading, and by the late '30s it is eliminated, and the stage is built out over the old pit.

Despite protests from the NAACP and others, the comics say they feel naked without it.

THE APOLLO BOASTS A VIRTUAL STOCK COMPANY OF THE *FINEST* COMEDIANS.

DUSTY FLETCHER

JOHN "SPIDER BRUCE" MASON

JOHNNY LEE LONG

JIMMIE BASKETTE

SPO-DEE-O-DEE

TIM "KINGFISH" MOORE

They're presented in sketches or skits involving up to a half dozen people or more.

I CALL THEM *LEBENSBILDER* . . . PICTURES OF LIFE.

FRANK SCHIFFMAN

DEWEY "PIGMEAT" MARKHAM PROBABLY PLAYS THE APOLLO MORE OFTEN THAN ANY OTHER PERFORMER INTO THE '70S.

During the '30s he is on the bill every week for four years.

HE IS MOST FAMOUS FOR THE *"**HERE COME THE JUDGE**"* ROUTINE.

INTRODUCED IN 1929, IT'S MADE NATIONALLY FAMOUS BY SAMMY DAVIS JR. IN THE LATE '60S.

MARKHAM ALSO CLAIMS TO HAVE INVENTED THE COMICAL DANCE MOVE *"**TRUCKIN'**."*

IT WAS THE BIGGEST THING IN THE COUNTRY!

THEN ONE DAY I SAW AN AL JOLSON MOVIE, AND THERE IN A BIG COLORED SEQUENCE WAS CAB CALLOWAY AND HIS BAND TRUCKIN' ALL OVER HEAVEN.

BUT OF ALL THE EARLY COMEDIANS, PROBABLY THE MOST BELOVED AND MOST SUCCESSFUL IS *JACKIE "MOMS" MABLEY*.

THERE WAS MY TRUCK GONE DOWN THE DRAIN, JUST LIKE *"**HERE COME THE JUDGE**."*

A regular for years at Connie's Inn, Moms starts at the Apollo in the early days at eighty-five dollars a week . . .

. . . becomes a headliner in black theaters and white nightclubs . . .

APOLLO

FEATURING "MOMS" MABLEY!

. . . and by the early '70s commands a salary of $8,500 a week at the Apollo.

LORETTA MARY AIKEN IS KNOWN TO EVERYONE AS "MOMS."

One of the early monologists, she delights the Apollo with folksy tales.

MY CHILDREN!

YEAH, MOMS, YOU RIGHT!

SHE PLAYS A SILLY, RANDY, BUT SAGE OLD BAT WHOSE *"MOMS' SHUFFLE"* IS ALMOST AS WELL KNOWN AS PIGMEAT'S TRUCKIN'.

AN OLD MAN CAN'T DO NOTHIN' FOR ME BUT BRING ME A MESSAGE FROM A YOUNG ONE.

MY SLOGAN IS, BY ALL MEANS DO WHAT YOU WANT TO DO, BUT KNOW WHAT YOU'RE DOIN'.

DANCE LEGEND *HONI COLES* IS ANOTHER KEY FIGURE WHO IS A PART OF THE APOLLO FOR MOST OF ITS HISTORY.

AT ONE TIME IN THE WORLD OF SHOW BUSINESS, THE TAP DANCER, OR HOOFER, WAS PROBABLY THE MOST IMPORTANT ACT ON THE AVERAGE BILL.

HE WAS THE BEST DRESSED, THE BEST CONDITIONED, THE MOST CONSCIENTIOUS PERFORMER ON ANY BILL.

In the early '30s, he develops a style known as *"high-speed rhythm tap."*

HE TALKS ABOUT THE EARLY DAYS OF DANCE AT THE APOLLO IN THE *AMSTERDAM NEWS*:

HE COULD OPEN THE SHOW, CLOSE IT, OR FILL ANY SPOT, ESPECIALLY THE TROUBLE SPOTS.

AND IN SPITE OF BEING THE LEAST PAID, HE WAS THE ACT TO "STOP THE SHOW."

COLES MEETS **CHOLLY ATKINS** WHILE TRAVELING WITH CAB CALLOWAY'S BAND.

After World War II, they form the team of Coles and Atkins.

But by that time the golden era of the dancers and the big bands has passed, making the duo "the last of the class acts."

FRANK SCHIFFMAN IS A TREMENDOUS FAN.

Through the '50s, Coles and Atkins traditionally reopen the Apollo, with Billy Eckstine, in August, after its usual summer break for renovations.

IN THE EARLY '60S, COLES BECOMES THE APOLLO'S **PRODUCTION MANAGER**.

Along with Atkins, he's an important mentor to all types of performers until his death in 1992.

IN THE '30S, AND FOREVER THEREAFTER, **DANCE** IS A VITAL PART OF THE APOLLO EXPERIENCE.

A LOT OF DANCERS WERE CHALLENGED RIGHT THERE ONSTAGE!

WANTA-BE TAP DANCERS, GONNA-BE TAP DANCERS, TRIED-TO-BE TAP DANCERS.

SANDMAN SIMS

WHEN BIG-NAME DANCERS PLAYED THE APOLLO, THERE WAS NOTHING IN THE AUDIENCE BUT DANCERS WITH THEIR TAP SHOES.

UP IN THE BALCONY, DANCERS—AND THE FIRST SIX ROWS, YOU SAW NOTHING BUT TAP DANCERS.

HEY, MAN, YOU AIN'T DOING NUTHIN'.

LET ME COME UP THERE AND SEE WHAT YOU CAN REALLY DO.

COMPETITION FORCES DANCERS INTO MORE AND MORE ACROBATIC STUNTS, AS EACH ACT TRIES TO OUTDO THE OTHER.

Debilitating injuries shorten careers and sometimes leave dancers crippled.

PERHAPS THE MOST SPECTACULAR DANCE ACTS OF ALL TIME ARE THE **BERRY BROTHERS** AND THE **NICHOLAS BROTHERS**.

Known as "*flash acts*" because of their blinding speed and fancy steps, they are among only a handful of dance acts that can headline an Apollo show.

ONCE, TO TOP THE NICHOLAS BROTHERS IN A 1936 CHALLENGE MEET, ANANIAS BERRY DEVISES A FINALE WHERE HE AND BROTHER JIMMY LEAP FROM THE BANDSTAND . . .

. . . AS THE BAND PLAYS ITS FINAL NOTE, AND CRASH TWELVE FEET DOWN INTO TENDON-RIPPING SPLITS ON BOTH SIDES OF BROTHER WARREN . . .

. . . WHO ALSO DOES A SPLIT AFTER COMPLETING A TWISTING BACK SOMERSAULT.

THE BERRY BROTHERS BEGIN WITH ELLINGTON AT THE COTTON CLUB, TOUR ABROAD, HELP OPEN RADIO CITY MUSIC HALL IN 1932, AND ALSO WORK IN HOLLYWOOD.

HAROLD AND FAYARD NICHOLAS— EIGHT AND FOURTEEN—OPEN AT THE COTTON CLUB.

Ananias, weakened by years of bodily abuse in pursuit of his art, dies in 1951. He is just thirty-nine.

The boys, clad in top hats and evening clothes, become the darlings of Harlem.

WHEN THEY DEBUT AT THE APOLLO ON MARCH 2, 1934, THEY HAVE ALREADY MADE THE FILM *KID MILLIONS* WITH EDDIE CANTOR—WHICH WOULD COME OUT LATER THAT YEAR— AND STARRED IN THE ZIEGFELD FOLLIES ON BROADWAY.

THE NICHOLAS BROTHERS ARE AN ALL-AROUND ACT, COMBINING WILD AIRBORNE SPLITS WITH TASTY TAPPING AND SINGING.

HAROLD EVEN DOES IMITATIONS OF CAB CALLOWAY AND LOUIS ARMSTRONG.

HOWEVER, THE ONES TO WHOM ALL THE APOLLO'S DANCERS OWE THE GREATEST DEBT ARE **BILL "BOJANGLES" ROBINSON** AND **JOHN BUBBLES**.

BILL ROBINSON BEGINS HIS CAREER AS A "PICK"—FROM THE DEROGATORY TERM FOR A SMALL BLACK CHILD: PICKANINNY.

These fast-stepping black children are employed as surefire *showstoppers* to bolster the white star's vaudeville act.

STARDOM DOESN'T COME UNTIL THE SMASH HIT 1928 STAGE PRODUCTION OF LEW LESLIE'S *BLACKBIRDS*, WHEN BOJANGLES IS FIFTY YEARS OLD . . .

SUDDENLY, HARLEM WAS CRAZY ABOUT BOJANGLES.

THE LEGENDARY **ETHEL WATERS**

EVERYBODY IN HARLEM SAID BOJANGLES WAS A MAGNIFICENT DANCER.

BO, BO!

THE YEAR SCHIFFMAN TAKES OVER THE APOLLO, BOJANGLES ACHIEVES HIS GREATEST FAME, STARRING WITH AND COACHING SHIRLEY TEMPLE IN THE FILM *THE LITTLE COLONEL*.

JOHN BUBBLES INVENTS **RHYTHM TAP**—THE STYLE HONI COLES MASTERS AND SPEEDS UP.

BUBBLES AND PARTNER **FORD L. "BUCK" WASHINGTON** BRING "DOWNTOWN" STYLE TO THE APOLLO.

Buck and Bubbles are already headliners on Broadway: In 1935, Bubbles is George Gershwin's personal choice to play Sportin' Life in *Porgy and Bess*.

WE WERE AN "AW!" ACT. WE WALKED ON THE STAGE UPTOWN IN A DOWNTOWN STYLE, THEY LOOKED AT US AND SAID, "AW!"

AT THE SAME TIME, BUCK PLAYS STOP-TIME ON THE PIANO IN THE LAZIEST MANNER IMAGINABLE.

HE FALLS OFF THE STOOL, REMEMBERING TO REACH UP FROM THE FLOOR JUST IN TIME TO PLUNK ONE NOTE EVERY SIXTEEN BARS.

DANCER PAUL DRAPER DESCRIBES THEM IN MARSHALL AND JEAN STEARNS'S BOOK, *JAZZ DANCE*:

PAUL DRAPER

BUBBLES HAS A CASUAL APPROACH TO THE COMPLICATED STEPS HE EXECUTES. HIS NONCHALANT MANNER CONTRADICTS THE INCREDIBLE THINGS HIS FEET ARE DOING.

YOU THINK HE IS JUST GOING TO STROLL AROUND THE STAGE, WHEN PRESTO, HE'LL TOSS OFF A BURST OF SIGHT AND SOUND THAT YOU JUST CAN'T BELIEVE.

DURING THE 1930S, THERE ARE AS MANY AS FIFTY TOP DANCE ACTS PLAYING REGULARLY AT THE APOLLO . . .

. . . ALONG WITH DOZENS OF OTHER COMEDIANS, SINGERS, EVEN ACROBATS CONTRIBUTING TO FRANK SCHIFFMAN'S TREASURED *VAUDEVILLE-VARIETY FORMAT*.

And, the Apollo continues the process of "nurturing" them, begun in the 1920s at the Lafayette.

SCHIFFMAN HAS A CIRCLE OF COLLEAGUES IN NIGHTCLUBS AND THEATERS WHO BREAK IN ACTS FOR THE APOLLO.

SOME CHARACTERIZE THE ARRANGEMENT LESS CHARITABLY.

THE APOLLO HAD A WORKING ARRANGEMENT WITH THE HOWARD THEATER IN WASHINGTON, THE ROYAL IN BALTIMORE, AND THE EARLE IN PHILLY.

IF YOU WANTED TO PLAY THE APOLLO, YOU HAD TO GET BOOKED FOR THE LOWER PRICE AT THE OTHER THEATERS.

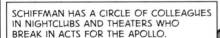

SANDMAN SIMS

JOHN HAMMOND

HE WOULD TAKE YOU OUT AND HOLD YOU AWHILE. GROOM YOU AND WORK YOU AROUND TILL YOU GOT A REAL GOOD ACT. BUILD YOUR ACT UP, AND BRING IT BACK TO THE APOLLO.

No doubt, Schiffman, the wily competitor, has a financial motive—and the theater owners regularly share contract prices, box office numbers, and critical reviews.

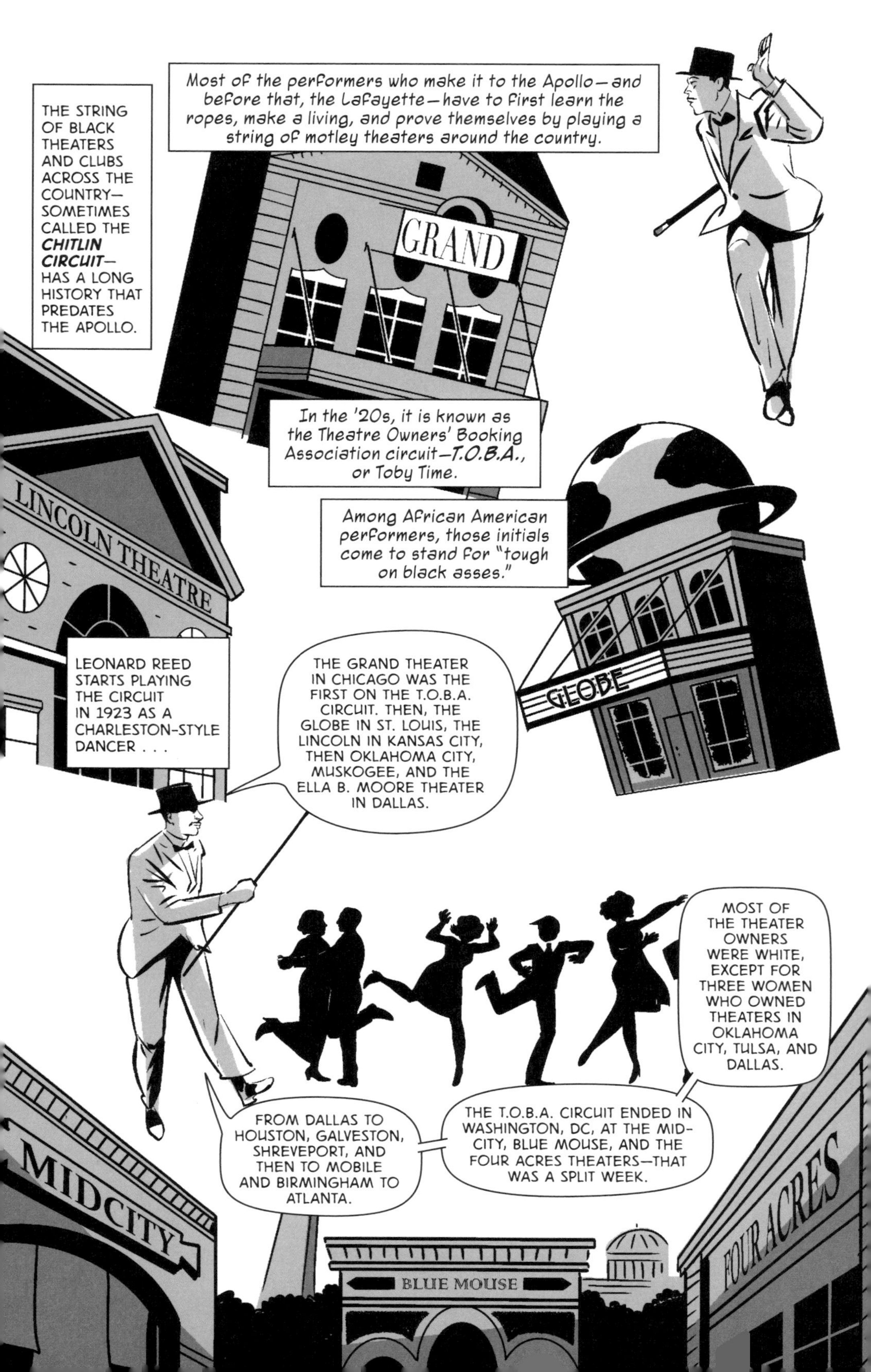
THE STRING OF BLACK THEATERS AND CLUBS ACROSS THE COUNTRY—SOMETIMES CALLED THE ***CHITLIN CIRCUIT***—HAS A LONG HISTORY THAT PREDATES THE APOLLO.
Most of the performers who make it to the Apollo—and before that, the Lafayette—have to first learn the ropes, make a living, and prove themselves by playing a string of motley theaters around the country.
GRAND
In the '20s, it is known as the Theatre Owners' Booking Association circuit—*T.O.B.A.*, or Toby Time.
LINCOLN THEATRE
Among African American performers, those initials come to stand for "tough on black asses."
LEONARD REED STARTS PLAYING THE CIRCUIT IN 1923 AS A CHARLESTON-STYLE DANCER . . .
THE GRAND THEATER IN CHICAGO WAS THE FIRST ON THE T.O.B.A. CIRCUIT. THEN, THE GLOBE IN ST. LOUIS, THE LINCOLN IN KANSAS CITY, THEN OKLAHOMA CITY, MUSKOGEE, AND THE ELLA B. MOORE THEATER IN DALLAS.
GLOBE
MOST OF THE THEATER OWNERS WERE WHITE, EXCEPT FOR THREE WOMEN WHO OWNED THEATERS IN OKLAHOMA CITY, TULSA, AND DALLAS.
FROM DALLAS TO HOUSTON, GALVESTON, SHREVEPORT, AND THEN TO MOBILE AND BIRMINGHAM TO ATLANTA.
THE T.O.B.A. CIRCUIT ENDED IN WASHINGTON, DC, AT THE MID-CITY, BLUE MOUSE, AND THE FOUR ACRES THEATERS—THAT WAS A SPLIT WEEK.
MIDCITY
BLUE MOUSE
FOUR ACRES

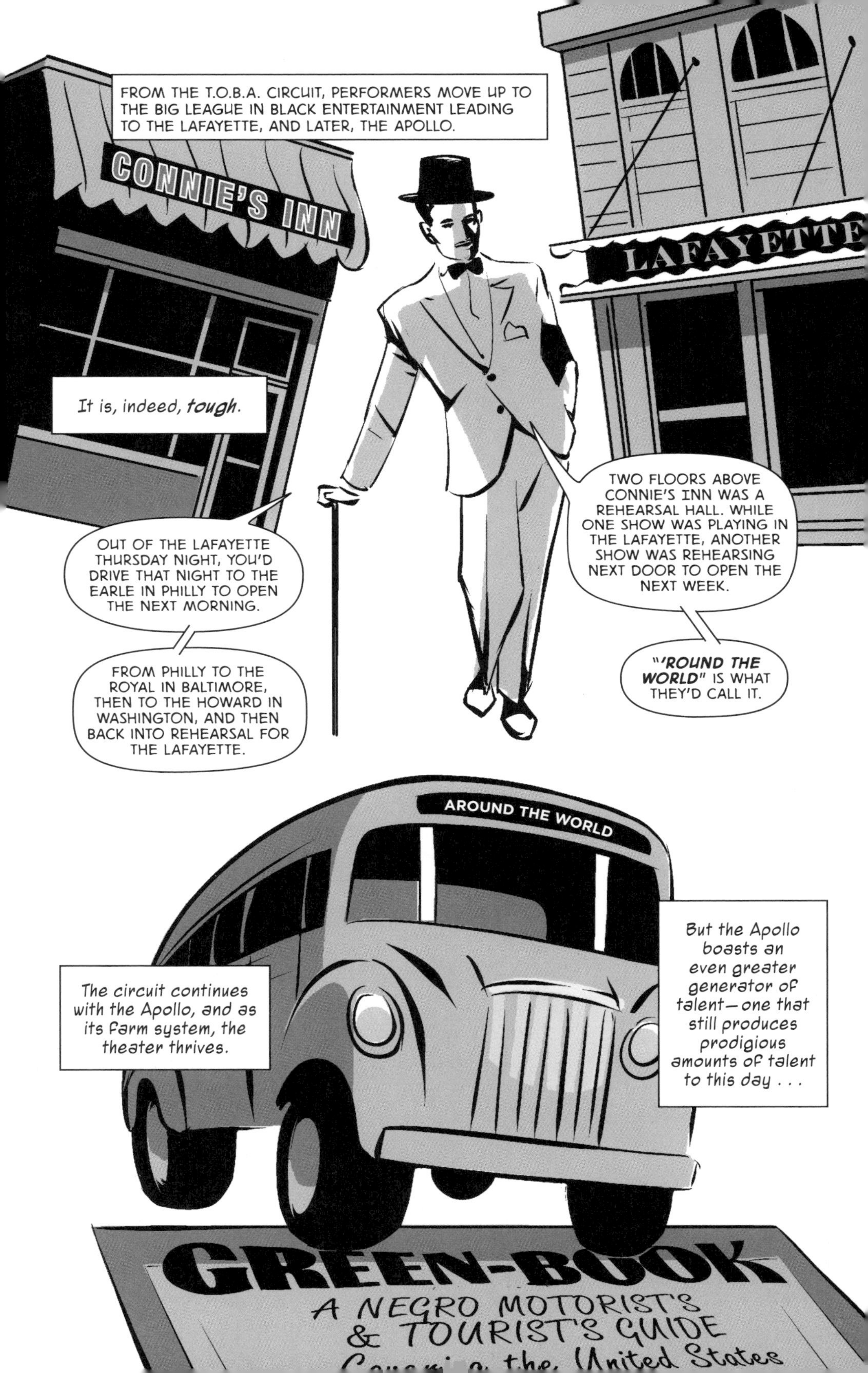
FROM THE T.O.B.A. CIRCUIT, PERFORMERS MOVE UP TO THE BIG LEAGUE IN BLACK ENTERTAINMENT LEADING TO THE LAFAYETTE, AND LATER, THE APOLLO.
CONNIE'S INN
LAFAYETTE
It is, indeed, *tough*.
OUT OF THE LAFAYETTE THURSDAY NIGHT, YOU'D DRIVE THAT NIGHT TO THE EARLE IN PHILLY TO OPEN THE NEXT MORNING.
FROM PHILLY TO THE ROYAL IN BALTIMORE, THEN TO THE HOWARD IN WASHINGTON, AND THEN BACK INTO REHEARSAL FOR THE LAFAYETTE.
TWO FLOORS ABOVE CONNIE'S INN WAS A REHEARSAL HALL. WHILE ONE SHOW WAS PLAYING IN THE LAFAYETTE, ANOTHER SHOW WAS REHEARSING NEXT DOOR TO OPEN THE NEXT WEEK.
"***'ROUND THE WORLD***" IS WHAT THEY'D CALL IT.
AROUND THE WORLD
The circuit continues with the Apollo, and as its farm system, the theater thrives.
But the Apollo boasts an even greater generator of talent—one that still produces prodigious amounts of talent to this day . . .
GREEN-BOOK
A NEGRO MOTORIST'S
& TOURIST'S GUIDE

CHAPTER 4

Amateur Night and the Apollo Audience

AMATEUR NIGHT, THE GREAT APOLLO TRADITION THAT HAS PRODUCED SO MUCH TALENT, COMES TO TELEVISION IN 1987 ON THE POPULAR LATE-NIGHT SERIES *SHOWTIME AT THE APOLLO*.

The long-running show keeps Amateur Night alive for new generations.

IT'S FUN AND EXCITING!

HOST
STEVE HARVEY

WE LOVE THE IDEA OF HELPING DISCOVER GREAT NEW TALENT.

AND WE GET A SLIGHTLY PERVERSE PLEASURE SEEING A HAPLESS AMATEUR BOOED OFFSTAGE.

However, the TV broadcast reflects a very different era.

Now, the sky's the limit, and urban music and urban popular culture rule.

Top stars emerge from everywhere, thanks to the Internet.

But back in the pre-television days, it's a very different environment for generations of African American hopefuls.

The legend of Amateur Night at the Apollo builds over decades, from thousands of individual stories . . .

JAMES BROWN, MEET SANDMAN SIMS.

I GAVE HIM A PAIR OF WHITE SNEAKERS.

SOME OTHER GUY GAVE HIM A PAIR OF PANTS. ANOTHER GUY GAVE HIM A SHIRT TO DO THE AMATEUR SHOW THAT NIGHT.

IN THE '50S, JAMES BROWN CAME TO NEW YORK, AND HE DIDN'T HAVE NO SHOES, NOTHING TO DANCE IN, NOTHING TO SING IN.

Harlem or Bust?

LEONARD REED IS THE APOLLO'S MANAGER AT THE TIME.

HE **BEGGED** ME TO PUT HIM ON THE AMATEUR HOUR.

NO, WE'RE FILLED UP!

I'M BETTER THAN ANYBODY ON THE SHOW! I'M BETTER THAN LITTLE WILLIE JOHN!

OK, WE'LL SEE . . .

I Criiiiied, I Criiiiiied,

HE **RIPPED** THAT SHOW APART!

THROUGHOUT THE APOLLO'S HISTORY, THE INNER CITIES, FACTORY TOWNS, AND DUSTY CROSSROADS OF AMERICA ARE FILLED WITH DREAMERS.

THESE COMMUNITIES OFFER LITTLE TO STIMULATE YOUNGSTERS WITH IMAGINATION, AND—DARE THEY HOPE IT—TALENT.

WHILE STARSTRUCK WHITE KIDS TRADITIONALLY HEAD FOR HOLLYWOOD OR BROADWAY . . .

. . . THEIR BLACK COUNTERPARTS BUCK THE ODDS AND BEAT A PATH FOR HARLEM AND THE WEDNESDAY NIGHT AMATEUR SHOW AT THE APOLLO.

THEY KNOW THEY WILL FACE THE TOUGHEST AND MOST DEMANDING AUDIENCE IN THE WORLD . . .

. . . A CROWD NOTORIOUS, ESPECIALLY ON AMATEUR NIGHT, FOR ITS VOCAL AND SOMETIMES PHYSICAL DEMONSTRATIONS OF DISPLEASURE.

THEY KNOW ABOUT *PORTO RICO*, THE CRAZY STAGEHAND WHO SERVES AS THE AUDIENCE'S HIT MAN AND EXECUTIONER.

THEY KNOW THEY MIGHT NOT EVEN PASS THE PRE-SHOW AUDITION, MUCH LESS WIN THE CONTEST.

THEY HAVE FAITH IN THEMSELVES, AND THEY KNOW THE APOLLO AUDIENCE IS AN ASTUTE JUDGE OF TALENT AND THE MOST APPRECIATIVE AUDIENCE IN THE WORLD.

AND, OF COURSE, THEY KNOW THAT FOUR FIRST-PLACE WINS GUARANTEES A WEEK'S PROFESSIONAL ENGAGEMENT AT THE THEATER.

YET THEY SHOW UP AND TRY—AN ESTIMATED 15,000, JUST IN THE FIRST TWENTY YEARS OF AMATEUR NIGHT AT THE APOLLO.

IF THEY CAN PLEASE THE AUDIENCE AT THE APOLLO, THEY CAN PLEASE ANY CROWD.

THE GREAT SOUL STAR **JOE TEX** IS KNOWN AS JOE ARRINGTON JR. IN 1955 WHEN HE DECIDES TO TAKE HIS CHANCE.

NEWLY ARRIVED FROM BAYTOWN, TEXAS, JOE SETTLES IN A DINGY ROOMING HOUSE, GETS A JOB IN A CLOTHING STORE, AND FILLS HIS EVENINGS SINGING ON STREET CORNERS WITH HIS BUDDIES.

HEMPSTEAD, LONG ISLAND.

YOU'RE GREAT, MAN! YOU OUGHTA GIVE THE APOLLO A TRY.

NAW . . .

SORRY, THERE'S A THREE-MONTH WAITING LIST.

ALL I WANT IS A **CHANCE**.

AUDITIONS

WE'LL SEND YOU A POSTCARD WHEN IT'S YOUR TURN. COME BACK NEXT MONDAY AND SIGN UP.

THE BASEMENT REHEARSAL HALL WAS ORIGINALLY A WHITE CLUB—JOE WARD'S COCONUT GROVE, SAID TO BE THE SITE OF LOUIS ARMSTRONG'S FIRST NEW YORK GIG.

When the Coconut Grove closed in 1930, it became the Rathskeller. Hence the leftover fake stone buttresses, exposed wood beams, and Germanic cityscapes.

THERE BOBBY SCHIFFMAN JUST HAPPENS TO SIT NEXT TO JOE, AND HE GETS AN EARFUL.

OK, KID, OK! I'LL GIVE YOU A SHOT TONIGHT. BE HERE AT TEN SHARP.

MAN, I'M GOING TO BE AT THE APOLLO TONIGHT! I'M GOING TO BE ON AMATEUR NIGHT! CHECK ME OUT!

WAITING TO GO ON, JOE SPOTS A SHORT, POLISHED TREE STUMP SITTING ON A PEDESTAL.

It is the remains of the fabled *Tree of Hope*—a chestnut tree that once stood outside the stage doors for the Lafayette Theater and Connie's Inn . . .

73

Before the tree is cut down to widen Seventh Avenue in 1933, it is a favorite gathering place for out-of-work performers.

BOOKING AGENTS REALIZE IT IS A GOOD, INFORMAL HIRING HALL, AND MANY JOBS ARE LANDED THERE.

The tree becomes a lucky charm for entertainers.

MANY GET A PIECE OF THE TREE OF HOPE WHEN IT IS CUT DOWN.

Ralph Cooper brings the largest chunk to the Apollo.

WAIT JUST A MINUTE, YOUNG MAN. YOU FORGOT TO TOUCH THE TREE OF HOPE!

IT BECOMES A SACRED AMATEUR NIGHT TRADITION—AMATEURS MUST TOUCH THE STUMP BEFORE GOING ON.

Joe wins the twenty-five-dollar first prize that night, then three more times, and gets a week's professional booking.

HENRY GLOVER OF KING RECORDS CATCHES JOE AT THE APOLLO AND SIGNS HIM.

Joe Tex goes on to become James Brown's labelmate and rival, and boasts million-selling hits such as "Hold What You've Got" and "Skinny Legs and All."

ALSO NEWLY ARRIVED IN NEW YORK, YOUNG PEARL BAILEY—WHO WOULD ONE DAY BOAST THE APOLLO BOX OFFICE RECORD—DECIDES TO GIVE AMATEUR NIGHT A TRY IN 1934.

So she heads down the street to the Apollo.

She first tries the Harlem Opera House's amateur contest, but arrives too late.

ERSKINE HAWKINS'S BAMA STATE COLLEGIANS

WHEN THE HAND WAS HELD OVER THE HEADS, I WON . . . FOR "IN MY SOLITUDE," ARRANGEMENT HOMEMADE.

IN HER AUTOBIOGRAPHY, *THE RAW PEARL*, PEARL BAILEY REMEMBERS BEING LUCKY IN MORE WAYS THAN ONE . . .

FOR THERE—THAT NIGHT—A YOUNG GIRL WALKED ON STAGE, OPENED HER MOUTH, AND THE AUDIENCE THAT HAD STARTED TO SNICKER ENDED UP CHEERING.

HER NAME WAS ELLA FITZGERALD. SHE WON, AND THAT VOICE WILL GO DOWN IN HISTORY.

I'M GRATEFUL I DIDN'T GO DOWN THE STREET TO THE OPERA HOUSE. I *DOUBT* I WOULD HAVE MADE IT THERE.

IT IS IMPOSSIBLE TO SAY WHICH AMATEUR NIGHT TRIUMPH IS THE MOST SIGNIFICANT.

SHE IS ONLY SIXTEEN YEARS OLD, A SINGER IN THE CHOIR AT THE MOUNT ZION BAPTIST CHURCH IN NEWARK, NEW JERSEY.

THE **COOTIE WILLIAMS** BAND WITH LEAD VOCALIST **EDDIE "CLEANHEAD" VINSON**

I REMEMBER HER STANDING BEHIND US, TREMBLING, SCARED TO COME ON.

But a leading contender surely is **Sarah Vaughan**'s in October 1942.

SARAH VAUGHAN DID "BODY AND SOUL." I'LL NEVER FORGET THAT. SHE BROKE THE HOUSE UP!

BILLY ECKSTINE—THE "FABULOUS MR. B"—IS IN THE APOLLO THAT EVENING CASHING HIS PAYCHECK FROM THE **EARL HINES** BAND.

GO ON OUT THERE, EVERYTHING'S GONNA BE ALL RIGHT. DO YOUR BEST, DON'T BE AFRAID.

Body and Sooooooul...

HE DECIDES TO STAY AND CATCH THE AMATEUR SHOW.

IT WAS LIKE A GRADE-B MOVIE . .

I RUSHED BACKSTAGE AND TOLD HER SHE MUST TRY OUT FOR THE EARL HINES BAND!

The "Divine Sarah" wins Hines over, too, and goes on to become one of the most important female jazz vocalists of all time.

Apollo Amateur Night Winners Hall of Fame

SARAH VAUGHN

PEARL BAILEY

GLADYS KNIGHT

RUTH BROWN

LESLIE UGGAMS

JIMI HENDRIX

DIONNE WARWICK

MICHAEL JACKSON

SCREAMIN' JAY HAWKINS

BILLY WARD OF THE DOMINOES

KING CURTIS

FRANKIE LYMON

BILL KENNY OF THE INKSPOTS

WILSON PICKETT

JAMES BROWN

"OF THE MAJOR BLACK ATTRACTIONS THAT ARE WORKING TODAY, 30 TO 40 PERCENT WERE LAUNCHED AT THE APOLLO'S AMATEUR NIGHT." —BOBBY SCHIFFMAN, 1975

OF COURSE, NOT EVERY CONTESTANT IS A BUDDING JAMES BROWN OR SARAH VAUGHAN.

GET OFF THE STAGE! *BOOOO!*

SHOOT HIM OFF!

But the audience knows that justice will be done—and calling in their own executioner becomes part of the Wednesday night ritual.

NORMAN MILLER IS THE STAGEHAND IN CHARGE OF SOUND.

BUT ON WEDNESDAY NIGHTS HE BECOMES **PORTO RICO**, THE CRAZED, WILDLY DRESSED NEMESIS OF EVERY TERRIFIED AMATEUR AND THE SAVIOR OF THE DISQUIETED APOLLO CROWD.

Legend has it that at one early Amateur Night show, Miller—his soundman's sensitive ears abused by a struggling crooner's singing attempt—runs onstage, fires a cap pistol, and chases the wretched amateur off.

The audience loves it, and a new **Apollo tradition** is born.

ANOTHER AMATEUR NIGHT FIXTURE, **DAVID "POP" JOHNSON**, SITS IN THE SAME BOX EVERY WEDNESDAY NIGHT.

In 1947, he claims he hasn't missed a show in thirteen years.

BLOW YOUR WHISTLE, POP!

When an amateur displeases him, he drapes a white handkerchief over his head.

Blowing his whistle summons Porto Rico.

EVENTUALLY, THE APOLLO HIRES **SANDMAN SIMS** TO TAKE OVER POP'S ROLE.

SANDMAN CAN ALSO BREAK UP A FAILING ROUTINE BY CALLING IN HIS SIDEKICK, **GEECH**, AN OLD RUBBER-LEGGED COMEDIAN.

Geech cracks up the audience by squawking for his girlfriend, Hester.

HESSSSTER?! HESTER, WHERE ARE YOU, GIRL?

Sandman cues Porto Rico by flashing the lights on his sombrero and wailing on his dilapidated trombone.

YOU HAD TO WEAR A DISGUISE FOR PROTECTION, TOO.

IS THAT GUY COMING OUT?

YEAH, HE'LL BE OUT IN A FEW MINUTES.

MANY A NIGHT I HAD SOMEONE WHO WANTED TO KNOW WHO WAS THAT GUY THAT BOOED THEM OFF.

THEY'D WAIT TO GO GET "HIM."

ONCE I CHANGED CLOTHES, THEY'D WALK RIGHT BY ME.

Much of the fun at Amateur Night is watching some poor soul fail miserably.

IN THE OLD DAYS, ONE FAILED AMATEUR'S PATHOS PROVIDED HYSTERICAL FODDER FOR THE HARLEM GRAPEVINE FOR WEEKS. TODAY, IT RESULTS IN MILLIONS OF HITS ON YOUTUBE. JUST ASK *LAURYN HILL*.

WHAT SONG ARE YOU SINGING?

"WHO'S LOVING YOU?"

THIRTEEN-YEAR-OLD LAURYN HILL SEEMS FINE TALKING TO HOST *RICK AVILES*.

COME ON, LAURYN. WE'RE GOING TO LOVE YOU!

NOT SO FAST.

The youngster starts out off-key and nervous. And the boos rain down.

HOWEVER, SHE MAINTAINS HER COMPOSURE AND FINISHES.

And despite the rough start, she becomes one of the greatest stars of the '90s, winning multiple Grammy Awards including Album of the Year in 1999.

COMEDIAN *DAVE CHAPPELLE*, JUST SIXTEEN WHEN HE TAKES HIS SHOT, TELLS HIS TALE OF WOE ON *INSIDE THE ACTORS STUDIO*:

I SAID, I'M GOING TO GO TO THE APOLLO AND RIP THAT MOTHER!

SANDMAN! I WANTED TO CHOKE HIM!

THAT WAS THE *BEST* THING THAT EVER HAPPENED TO ME . . . AFTER THAT, I WAS FEARLESS. THAT NIGHT WAS *LIBERATING*.

I STILL REMEMBER THAT BOO. I HAD NEVER BEEN BOOED OFF STAGE BEFORE. I JUST REMEMBER LOOKING OUT AND SEEING EVERYBODY BOOING. EVERYBODY! EVEN OLD PEOPLE.

WHO BOOS A CHILD PURSUING HIS DREAMS? THIS IS THE *MEANEST* CROWD IN THE WORLD!

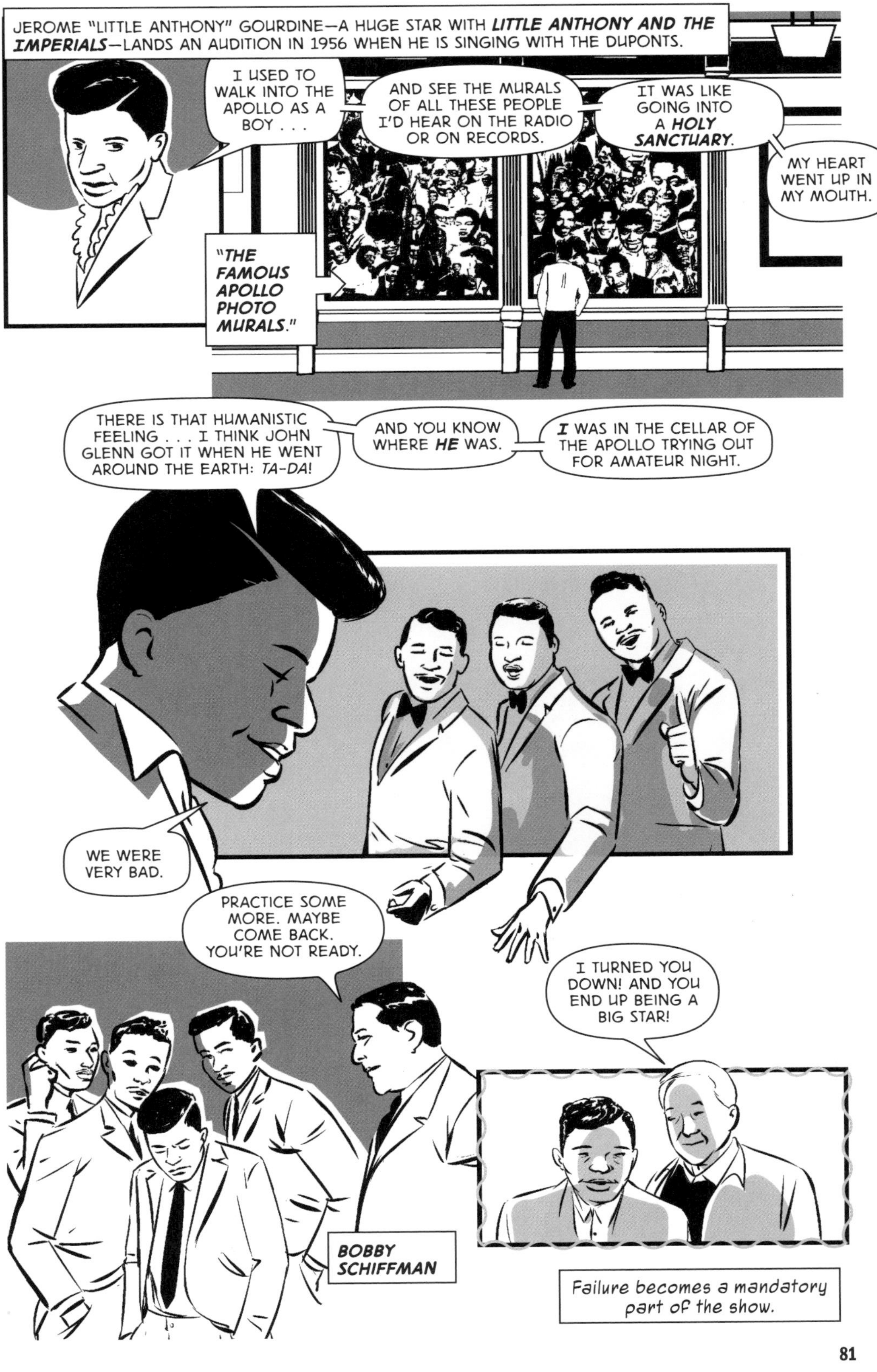

JEROME "LITTLE ANTHONY" GOURDINE—A HUGE STAR WITH **LITTLE ANTHONY AND THE IMPERIALS**—LANDS AN AUDITION IN 1956 WHEN HE IS SINGING WITH THE DUPONTS.
I USED TO WALK INTO THE APOLLO AS A BOY . . .
AND SEE THE MURALS OF ALL THESE PEOPLE I'D HEAR ON THE RADIO OR ON RECORDS.
IT WAS LIKE GOING INTO A **HOLY SANCTUARY**.
MY HEART WENT UP IN MY MOUTH.
"**THE FAMOUS APOLLO PHOTO MURALS**."
THERE IS THAT HUMANISTIC FEELING . . . I THINK JOHN GLENN GOT IT WHEN HE WENT AROUND THE EARTH: *TA-DA*!
AND YOU KNOW WHERE **HE** WAS.
I WAS IN THE CELLAR OF THE APOLLO TRYING OUT FOR AMATEUR NIGHT.
WE WERE VERY BAD.
PRACTICE SOME MORE. MAYBE COME BACK. YOU'RE NOT READY.
I TURNED YOU DOWN! AND YOU END UP BEING A BIG STAR!
BOBBY SCHIFFMAN
Failure becomes a mandatory part of the show.

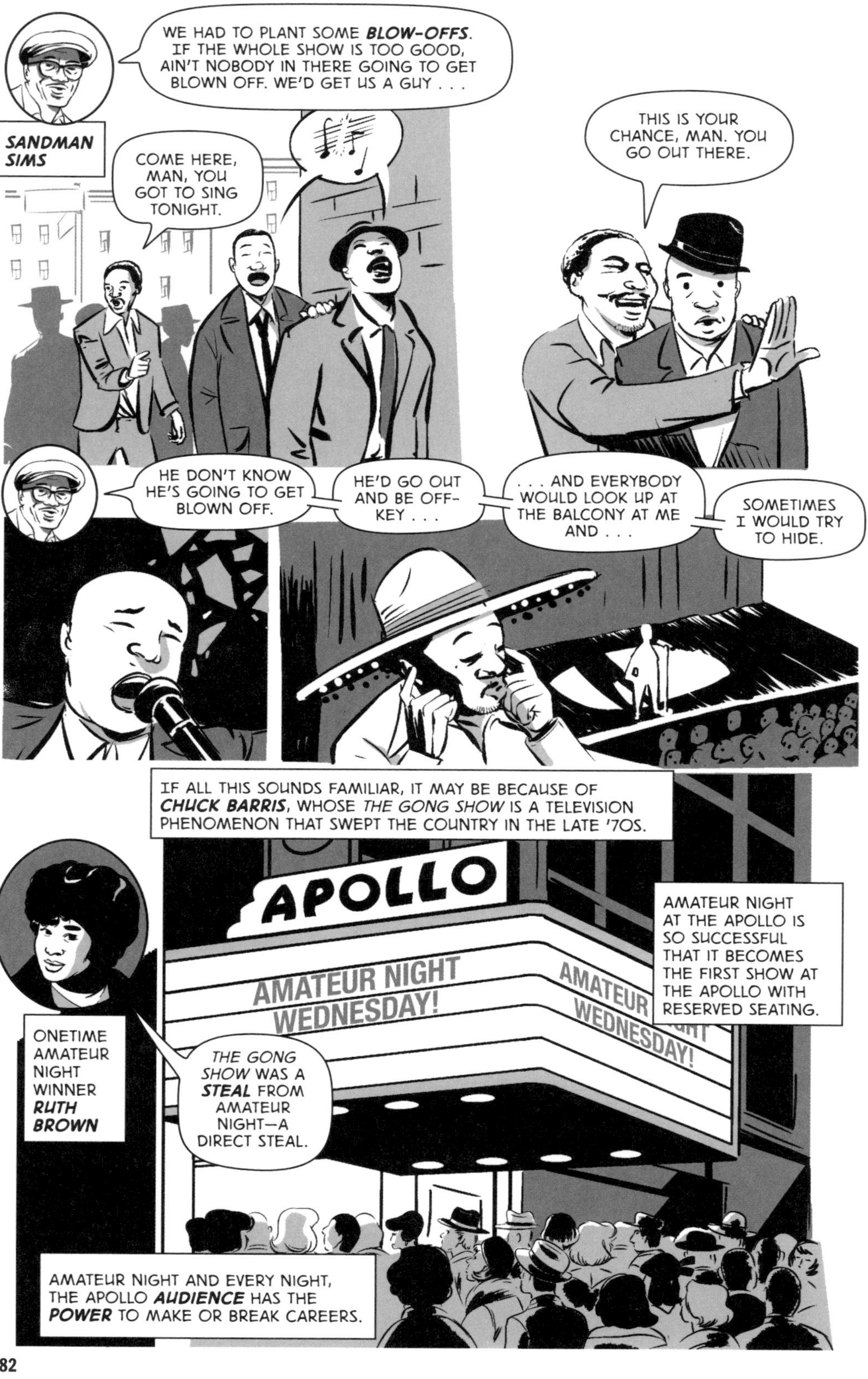
WE HAD TO PLANT SOME **BLOW-OFFS**. IF THE WHOLE SHOW IS TOO GOOD, AIN'T NOBODY IN THERE GOING TO GET BLOWN OFF. WE'D GET US A GUY . . .
SANDMAN SIMS
COME HERE, MAN, YOU GOT TO SING TONIGHT.
THIS IS YOUR CHANCE, MAN. YOU GO OUT THERE.
HE DON'T KNOW HE'S GOING TO GET BLOWN OFF.
HE'D GO OUT AND BE OFF-KEY . . .
. . . AND EVERYBODY WOULD LOOK UP AT THE BALCONY AT ME AND . . .
SOMETIMES I WOULD TRY TO HIDE.
IF ALL THIS SOUNDS FAMILIAR, IT MAY BE BECAUSE OF **CHUCK BARRIS**, WHOSE *THE GONG SHOW* IS A TELEVISION PHENOMENON THAT SWEPT THE COUNTRY IN THE LATE '70S.
APOLLO
AMATEUR NIGHT WEDNESDAY!
AMATEUR NIGHT AT THE APOLLO IS SO SUCCESSFUL THAT IT BECOMES THE FIRST SHOW AT THE APOLLO WITH RESERVED SEATING.
ONETIME AMATEUR NIGHT WINNER **RUTH BROWN**
THE GONG SHOW WAS A **STEAL** FROM AMATEUR NIGHT—A DIRECT STEAL.
AMATEUR NIGHT AND EVERY NIGHT, THE APOLLO **AUDIENCE** HAS THE **POWER** TO MAKE OR BREAK CAREERS.

BUT IT IS MUCH MORE THAN THAT.

The audience is the embodiment of the spirit of Harlem.

The **Force** that truly makes the Apollo **great**.

Bereft of political power, housed in society's castoffs, and denied access to many cultural institutions, they take great pride in their fabled establishment.

The Apollo audience thus enforces a standard of excellence.

It is the **power** of the **powerless**.

THE SCHIFFMANS LOOK TO THE BLACK COMMUNITY TO LEARN WHAT THEY SHOULD BRING INTO THE APOLLO.

AND RECORD COMPANY EXECUTIVES, TALENT AND BOOKING AGENCIES, LOOK TO THE APOLLO AUDIENCE AS EARLY ADOPTERS WHO CAN GUIDE THEM TO WHAT MIGHT WORK IN THE WORLD AT LARGE.

ATLANTIC RECORDS' **AHMET ERTEGUN**

WE SAW EVERY SHOW FOR TWENTY YEARS. TWICE A WEEK.

OSCAR COHEN AND **JOE GLASER** OF ASSOCIATED BOOKING

AUDIENCES COME TO EXPECT THE **BEST**, AND GENERALLY THEIR WILD ENTHUSIASM INSPIRES THE BEST.

THEIR DISPLEASURE WITH THOSE WHO DON'T MEET THEIR EXPECTATIONS PRODUCES A REACTION FEW PERFORMERS WHO EXPERIENCE IT EVER FORGET.

THOSE WHO FAIL TO GIVE THE APOLLO CROWD THEIR ALL, OR ATTEMPT TO ELEVATE THEMSELVES AT THE AUDIENCE'S EXPENSE, ALWAYS REGRET IT.

NINA SIMONE WAS A VERY HOT COMMODITY WHO HAD A SUPER-BIG RECORD CALLED "PORGY."

IT'S AMATEUR NIGHT. THE THEATER IS JAMMED WITH PEOPLE.

SHE CAME WITH A VERY HIGHFALUTIN' ATTITUDE TOWARD HER PEOPLE.

ABOUT THE FIFTH NUMBER IN THE SHOW, SHE STILL HADN'T DONE "PORGY." THE PEOPLE IN THE BACK STARTED TO YELL . . .

SING "PORGY"! COME ON, SING "PORGY"!

I'LL SING "PORGY" WHEN AND IF I GET READY TO SING "PORGY."

I KNEW THAT THIS WAS AMATEUR NIGHT. THE INTERESTING THING IS, THE AMATEURS ARE NOT BACKSTAGE. YOU'RE THE AMATEURS!

THE AUDIENCE GOT UP AND WALKED OUT EN MASSE.

THE NEXT TIME NINA SIMONE CAME TO THE THEATER, ON THE FIRST SHOW, THREE WOMEN GOT UP FROM THE AUDIENCE, WALKED DOWN THE AISLE, THREW HANDFULS OF PENNIES ON THE STAGE, AND WALKED OUT.

THE APOLLO TAUGHT ME HUMILITY.

IT TAUGHT ME NOT TO BE SO GRAND, NOT TO GET SO CARRIED AWAY THAT YOU FEEL THESE PEOPLE ARE IDIOTS THAT ARE COMING OUT HERE TO WATCH YOU—BECAUSE THAT IS NOT THE CASE.

IT TAUGHT ME THAT MY AUDIENCE WAS ALWAYS *FIRST* AND *FOREMOST.*

RUTH BROWN

AT THE OPENING SHOW—WHEN THE BAND STARTED PLAYING THE THEME SONG, AND THE HOUSE LIGHTS WOULD COME UP ON THE CURTAIN—YOU'D START TO GET THE ITCHY FEELING AND NERVOUSNESS. BECAUSE IT SEEMED LIKE A DUAL THING.

IT WASN'T JUST BEING *ACCEPTED* AS A PERFORMER.

SAMMY DAVIS JR.

IT WAS BEING ACCEPTED BY YOUR OWN *PEOPLE.*

WHEN PERFORMERS HIT THE APOLLO STAGE, NO MATTER HOW SUCCESSFUL THEY WERE, THEY WERE *NERVOUS.*

EVERY PERFORMER WAS, BUT IT KEYED THEM UP. IT SPURRED THEM ON TO DO THE BEST THEY POSSIBLY COULD.

THEY PUT OUT EVERY FIBER OF THEIR ENERGY, EMOTION, AND ABILITY TO PLEASE THAT AUDIENCE. THEY KNEW THAT IF THEY DIDN'T GIVE THEIR *ALL*, THE AUDIENCE WOULD JUMP RIGHT ON THEM.

BOBBY SCHIFFMAN

THERE WAS A RUNNING JOKE AT THE APOLLO: WHEN A GUY WALKS ONSTAGE, HE'S SUPPOSED TO *OWN* IT.

AND IF SOMEBODY'S COMING ONSTAGE AFTER YOU, YOU'RE SUPPOSED TO GIVE IT TO THE POINT THAT THEY CAN'T FOLLOW YOU. THAT'S CONSUMMATE PERFORMANCE.

DIONNE WARWICK

YOU PASSED THAT PERSON GOING ONSTAGE, AND YOU HAVE TO TAKE A HOSE— COOL THAT STAGE OFF.

I THINK THE *GREATEST* PERFORMANCES OF ANYBODY HAVE BEEN AT THE APOLLO THEATER.

IF AN ACT WOULD COME OFF, AND THEY GOT A STANDING OVATION, THEY'D WALK OFFSTAGE LIKE THIS . . .

THE FIRST ACT WOULD SET THE PACE FOR THE REST OF THE SHOW. THAT'S WHY OPENING ACTS WERE SO DARNED GOOD: THEY KNEW THEY HAD TO COME OUT **SMOKING**.

YOU BETTER CALL THE FIRE DEPARTMENT. I FEEL **SORRY** FOR YOU COMING BEHIND ME.

IF THE AUDIENCE LIKED THE OPENING ACT, BEFORE THE END OF THE WEEK, THAT ACT WAS NOT THE OPENER.

LITTLE ANTHONY

I REMEMBER SCHIFFMAN SENDING DOWN A NOTICE: "THE IMPERIALS CAN'T BE THIRD, MOVE THEM TO FIFTH."

WE WERE **KILLING** THE ACT THAT WAS COMING DOWN AFTER US, AND THEY COULDN'T HANDLE IT.

THERE WAS A COMPETITIVE HIGH AS PERFORMERS, BUT THEY WERE VERY LIBERAL AND NICE AFTER THE PERFORMANCE.

HEY, MAN, DON'T BE LOOKING STRAIGHT OUT LIKE THAT.

YOU SEE THEM GIRLS OVER THERE AT THE TOP? NOW, YOU GOT TO PLAY TO **THEM**.

THE **DELLS** OF "OH, WHAT A NIGHT" FAME.

KILL! GO OUT THERE AND WIPE 'EM OUT.

WE WERE **PROUD** WHEN WE CAME ONSTAGE.

OR WE COULD SAY TO EACH OTHER, "HEY, MAYBE IF YOU DO THIS LIKE THIS, IT MIGHT GO OVER BETTER."

GLADYS KNIGHT

IT WAS A SCHOOL, THAT'S WHAT IT WAS. MAYBE MORE THAN A THEATER, IT WAS A SCHOOL.

THE IMPLICIT LINK WITH THE PERFORMERS ONSTAGE CREATES A CHARGE LIKE THAT BETWEEN THE TWO POLES OF A BATTERY, AND IT **ELECTRIFIES** THE ATMOSPHERE AT THE APOLLO.

To be a part of the Apollo audience is to be a part of the show.

SOME ANTHROPOLOGISTS HAVE LINKED THIS SORT OF INTERACTION WITH THE AFRICAN PAST, WHEN ART WAS REGARDED AS AN INSEPARABLE PART OF LIFE THAT WAS NOT TO BE PURCHASED FOR A TWO-DOLLAR TICKET.

PROFESSOR **PHYL GARLAND**

While the Schiffmans run the theater, even they acknowledge that the audience is the **real** boss . . .

OH, MAN, THEY CUT LOOSE ON THIS GUY. HE STRUGGLED THROUGH HIS ACT, AND HE ACTUALLY WAS **BAD**.

BOO!!

BOO!!

JOHNNY OTIS

IF THERE IS SOME TRUTH TO THIS, NOWHERE IN MODERN-DAY AMERICA IS IT MORE APPARENT THAN AT THE APOLLO.

YOU SEE, MR. OTIS, I HIRED HIM IN GOOD FAITH, BUT THE PEOPLE **OVERRULED** ME, AND THEY FIRED HIM.

SCREW THEM. I WOULDN'T WORK HERE IF THEY PAID ME A MILLION DOLLARS.

WHEN SUPERSTARS LIKE JAMES BROWN APPEAR, EAGER FANS WAIT OUTSIDE, IN ANY WEATHER, FOR HOURS.

BECAUSE OF THE THEATER'S GENERAL ADMISSION, STAY-ALL-DAY POLICY IN THE EARLY DAYS, THE THEATER DOES NOT NORMALLY CLEAR AFTER EACH SHOW.

You might say standing in line toughens up the Apollo's patrons, sharpens their critical attitude, and tests their patience.

Ushers queue them up in two lines.

THE OTHER STRETCHES EAST AND AROUND THE CORNER ON SEVENTH AVENUE TO THE OLD ALHAMBRA THEATER.

ONE GOES WEST DOWN 125TH STREET, AROUND THE CORNER, AND UP EIGHTH AVENUE TO THE BRADDOCK HOTEL.

There are usually people waiting to take seats as they became available.

WE HAD A FILM CALLED *THE RIVER*—A DOCUMENTARY OF ALL THE MAIN RIVERS IN THE COUNTRY.

THE RIVER

TO MOVE PEOPLE OUT, THE APOLLO'S MANAGEMENT GETS CREATIVE.

DOLL THOMAS

LOOK AT TWENTY MINUTES OF ALL THAT WATER FALLING, AND THEY'RE GOING TO WANT GO TO THE BATHROOM.

THE MINUTE THEY GOT UP, WE PUT SOMEONE IN THEIR SEAT.

LADIES AND GENTLEMEN, IT'S SHOWTIME AT THE APOLLO!

A performer hitting the stage then is greeted by a frenzied scene as the film ends . . .

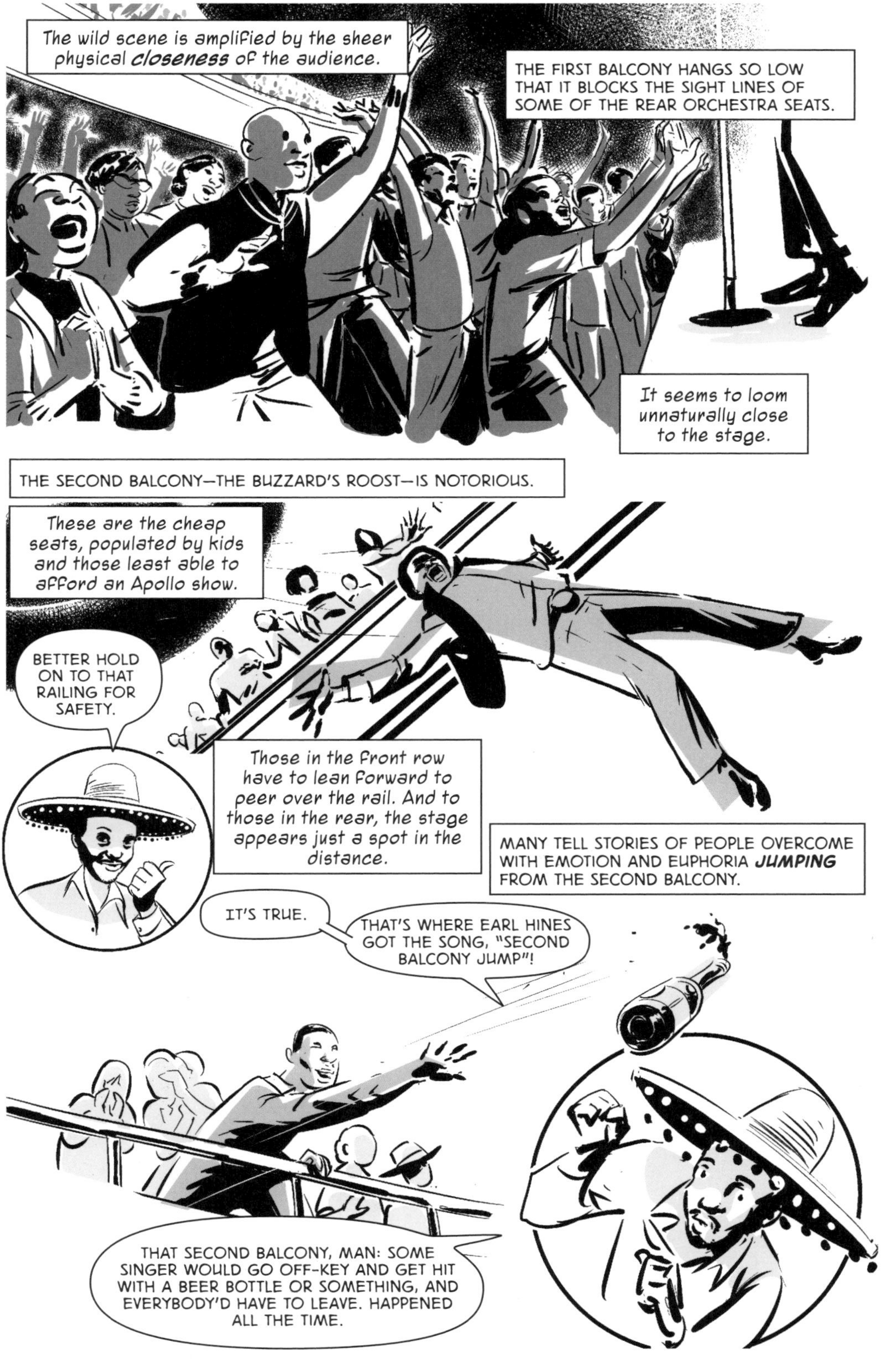
The wild scene is amplified by the sheer physical *closeness* of the audience.
THE FIRST BALCONY HANGS SO LOW THAT IT BLOCKS THE SIGHT LINES OF SOME OF THE REAR ORCHESTRA SEATS.
It seems to loom unnaturally close to the stage.
THE SECOND BALCONY—THE BUZZARD'S ROOST—IS NOTORIOUS.
These are the cheap seats, populated by kids and those least able to afford an Apollo show.
BETTER HOLD ON TO THAT RAILING FOR SAFETY.
Those in the front row have to lean forward to peer over the rail. And to those in the rear, the stage appears just a spot in the distance.
MANY TELL STORIES OF PEOPLE OVERCOME WITH EMOTION AND EUPHORIA ***JUMPING*** FROM THE SECOND BALCONY.
IT'S TRUE.
THAT'S WHERE EARL HINES GOT THE SONG, "SECOND BALCONY JUMP"!
THAT SECOND BALCONY, MAN: SOME SINGER WOULD GO OFF-KEY AND GET HIT WITH A BEER BOTTLE OR SOMETHING, AND EVERYBODY'D HAVE TO LEAVE. HAPPENED ALL THE TIME.

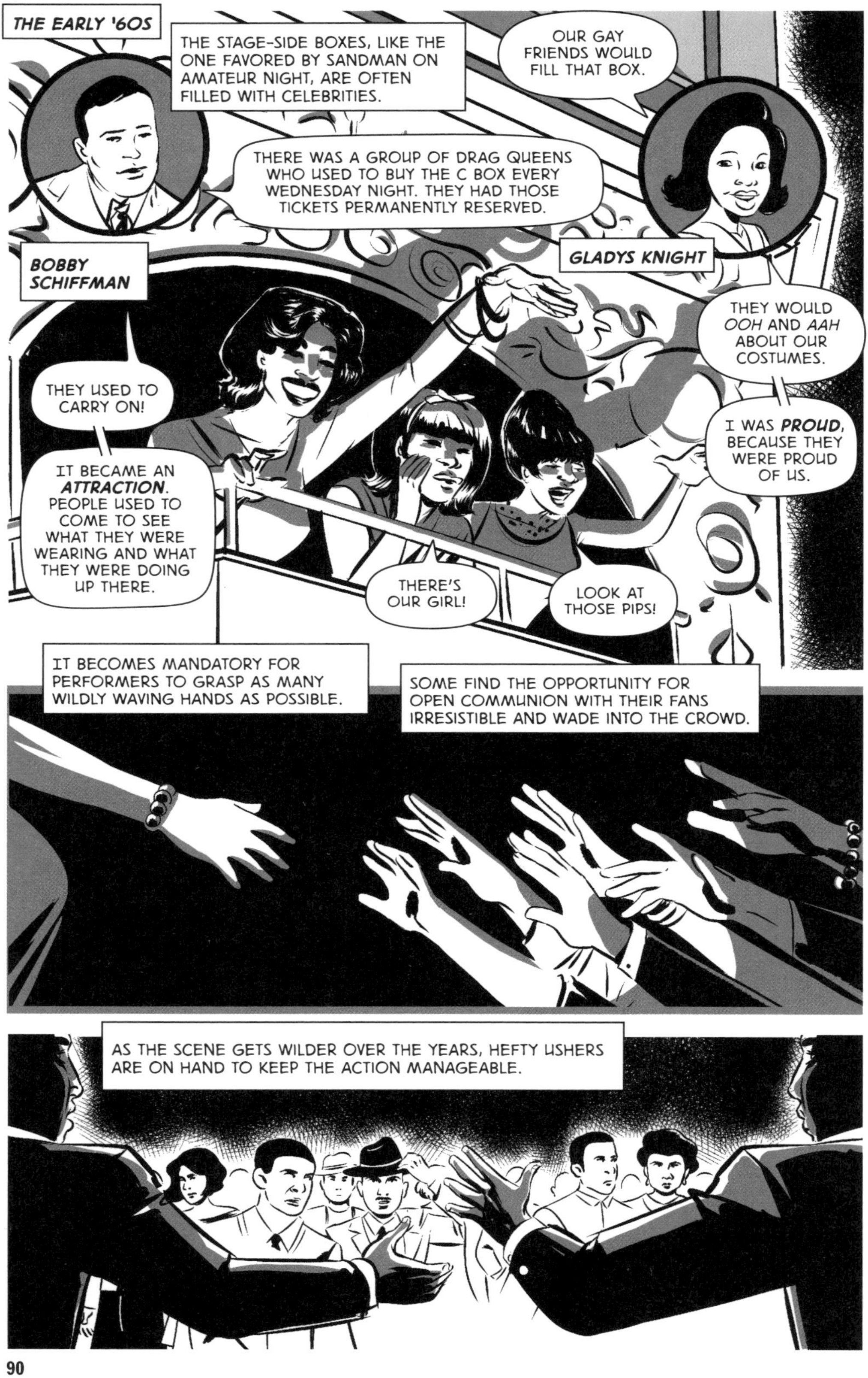

THE EARLY '60S
THE STAGE-SIDE BOXES, LIKE THE ONE FAVORED BY SANDMAN ON AMATEUR NIGHT, ARE OFTEN FILLED WITH CELEBRITIES.
OUR GAY FRIENDS WOULD FILL THAT BOX.
THERE WAS A GROUP OF DRAG QUEENS WHO USED TO BUY THE C BOX EVERY WEDNESDAY NIGHT. THEY HAD THOSE TICKETS PERMANENTLY RESERVED.
BOBBY SCHIFFMAN
GLADYS KNIGHT
THEY USED TO CARRY ON!
IT BECAME AN ***ATTRACTION***. PEOPLE USED TO COME TO SEE WHAT THEY WERE WEARING AND WHAT THEY WERE DOING UP THERE.
THEY WOULD *OOH* AND *AAH* ABOUT OUR COSTUMES.
I WAS ***PROUD***, BECAUSE THEY WERE PROUD OF US.
THERE'S OUR GIRL!
LOOK AT THOSE PIPS!
IT BECOMES MANDATORY FOR PERFORMERS TO GRASP AS MANY WILDLY WAVING HANDS AS POSSIBLE.
SOME FIND THE OPPORTUNITY FOR OPEN COMMUNION WITH THEIR FANS IRRESISTIBLE AND WADE INTO THE CROWD.
AS THE SCENE GETS WILDER OVER THE YEARS, HEFTY USHERS ARE ON HAND TO KEEP THE ACTION MANAGEABLE.

WHEN ACTS LIKE LIONEL HAMPTON AND JAMES BROWN BEGIN DEMANDING A PERCENTAGE OF THE HOUSE RECEIPTS, THE APOLLO STARTS CLEARING THE HOUSE AFTER EACH SHOW.

THE MOMENT THE LAST ACT WAS OVER, THEY'D TURN THE LIGHTS UP.

HAROLD CROMER

THE USHERS WOULD RUN UP AND DOWN THE AISLES GETTING EVERYBODY OUT.

THEY'D SEND THEM OUT THE SIDE DOOR ONTO 126TH STREET.

EVERYBODY PLEASE CLEAR THE THEATER!

THEY'D HAVE A FIGHT, BUT THEY'D GET THEM OUT.

HEY, MAN, I PAID MY MONEY. I CAN STAY IN THIS MOTHER ALL DAY.

THE MOST **VOCAL** SEGMENT OF THE AUDIENCE IS THE **KIDS**.

WE WERE ON LINE AT NINE IN THE MORNING ON SATURDAY WAITING FOR THE THEATER TO OPEN AT NOON, IN ORDER TO BE IN THE FRONT SEATS.

THOSE FIRST THREE ROWS, EVERYONE WANTED TO BE THERE, BECAUSE WHEN THE ARTIST CAME DOWN AND PUT THEIR HAND OUT, YOU COULD SAY, "OH, I TOUCHED HIM, WOW!"

As rhythm and blues, and then soul music, become dominant at the Apollo, the kids increasingly dominate the audience.

"LITTLE" LESLIE UGGAMS

COMEDIAN **SCOEY MITCHELL**

As long as it is at the Apollo, the audience accepts and encourages quality entertainment of any type.

PERHAPS BILLIE HOLIDAY EXPRESSED IT BEST IN HER AUTOBIOGRAPHY:

THERE'S NOTHING LIKE AN AUDIENCE AT THE APOLLO.

THAT'S ONE THING ABOUT THE APOLLO: YOU COULD BE AN OPERA SINGER AND COME IN THE APOLLO . . .

. . . AND THOUGH THEY MAY NOT REALLY UNDERSTAND THE FACT THAT YOU'RE SINGING IN ITALIAN, IF YOU WERE SINGING GOOD, THEY'D LET YOU KNOW IT.

THEY DIDN'T ASK ME WHAT MY STYLE WAS, WHO I WAS, WHERE I'D COME FROM, WHO INFLUENCED ME, OR ANYTHING.

THEY JUST BROKE THE HOUSE UP.

91

CHAPTER 5

The 1940s: Boppin'

Hawkins is onto something *new*. He's expanding the presumed capabilities of his instrument.

THEY CALL HIM "BEAN." IN 1940, **COLEMAN HAWKINS** IS THE HOTTEST SAX MAN IN THE WORLD.

MUSICIANS WEAR OUT COPIES OF "BODY AND SOUL" TRYING TO FIGURE OUT BEAN'S PHENOMENAL SOLO.

WHAT THE? SPIN IT AGAIN, MAN.

HAWKINS PLAYS THE APOLLO AND TOURS THE COUNTRY WITH HIS SIXTEEN-PIECE BAND, BUT HIS ARTISTIC JOURNEY FORESHADOWS A MAJOR SHAKE-UP OF THE BIG BAND SCENE.

His inventiveness rips apart the complacent world of swing.

AS WITH SO MANY KEY MOMENTS IN MUSIC AND POPULAR CULTURE, THE APOLLO IS THE SITE OF THIS REMARKABLE SCENE IN 1940.

BUNNY BERIGAN

JACK JENNEY

TOMMY DORSEY

COLEMAN HAWKINS

HARRY JAMES

Hawkins has just completed his week at the Apollo, headlining with Ralph Cooper and Pigmeat Markham.

On this very early Friday morning in late June, Bean celebrates by calling a few friends up onstage for a jam on Fats Waller's "Honeysuckle Rose."

JOHN KIRBY

COUNT BASIE

GENE KRUPA

JOE MARSALA

CARMEN MASTREN

WHAT A MARVELOUS **RELEASE** FOR THESE MUSICIANS: SWING MUSIC IS AT ITS PEAK POPULARITY, BUT IT IS BECOMING HIDEBOUND AND COMMERCIALIZED.

These Friday morning impromptu get-togethers have become quite popular at the Apollo.

SORRY, BOYS, YOU CAN'T BE PLAYING WITHOUT A CONTRACT. WE'VE GOT TO PROTECT THE UNION.

The Musician's Union begins handing out fines of $100 to $500 to musicians for playing without a contract.

THE APOLLO CONTINUES TO CONTRIBUTE TO THE NEW MUSIC SCENE EVEN AS THE INNOVATION MOVES UNDERGROUND TO SMALL CLUBS.

$100 FINE

WE'RE GOING TO *CLOSE* THESE SESSIONS DOWN.

TOO POPULAR.

Minton's, in particular, becomes the hip spot to jam, thanks to the club's new manager, ex-bandleader Teddy Hill.

MAN, WE'RE LUCKY TEDDY'S A UNION REP.

DIG, WE CAN GET BACK TO *JAMMIN'* WITHOUT WORRYIN' ABOUT THOSE FINES.

ON MONDAY NIGHTS, HILL HOSTS A "DOWN HOME" DINNER FOR EVERYONE IN THE FEATURED BAND AT THE APOLLO THAT WEEK.

BUT THE GREATEST ATTRACTION IS MINTON'S LITTLE HOUSE BAND.

These jam sessions produce a revolutionary new sound: *bebop*.

CHARLIE CHRISTIAN

JOE GUY

NICK FENTON

KENNY "KLOOK" CLARKE

FRANK SCHIFFMAN AND THE APOLLO ARE KEEPING A WATCHFUL EYE ON THESE NEW DEVELOPMENTS.

DIZZY GILLESPIE

THELONIOUS MONK

CHARLIE PARKER

In 1943, the Apollo becomes the first to book the experimental bebop band of *Earl Hines*—which showcases Dizzy Gillespie and *Charlie Parker*.

It is new music—aggressive, cynical, troubling, *modern*—for a new age.

A NEW AGE OF WAR.

NEARLY ONE MILLION AFRICAN AMERICANS SERVE IN WORLD WAR II.

The war effort affects everything.

Sometimes in ways that are coincidental but no less problematic for artists . . .

HOW'S OUR BAND GONNA GET TO GIGS WITH THIS *GAS RATIONING*?

THE BOSS CAN'T CHARTER BUSSES ANYMORE EITHER.

MANY WHITE BANDS TURN TO THE RAILS, BUT BLACK BANDS ARE HAMPERED BY RACIST JIM CROW RESTRICTIONS ON TRAINS IN THE SOUTH.

Finally, the NAACP prevails on the Office of Defense Transportation to ease its *charter bus ban* for black bands.

But only five buses are made available.

OTHER POLICIES MAKE IT HARDER FOR FANS TO GET OUT, TOO.

TICKETS GETTING HIGH WITH THIS 20 PERCENT *AMUSEMENT TAX* FOR THE WAR.

YEAH, AND GOTTA GET HOME BEFORE THAT BROWNOUT *CURFEW* AT MIDNIGHT!

NOT ENOUGH GAS IN THE TANK TO GET TO WORK AND A SHOW WITH THIS RATIONING.

THE APOLLO KEEPS BOPPIN'.

Paradoxically, swing becomes so popular that some top black bands break into formerly all-white territory, and play the Apollo less.

So the Apollo relies more on newer black bands like those of *Erskine Hawkins*, *Buddy Johnson*, *Cootie Williams*, and *Lucky Millinder*.

NO BAND CAN SURVIVE ON OCCASIONAL GIGS AT THE APOLLO, AND WORLD EVENTS ARE AFFECTING BANDS AROUND THE COUNTRY.

FEWER GIGS, AND CAN'T MAKE RECORDS SINCE THE UNION *RECORDING BAN* IN '42.

TWO YEARS LATER AND WE STILL AIN'T GETTING ROYALTIES.

WAR SERVICE CLAIMS MANY LEADERS AND SIDEMEN.

THE APOLLO SUPPORTS MEN AND WOMEN IN UNIFORM. AT THE HARLEM DEFENSE RECREATION CENTER, THIRTY-FIVE TICKETS FOR APOLLO SHOWS ARE SET ASIDE FOR SOLDIERS EACH DAY.

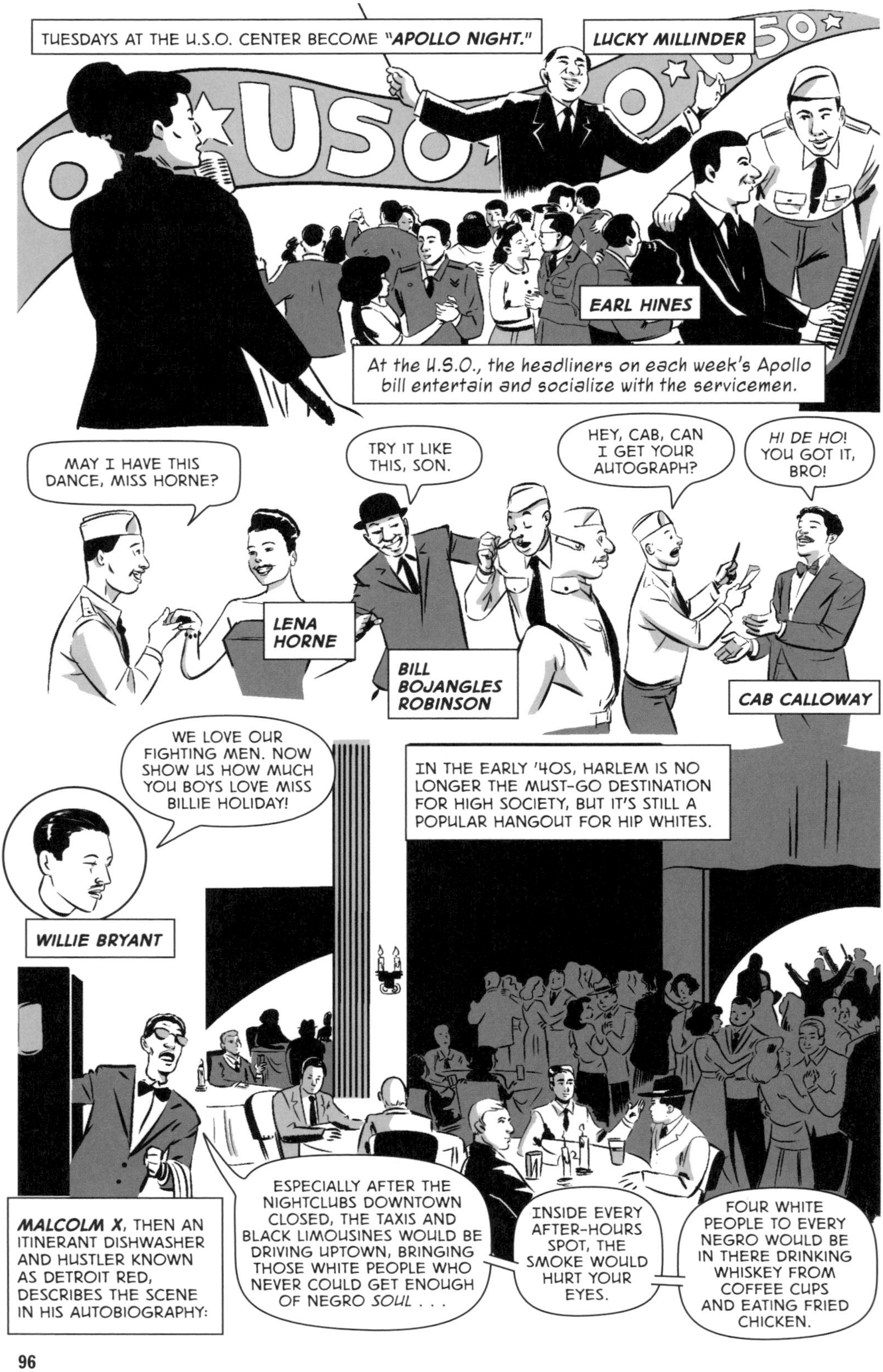
TUESDAYS AT THE U.S.O. CENTER BECOME "APOLLO NIGHT."
LUCKY MILLINDER
USO
EARL HINES
At the U.S.O., the headliners on each week's Apollo bill entertain and socialize with the servicemen.
MAY I HAVE THIS DANCE, MISS HORNE?
LENA HORNE
TRY IT LIKE THIS, SON.
BILL BOJANGLES ROBINSON
HEY, CAB, CAN I GET YOUR AUTOGRAPH?
HI DE HO! YOU GOT IT, BRO!
CAB CALLOWAY
WE LOVE OUR FIGHTING MEN. NOW SHOW US HOW MUCH YOU BOYS LOVE MISS BILLIE HOLIDAY!
WILLIE BRYANT
IN THE EARLY '40S, HARLEM IS NO LONGER THE MUST-GO DESTINATION FOR HIGH SOCIETY, BUT IT'S STILL A POPULAR HANGOUT FOR HIP WHITES.
MALCOLM X, THEN AN ITINERANT DISHWASHER AND HUSTLER KNOWN AS DETROIT RED, DESCRIBES THE SCENE IN HIS AUTOBIOGRAPHY:
ESPECIALLY AFTER THE NIGHTCLUBS DOWNTOWN CLOSED, THE TAXIS AND BLACK LIMOUSINES WOULD BE DRIVING UPTOWN, BRINGING THOSE WHITE PEOPLE WHO NEVER COULD GET ENOUGH OF NEGRO SOUL . . .
INSIDE EVERY AFTER-HOURS SPOT, THE SMOKE WOULD HURT YOUR EYES.
FOUR WHITE PEOPLE TO EVERY NEGRO WOULD BE IN THERE DRINKING WHISKEY FROM COFFEE CUPS AND EATING FRIED CHICKEN.

But frustration soon replaces optimism, and by the mid-'40s many African Americans are mired in disappointment.

During World War II, blacks fight in segregated units. When some finally are integrated, black soldiers usually serve in menial positions.

ON THE **HOME FRONT**, THOUSANDS OF AFRICAN AMERICANS FIND LUCRATIVE JOBS IN THE DEFENSE INDUSTRY.

For the first time their economic situation improves measurably.

STORIES OF BLACK SERVICEMEN BEATEN AND KILLED BY WHITE "CRACKERS" NEAR SOUTHERN MILITARY BASES TURN UP ALL TOO FREQUENTLY IN THE HARLEM NEWSPAPERS.

HARLEMITES ARE FURTHER UPSET WHEN MAYOR FIORELLO LA GUARDIA TEMPORARILY CLOSES THE SAVOY BALLROOM—HE SAYS TO PREVENT INCIDENTS ARISING OUT OF INTERRACIAL MINGLING.

The New York

Negro Serviceman Murdered Outside Georgia Army Base

EVENTS COME TO A HEAD ON THE NIGHT OF SUNDAY, AUGUST 1, 1943, IN THE **WORST** RIOT HARLEM HAS EVER EXPERIENCED.

A WHITE POLICEMAN ANSWERS A CALL FOR HELP AT THE **BRADDOCK HOTEL**.

It's a favorite hangout for Apollo entertainers at 126th Street near Eighth Avenue, just down from the theater's stage door.

97

A BLACK SOLDIER INTERVENES WHEN THE COP TRIES TO ARREST A WOMAN.

THE COP ARRESTS THE WOUNDED SOLDIER AND MARCHES HIM TO NEARBY SYDENHAM HOSPITAL.

A false rumor spreads.

HE'S DEAD! THEY KILLED HIM!

WAITING OUTSIDE THE HOSPITAL FOR WORD OF THE SOLDIER'S CONDITION, THE CROWD GROWS RESTLESS.

THE CROWD TURNS INTO A RAMPAGING MOB, GUTTING **HUNDREDS** OF WHITE-OWNED BUSINESSES ON AND AROUND 125TH STREET.

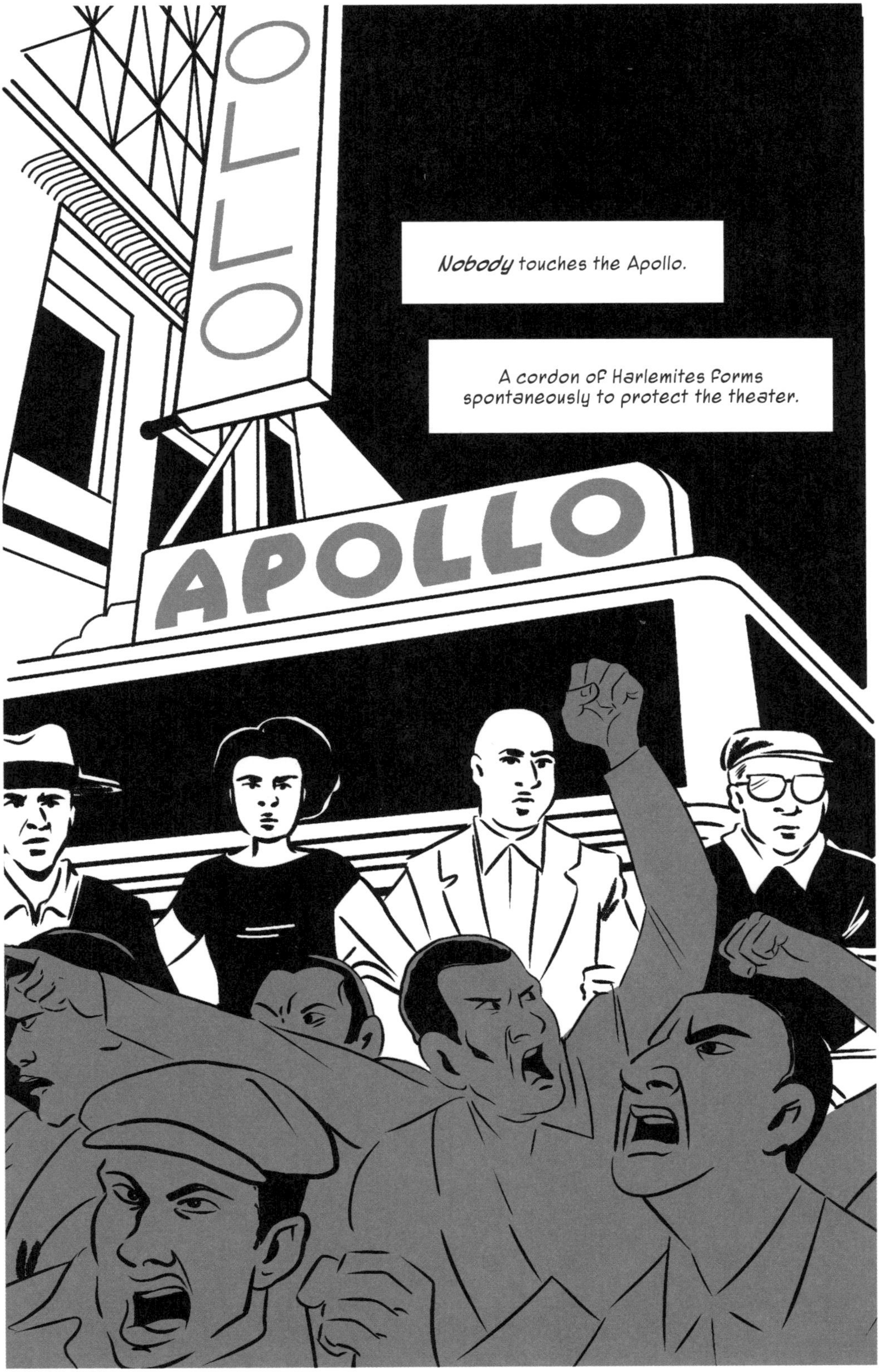
OLLO
Nobody touches the Apollo.
A cordon of Harlemites forms spontaneously to protect the theater.
APOLLO

The riot rages until dawn.

Hundreds are arrested, hundreds more are wounded, and at least six people die.

REV. ADAM CLAYTON POWELL SR., PASTOR OF HARLEM'S FAMOUS ABYSSINIAN BAPTIST CHURCH

IT WAS THE **HOTTEST HELL** EVER CREATED IN HARLEM.

MALCOLM X IN HIS AUTOBIOGRAPHY . . .

AFTER THE RIOT, THINGS GOT VERY TIGHT IN HARLEM.

IT WAS TERRIBLE FOR THE NIGHTLIFE PEOPLE, AND FOR THOSE HUSTLERS WHOSE MAIN INCOME HAD BEEN THE WHITE MAN'S MONEY.

THE 1935 RIOT HAD LEFT ONLY A RELATIVE TRICKLE OF THE MONEY WHICH HAD POURED INTO HARLEM DURING THE 1920S.

AND NOW THIS NEW RIOT ENDED EVEN THAT TRICKLE.

THE APOLLO GETS MORE THAN ITS SHARE OF THAT TRICKLE OF MONEY, HOWEVER.

WE'RE HANGIN' IN. DURING THE WEEK, THE AUDIENCE IS STILL ABOUT 40 PERCENT WHITE.

YES, AND AT THE AMATEUR NIGHT AND SATURDAY MIDNIGHT SHOWS, MAYBE 75 PERCENT.

MR. REED, WE WILL NEED TO INSTITUTE RESERVED SEATING FOR THOSE POPULAR SHOWS.

The Apollo is such a great deal that the crowds still come.

1945

APOLLO MANAGER **LEONARD REED**

FRANK SCHIFFMAN

Ticket prices top out at *one dollar*, and start at *fifty cents* before noon.

THE END OF THE WAR ALSO MARKS THE END FOR MANY OF THE BIG SWING BANDS—WHITE AND BLACK.

BENNY GOODMAN

ERSKINE HAWKINS

HARRY JAMES

BENNY CARTER

BUDDY JOHNSON

TOMMY DORSEY

IT WAS TOO EXPENSIVE TO KEEP THE BIG BANDS GOING.

DURING '47 IT STARTED PETERING OUT.

YOU HAD TELEVISION, AND PEOPLE WEREN'T GOING TO SHOWS AS MUCH. THAT KILLS A BIG BAND.

EDDIE "CLEANHEAD" VINSON

THERE WERE NO MORE JOBS. WE HAD TO **STRUGGLE** TOO HARD.

BILLY ECKSTINE AND I MET IN WASHINGTON, DC. HE HAD A BIG BAND AND I HAD A BIG BAND.

I'M BREAKING MY BAND DOWN. I'M SORRY.

BUT, IN THE END, OUR ART AND OUR ENTERTAINMENT IS A REFLECTION OF OUR WAY OF LIFE.

JOHNNY OTIS

BILLY ECKSTINE

WHEN I GOT HOME TO LOS ANGELES I WAS FORCED TO REDUCE THE SIZE OF MINE. I COULDN'T AFFORD FIFTEEN OR SIXTEEN GUYS.

IT WAS A CHANGE OF LIFESTYLE.

101

THE SEEDS OF THIS LIFESTYLE CHANGE ARE GROWING IN BILLY ECKSTINE'S NEW BAND.

GENE AMMONS

ART BLAKEY

FATS NAVARRO

Dizzy Gillespie

John Malachi

DEXTER GORDON

It boasts a *who's who* of modern jazz.

Charlie Parker

KENNY DORHAM

miles Davis

And makes its mark on the Apollo from 1944 to 1947, providing the indispensable *link* from the big band sound to bebop.

AND, OF COURSE, IT FEATURES ECKSTINE'S APOLLO AMATEUR NIGHT FIND: SARAH VAUGHAN.

DIZZY GILLESPIE AND CHARLIE PARKER ARE BEBOP'S BREAKOUT STARS AND GREATEST CHARACTERS.

Their Apollo appearances are major events for bop fans.

AS A PENNILESS, UNEMPLOYED MUSICIAN, DIZZY HANGS AROUND BACKSTAGE AT THE APOLLO.

HE MEETS HIS WIFE, LORRAINE WILLIS, AT THE THEATER, WHERE SHE IS A CHORUS GIRL.

He keeps his ears open for job opportunities and his eyes open for the chance to hustle a buck or two.

I GOT TO GET SERIOUS ABOUT MY BAND AND MAKE SOME DOUGH SO LORRAINE CAN *QUIT* THIS GIG.

BUT THAT IS AFTER THE LEGENDARY 1941 INCIDENT WITH BANDLEADER CAB CALLOWAY.

AFTER THE SHOW, DIZZY PROCLAIMS INNOCENCE AND IN THE ENSUING TUSSLE, HE STABS CALLOWAY IN THE BUTT WITH A PENKNIFE!

Calloway accuses Dizzy of being the spitball shooter.

The two later patch things up, become great friends, and frequently tell the story.

BACK IN 1939, BANDLEADER *LIONEL HAMPTON*, PREPARING FOR HIS LEGENDARY "HOT MALLETS" RECORDING SESSIONS, FIRST HEARS DIZ PLAYING WITH CALLOWAY AT THE APOLLO.

I ASKED HIM TO PLAY ON THIS SESSION I HAD.

The recordings are felt by many to be the *first* to feature the infant sounds of bebop.

HE CAME OUT WITH A DIFFERENT STYLE THAN WE'D EVER HEARD BEFORE.

DIZZY BECOMES A LEADER IN MORE WAYS THAN ONE.

LIONEL HAMPTON

His goatee, beret, and jive patter set the style for a generation that culminates with the Beats of the 1950s.

AS A BANDLEADER, HE IS RELAXED, YET ALWAYS IN CONTROL.

HEY, FELLAS, WHY YOU GUYS SO STIFF, MAN?

THIS IS A *SHOW*. DON'T BE SITTING UP THERE LIKE THAT.

DIZ KNOWS HE'S LICKED.

ALL RIGHT, FELLAS. THAT'S ENOUGH OF THE COMEDY.

LET'S GO BACK TO LIKE YOU WERE BEFORE. TIGHTEN UP AND TURN IT LOOSE!

WHEN CHARLIE PARKER LEAVES HIS HOMETOWN, KANSAS CITY, FOR NEW YORK WITH THE JAY MCSHANN BAND IN 1941, HE ATTRACTS RAPT ATTENTION FROM THE COGNOSCENTI.

If Dizzy Gillespie is the *light side* of the bebop revolution, Charlie "Bird" Parker is the *dark side*.

His is one of the most tragic stories in the cultural history of America, although the Apollo supports this genius even in his darkest hour.

Soon after leaving school, Charlie gets caught up in hard drugs, alcohol, and dissoluteness.

CHARLIE PARKER WAS A *GENIUS*.

BUT HE LIVES DAY TO DAY, HUSTLE TO HUSTLE, BED TO BED, FIX TO FIX.

Those who recognize Parker's greatness love him and forgive him his excesses.

He suffers devastating abuse from other musicians as he develops his revolutionary style at "cutting contests" all over Boss Pendergast's notoriously corrupt Kansas City.

Whenever his alto sax isn't in hock, he develops new musical ideas and modes of thought that continue to influence improvisational musicians today.

But his antics often get him into nonmusical jams.

ONE OF BIRD'S FAVORITE HANGOUTS IS THE BRADDOCK HOTEL BAR, WHERE APOLLO PERFORMERS OFTEN DROP IN BETWEEN SHOWS.

Bird takes advantage of its policy of two drinks for the price of one.

THERE HE GOES AGAIN.

Bird is so destitute thanks to his heroin habit that he can't even afford the price of the initial drink.

HIS FRIENDS DON'T MIND THE GAMBIT, BUT HE'S CAUGHT IN THE ACT BY A GROUP OF LOCAL HARD GUYS.

WHAT THE HELL?

YOU BUM, YOU OWE US A ROUND.

LUCKILY THE MCSHANN BAND IS PLAYING THE APOLLO, AND HIS FORMER BANDMATE, GENE RAMEY, BAILS HIM OUT.

MAN, I'M *BROKE*. BUT I'LL GET IT. WAIT, I'LL GET IT.

HIS WAY OF LIFE HELPS CREATE THE CHARLIE PARKER **LEGEND**, BUT HIS MUSIC MAKES HIM A **HERO**.

HIS APOLLO ENGAGEMENTS ARE EAGERLY AWAITED BY YOUNG ACOLYTES IN HARLEM LIKE **JACKIE MCLEAN**.

McLean, the great altoist deeply influenced by Bird's music—and unfortunately, Parker's drug habit as well—describes a 1948 Parker performance to A. B. Spellman in *Four Lives in the Bebop Business* . . .

WHEN BIRD WAS AT THE APOLLO, WE WOULD GO EARLY IN THE MORNING AND STAY AND WATCH THE SHOW ALL DAY LONG.

WE WOULD WATCH HIM FROM THE FIRST SHOW UNTIL AFTER THREE O'CLOCK, WHEN IT WAS TIME TO GO HOME FROM SCHOOL.

WE USED TO GO HOME AND PUT OUR BOOKS UP AND THEN TELL OUR PARENTS THAT WE WERE GOING TO THE APOLLO.

THEY'D LET US GO, AND WE'D SPLIT AND WATCH BIRD AGAIN UNTIL NINE, WHEN IT WAS TIME TO GO HOME AT NIGHT.

WE'D GET SOME HOT DOGS AT INTERMISSION, AND THAT WOULD BE ALL WE HAD TO EAT ALL DAY LONG.

A **CABARET CARD** IS REQUIRED TO PLAY IN NEW YORK ESTABLISHMENTS SERVING ALCOHOL. . .

THAT LEAVES THE APOLLO AS THE ONLY NEW YORK VENUE OPEN TO HIM. HE SEEMS TO HAVE **LOST HEART**.

His 1953 revue, "Charlie Parker and Strings," is a flop at the Apollo and elsewhere.

IN 1955 HE DIES, COUGHING UP BLOOD IN THE FIFTH AVENUE APARTMENT OF LEGENDARY BEBOP PATRON **BARONESS PANNONICA DE KOENIGSWARTER**.

Dizzy Gillespie pays for his funeral.

Department of Public Works
Cabaret and Dance Hall Employees
Identification Card

Name: Charlie Parker
Title: Musician

. . . But after years of problems, Charlie's is revoked. He can no longer play the bustling **52nd Street** jazz club scene.

The attending doctor estimates him to be between fifty and sixty, based on his physical condition.

Charlie Parker is thirty-four years old.

LIKE BIRD, WITH BILLIE HOLIDAY, GENIUS AND *HARD LIVING* GO HAND IN HAND.

A great blues singer, Billie also epitomizes the attractiveness of the pop singer in wartime America.

AND WHEN YOU SING IT, OTHER PEOPLE CAN FEEL SOMETHING, TOO.

GIVE ME A SONG I CAN FEEL, AND IT'S *NEVER* WORK.

IF YOU FIND A TUNE AND IT'S GOT SOMETHING TO DO WITH YOU, YOU FEEL IT.

After her early success at the Apollo in the '30s, Billie Holiday becomes one of the most critically acclaimed vocalists of the '40s.

THERE ARE A FEW SONGS I FEEL SO MUCH I CAN'T STAND TO SING THEM, BUT THAT'S SOMETHING ELSE AGAIN . . .

SHE IS TALKING ABOUT "STRANGE FRUIT," THE 1939 RECORDING THAT MAKES HER CAREER.

BILLIE, *PLEASE* DON'T SING IT. I SYMPATHIZE, BUT THIS SONG IS NOT APPROPRIATE.

This gripping song—*strange fruit* refers to lynched black bodies dangling from the limbs of trees—was written especially for Billie.

FRANK SCHIFFMAN

WHEN SHE FINISHES, THE ENTIRE THEATER FALLS SILENT, EXCEPT FOR THEIR COLLECTIVE SIGH.

Though vastly popular nationally, the troubled star is *busted* twice in the '40s for narcotics.

At the peak of her commercial success in 1947, a drug bust results, like Bird, in her Cabaret Card being pulled. Billie spirals into *chaos*.

BILLIE HOLIDAY
6/7/46 Armstrong Unit
Vocalist. Sings torch songs.
10/13/48 3000.00
8/26/49 2075.75
Unless a miraculous change takes 5/25/50 £500.00
place Billie's value to us is lost.
She has lost her public favor. She
seems unable to remain away from
stimulants.

BILLIE HOLIDAY
Terrible! She was sick, but she was also under the
effect of stimulants. Only a miracle can restore
this girl and make her worthwhile playing her again.

FRANK SCHIFFMAN'S INDEX CARD ON BILLIE TELLS THE END OF A SAD TALE OF DRUG ABUSE AND FAILING ABILITIES.

In 1959, Billie Holiday dies—cruelly arrested for drug possession and handcuffed even while laying terminally ill in her New York hospital bed.

IN HER PRIME, BILLIE IS AT THE FOREFRONT OF A WARTIME TREND THAT THE APOLLO EMBRACES AND ENCOURAGES.

THE POPULARITY OF THESE **"POP"** SONGS COINCIDES WITH THE LIFTING OF THE RECORDING BAN IN 1944.

Bars and restaurants stock their newfangled *jukeboxes*.

Inspired by the separations and sentimentality forced by World War II, Harlemites in the '40s want to hear *ballads*—love songs sung in intimate tones.

As home *record players* become more popular, consumers get in the habit of buying the latest top hits.

FOR AFRICAN AMERICANS, BILLY ECKSTINE IS PERHAPS THE GREATEST **SINGING IDOL** OF THE DECADE.

ECKSTINE'S SEAT-RUMBLING VIBRATO AND FACIAL CONTORTIONS REALLY GET TO THE APOLLO CROWD.

In 1945, Eckstine is also one of the few black singers to cross over from *Billboard's "Harlem Hit Parade"*— that became known as the black "R&B" chart—to the *"Honor Roll of Hits"* —the white "pop" chart.

Like Sinatra at the Paramount, Eckstine at the Apollo has a fanatical following of squealing adolescents who reverently refer to him as "Mr. B."

HE KNOWS JUST HOW TO QUIET THE THRONGS AT THE APOLLO WHEN THEY GET CARRIED AWAY.

STEADY NOW . . .

My destiny...

BOYS WEAR "MR. B" SHIRTS

IN THE LATE '40S, ECKSTINE REALLY TAKES OFF, AND FROM 1949 INTO THE EARLY '50S THE "SEPIA SINATRA" IS THE HOTTEST THING AT THE APOLLO, FUELED BY HITS LIKE "MY DESTINY."

TWO OTHER APOLLO HEARTTHROBS ARE **NAT KING COLE** AND **BILL KENNY** OF THE INK SPOTS.

If I didn't care...

Years later, Redd Foxx's TV character, Fred Sanford, loves to mimic Kenny's winsome high-pitched tenor.

THE NAT KING COLE TRIO SELL MILLIONS OF RECORDS IN THE MID-'40S.

When Cole goes solo in the late '40s, he is the top black act in show business.

125th APOLLO

NAT KING COLE

Held Over for a Second Smash Week!

...**HIS TRIO**

I DON'T CARE WHAT YOU HAVE TO DO, CLEAR NEXT WEEK.

YES, YES, I **KNOW** WE NEVER DO THAT.

PEARL BAILEY'S STAR IS ALSO ASCENDING BY THE LATE '40S, AFTER YEARS OF WORK WITH CAB CALLOWAY, COOTIE WILLIAMS, AND OTHERS SINCE HER 1934 AMATEUR NIGHT WIN.

BY 1953, HER SHOW WITH DUKE ELLINGTON GROSSES $40,000 AND SETS AN APOLLO **ATTENDANCE RECORD**.

"Pearly Mae" is a welcome tonic to war-weary Harlemites.

JOHN HAMMOND

PEARL BAILEY WAS THE APOLLO **IDEAL** OF A SINGER!

While her career later expands into nightclubs, Broadway, film, and television, Pearl always remains loyal to the Apollo.

HEY, BOBBY, WHEN CAN I COME **HOME**?

ANOTHER AMATEUR NIGHT WINNER, SARAH VAUGHAN, IS SIGNED BY ECKSTINE, ADORED BY BIRD, AND HAS HER FIRST SOLO RECORDING SESSION IN 1944, ARRANGED BY DIZZY GILLESPIE.

DIZ AND BIRD WERE THE BIGGEST AND MOST IMPORTANT CONTRIBUTORS TO MODERN JAZZ.

I'll wait and pray...

BUT, IN THE VOCAL FIELD, IT WOULD BE SARAH VAUGHAN.

BILLY ECKSTINE

HER **PERFECT PITCH** IS SOMETHING OF A PROBLEM AT THE APOLLO.

"Sassy" continually complains that the theater's piano is out of tune, even though Frank Schiffman has it tuned before every performance.

FORGET IT, POP, I'LL DO IT MYSELF.

Musicians love to play for the "Divine Sarah" because she uses her voice as an instrument, bending and coloring notes like a true improviser.

DINAH WASHINGTON COMBINES JAZZ STYLINGS WITH THE BLUES TO PRODUCE ONE OF THE GUTSIEST SOUNDS IN MUSIC.

But, she also has a great success with pop records like "Unforgettable" and "What a Difference a Day Makes."

LIONEL HAMPTON DISCOVERS HER IN THE WINDY CITY IN 1943.

MY MANAGER, JOE GLASER'S FRIEND, HAD A NIGHTCLUB IN THE LOOP.

Like Sarah Vaughan, Dinah Washington had **roots** in gospel music, having begun as a singer with church choirs in Chicago.

WHAT'S YOUR NAME, GIRL?

RUTH JONES.

I DON'T LIKE THAT NAME— CAN I CALL YOU SOMETHING ELSE?

I DON'T CARE WHAT YOU CALL ME, AS LONG AS YOU GIVE ME A JOB!

FROM NOW ON, YOUR NAME WILL BE DINAH WASHINGTON . . .

THEY HAD A YOUNG LADY WORKING IN THE LADIES' POWDER ROOM, AND EVERY TIME THE BAND WAS TO COME OUT TO PLAY, SHE WOULD POP HER HEAD OUT THE DOOR AND SING WITH THE BAND.

LADIE

1940s. While vocalists *overshadow* most of the bands, those of Lionel Hampton and Louis Jordan become the hottest African American attractions of their time.

Hamp gains fame in 1936 when Benny Goodman taps him to play vibes in Goodman's integrated group.

LIONEL HAMPTON

LOUIS JORDAN

Hamp brings his great sixteen-piece band into the Apollo in December 1940—to the delight of the Apollo crowd.

With such an outstanding lineup, Hampton begins letting his men work out on longer and wilder solos that often whip audiences into a frenzy.

DEXTER GORDON
SAX

ILLINOIS JACQUET
SAX

JOE NEWMAN
TRUMPET

IN "FLYING HOME," THE LIGHTS WOULD GO OUT, AND YOU'D SEE THE AIRPLANES PROJECTED ON THE SCRIM BEHIND THE BANDSTAND. YOU'D HEAR THE MOTOR HUMMING, AND THAT'S WHEN THE SAXOPHONE PLAYER STARTED PLAYING HIS FAMOUS SOLO . . .

"Flying Home," a number he writes and originally records with Goodman, becomes Hamp's showstopper.

Hampton has a penchant for clearing the Apollo, even if it means leading the audience out with his own band!

"FLYING HOME" WOULD GO ON FOR TWENTY MINUTES.

IT WAS A FANTASTIC THING TO SEE HAMP PERFORM.

HAMP WOULD JUMP ON HIS DRUM, THE APOLLO'S ELECTRICIAN, BOB HALL, WOULD PUSH A BUTTON, AND A SMUDGEPOT WOULD COME UP LIKE THE STAGE WAS BLOWING UP.

Sammy Davis Jr. works with Hampton when young Sammy is still a member of the Will Mastin Trio.

YOU'D LOOK UP AND HEAR HIM, AND THEN SUDDENLY HE'D DISAPPEAR . . .

AND THE ONLY PEOPLE LEFT ON STAGE WOULD BE THE DRUMMER AND A BASS PLAYER.

MILITARY DRUMSTICKS ARE BIG—PARADE STICKS.

BUT THAT WASN'T LOUD ENOUGH.

HAMP HAD TO TURN THE STICKS AROUND TO THE OTHER END TO KEEP THAT BEAT GOING.

HE'D GO PARADING OUT IN THE AUDIENCE . . .

AND RIGHT OUT THE THEATER ONTO 125TH STREET . . .

TO ENTERTAIN THE PEOPLE WAITING ON LINE!

WE JUST BLEW UP THE COMMUNITY WITH HAPPINESS AND JOY AND EXCITEMENT. FOURTH OF JULY EVERY DAY!

APOLLO

TONIGHT LIONEL HAMPTON

TONIGHT LIONEL HAMPTON

HAMP!

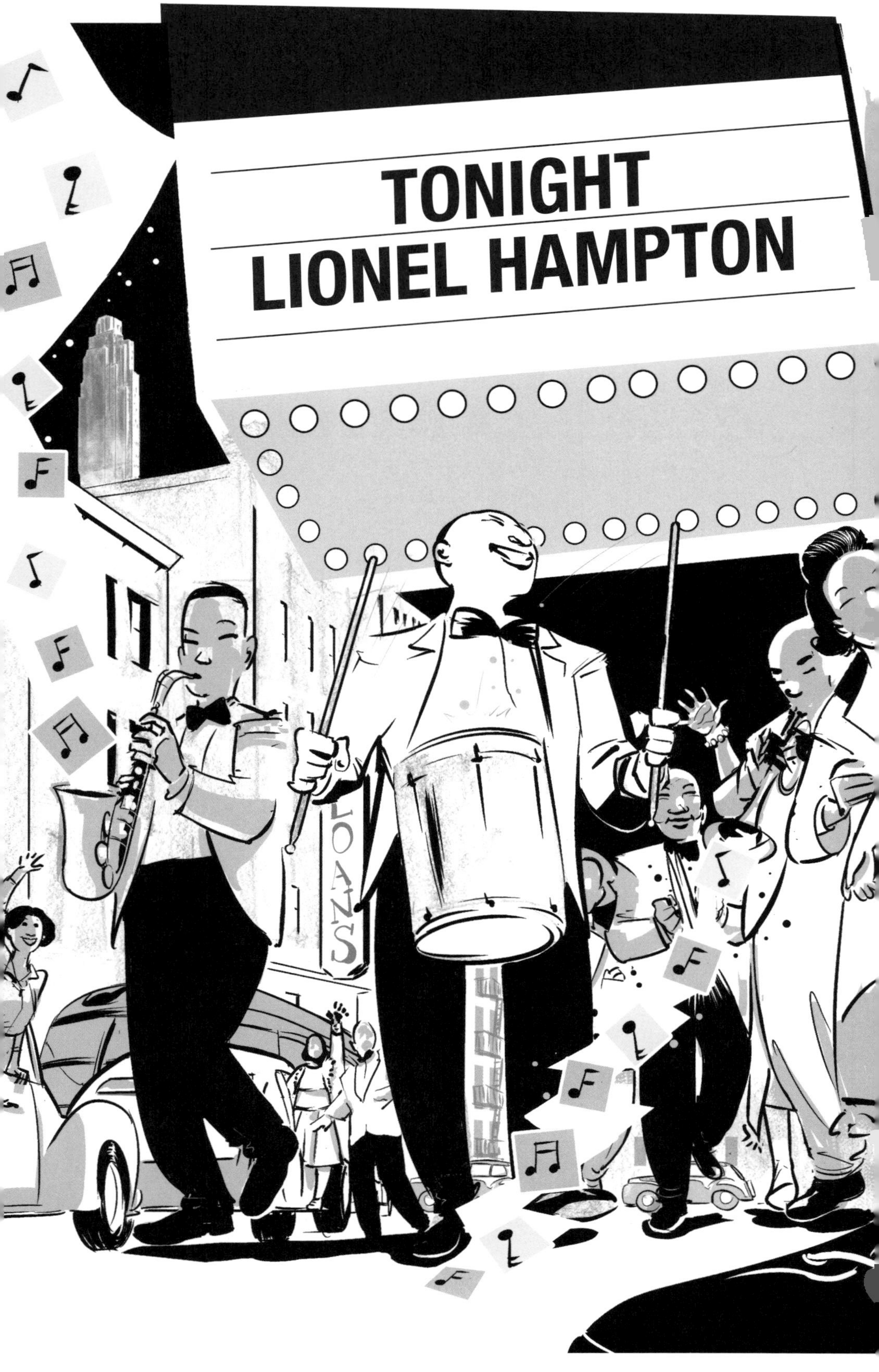
TONIGHT
LIONEL HAMPTON
LOANS

Hampton, with deep jazz roots, and Louis Jordan, who started with Chick Webb, would become great influences on the rhythm-and-blues and rock-and-roll revolutions to come.

JORDAN ALSO **SPEAKS** FOR THE PEOPLE AS AN INTERPRETER OF BLACK STREET LINGO TO THE WHITE WORLD.

LOUIS JORDAN

LIONEL HAMPTON

JAZZMEN PLAY MOSTLY FOR THEMSELVES. I WANT TO PLAY FOR THE **PEOPLE**!

ALL THAT ROCK-AND-ROLL STUFF. IT **ALL** STARTED WITH US. ALL THAT DANCING AND THINGS ONSTAGE. IT WAS ALL MY IDEAS.

Starting in 1942, Jordan is a regular on the "Harlem Hit Parade."

In 1946 alone, he scores eleven hits.

JORDAN MODELS HIMSELF AFTER CAB CALLOWAY, AND, LIKE HIS MENTOR, JORDAN ALSO CLOWNS IN FILMS.

JORDAN'S RELATIONSHIP WITH THE APOLLO AUDIENCE IS BLISSFUL. IN 1948, HE JOINS NAT COLE AS ONE OF FEW ARTISTS **HELD OVER** FOR A SECOND WEEK.

His early two-reeler films have been called the first rock-and-roll films, and precursors to music videos.

AS LATE AS 1960, JORDAN CAN STILL PACK THEM IN, AND RUNS A "LOUIS JORDAN FOR PRESIDENT" CAMPAIGN FROM THE APOLLO.

SAMMY DAVIS JR. GROWS UP IN A FAMILY OF VAUDEVILLIANS WHO CONSTANTLY TOUR THE COUNTRY AS PART OF THE ACT OF HIS FATHER AND HIS ADOPTED UNCLE, **WILL MASTIN**.

BILL "BOJANGLES" ROBINSON IS SO IMPRESSED WITH SAMMY THAT HE VOLUNTEERS TO TUTOR THE BOY.

HE'S A PERFECTIONIST.

EVERYONE KNEW MY MOTHER. SHE WAS A CHORUS GIRL AT THE APOLLO.

WHEN I FIRST CAME IN WITH THE WILL MASTIN TRIO, I WAS BABY SANCHEZ'S SON: BE NICE TO HIM.

When Sammy Davis Jr. first appears at the Apollo in 1947 with his father and uncle, they split $650 for the week.

113

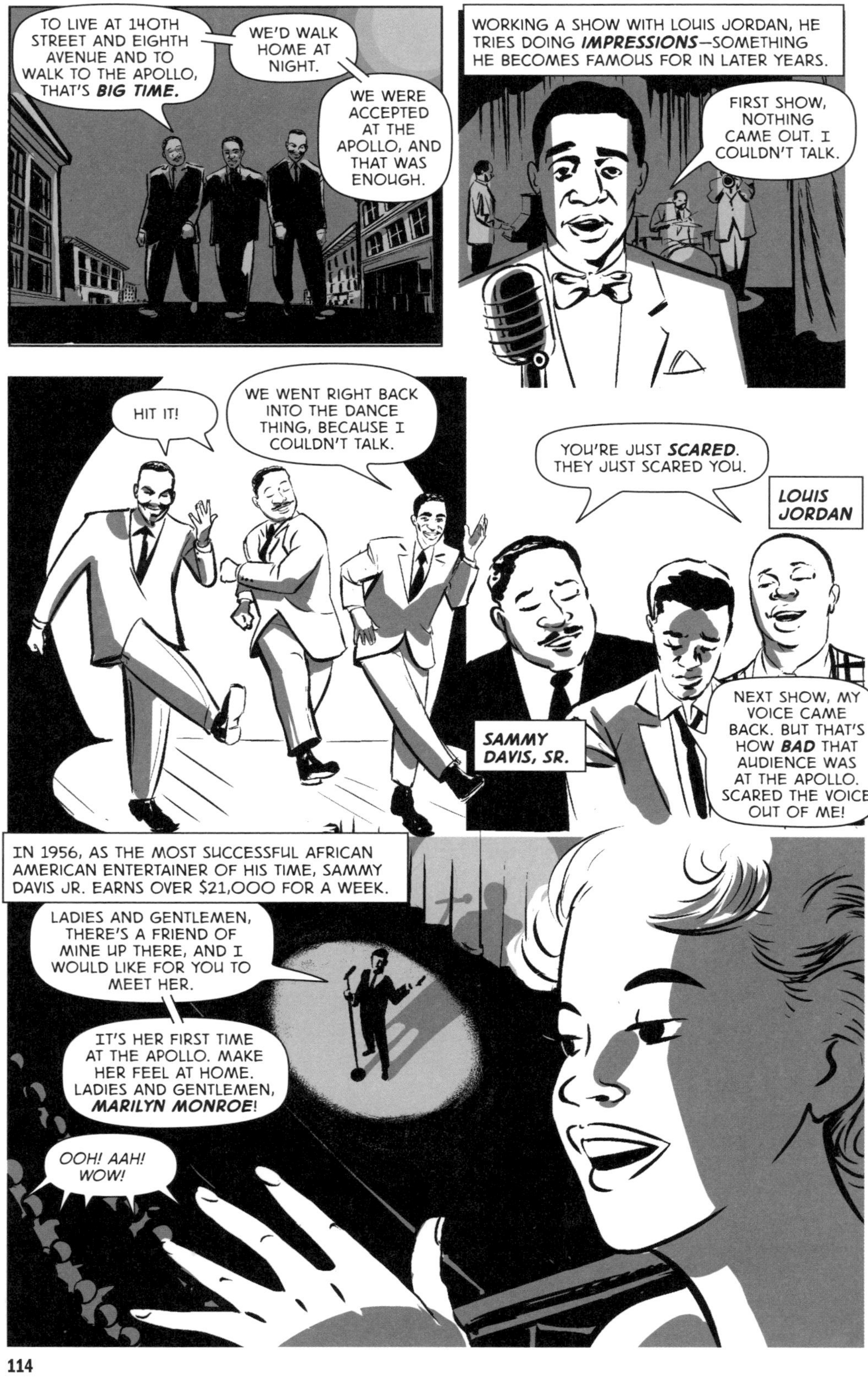

TO LIVE AT 140TH STREET AND EIGHTH AVENUE AND TO WALK TO THE APOLLO, THAT'S **BIG TIME.**
WE'D WALK HOME AT NIGHT.
WE WERE ACCEPTED AT THE APOLLO, AND THAT WAS ENOUGH.
WORKING A SHOW WITH LOUIS JORDAN, HE TRIES DOING **IMPRESSIONS**—SOMETHING HE BECOMES FAMOUS FOR IN LATER YEARS.
FIRST SHOW, NOTHING CAME OUT. I COULDN'T TALK.
HIT IT!
WE WENT RIGHT BACK INTO THE DANCE THING, BECAUSE I COULDN'T TALK.
YOU'RE JUST **SCARED**. THEY JUST SCARED YOU.
LOUIS JORDAN
SAMMY DAVIS, SR.
NEXT SHOW, MY VOICE CAME BACK. BUT THAT'S HOW **BAD** THAT AUDIENCE WAS AT THE APOLLO. SCARED THE VOICE OUT OF ME!
IN 1956, AS THE MOST SUCCESSFUL AFRICAN AMERICAN ENTERTAINER OF HIS TIME, SAMMY DAVIS JR. EARNS OVER $21,000 FOR A WEEK.
LADIES AND GENTLEMEN, THERE'S A FRIEND OF MINE UP THERE, AND I WOULD LIKE FOR YOU TO MEET HER.
IT'S HER FIRST TIME AT THE APOLLO. MAKE HER FEEL AT HOME. LADIES AND GENTLEMEN, **MARILYN MONROE**!
OOH! AAH! WOW!

SAMMY SUCCESSFULLY DANCES HIS WAY INTO THE FUTURE. BUT SOME OF THE GREATEST DANCERS OF THE '40S—*BUNNY BRIGGS*, *BABY LAURENCE*, AND *TEDDY HALE*—HAVE BEEN CALLED THE DYING BREED.

As bop gains dominance in the '40s, even the greatest dancers find themselves *subordinate* to music that is more complex and less danceable.

BUNNY BRIGGS

BABY LAURENCE

TEDDY HALE

TRAGICALLY, TEDDY HALE AND BABY LAURENCE ALSO FALL VICTIM TO BOP'S GREATEST *SCOURGE*—HEROIN.

GREGORY HINES

BUNNY BRIGGS

SAVION GLOVER

BUNNY BRIGGS ADAPTS, BECOMES A MENTOR TO NEW DANCERS, AND LONG WORKS SUCCESSFULLY, APPEARING ON BROADWAY IN *BLACK AND BLUE* IN 1989, RECEIVING A TONY AWARD NOMINATION.

But for dancers—once the *backbone* of the Apollo's vaudeville-variety format—and for other acts dependent on that format, the 1940s are a transitional time.

115

COMEDY AT THE APOLLO IS RELUCTANTLY COMING TO TERMS WITH MODERN TIMES.

THE OLDER GUYS WERE ALL DOING BLACKFACE WHEN I CAME ALONG IN 1944.

IT'S TIME TO GET THE BLACK OFF YOUR FACE. YOU DON'T NEED IT.

JOHN "ASHCAN" LARUE

TIMMIE ROGERS

WHO IN HELL DO YOU THINK YOU ARE? YOU JUST STARTED YOUR COMEDY ACT. WE'VE BEEN DOIN' THIS FOR FORTY YEARS, SON.

JOHN VIGAL

WE *KNOW* COMEDY. YOU HAVE TO *LEARN* IT.

I'VE LEARNED ONE THING: YOU DON'T NEED TO BE BLACKIN' YOUR FACE!

SUPPOSE YOU WERE ON RADIO? WOULD YOU WEAR BLACK ON YOUR FACE?

THAT STOPPED THEM *COLD*.

BUT IT WAS TRADITION. A MASK TO HIDE BEHIND.

ABOUT TWO YEARS LATER THEY ALL TOOK THE BLACK OFF THEIR FACES, AND THEY WERE JUST AS FUNNY WITHOUT BLACKFACE.

BECAUSE THE MAKEUP, THE CLOTHES, DON'T MAKE YOU. WHAT YOU *SAY* MAKES YOU.

COMING SOON: SOMETHING NEW!

As the '40s come to a close, the Apollo is about to enter a dynamic new phase.

The whole entertainment scene is *changing*, and with it the Apollo's treasured vaudeville variety format.

And for the entertainers dependent upon this format, there would be nothing funny in that at all.

CHAPTER 6

The 1950s: Rockin'

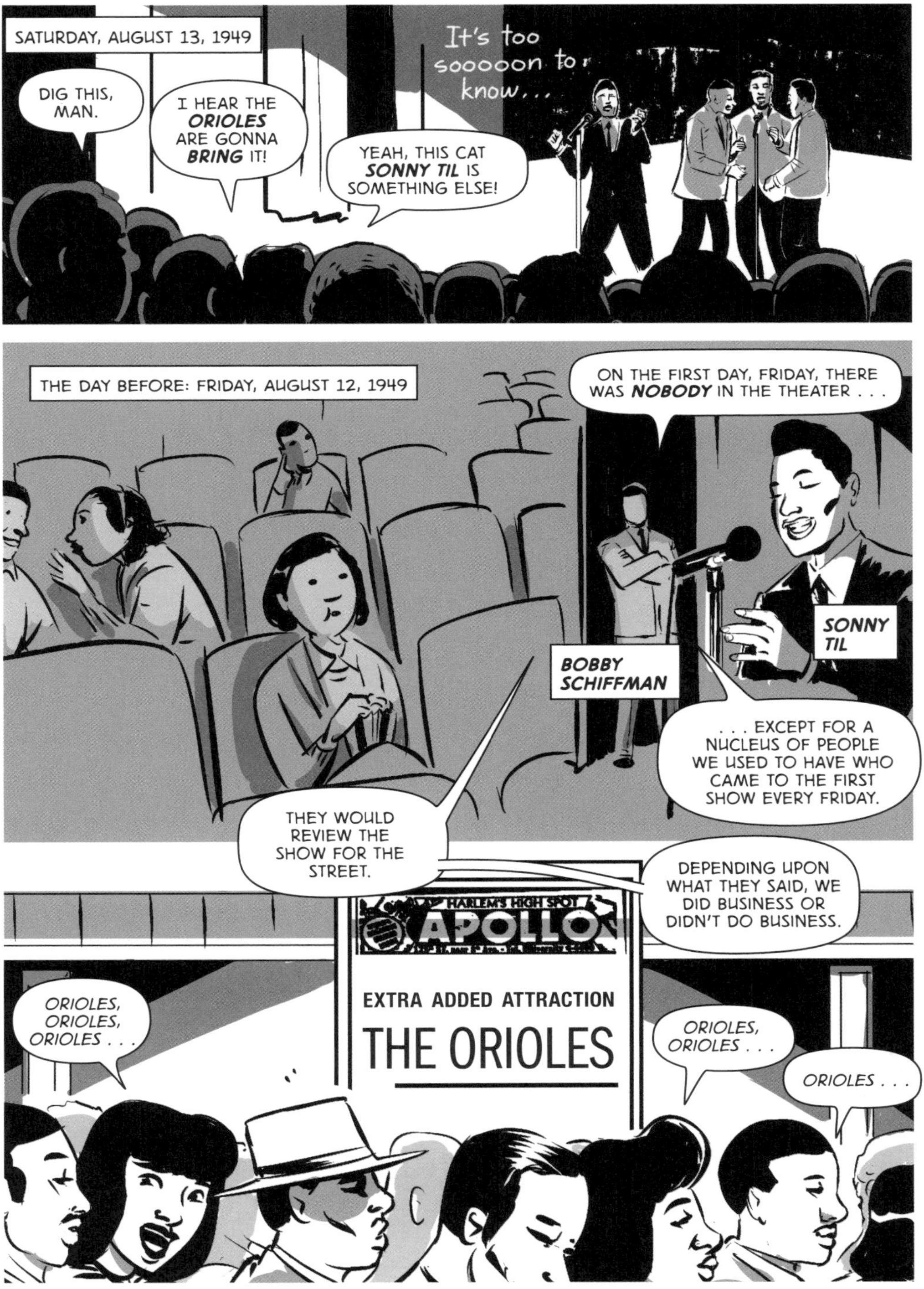
SATURDAY, AUGUST 13, 1949
DIG THIS, MAN.
I HEAR THE ORIOLES ARE GONNA BRING IT!
YEAH, THIS CAT SONNY TIL IS SOMETHING ELSE!
It's too sooooon to know, . . .
THE DAY BEFORE: FRIDAY, AUGUST 12, 1949
ON THE FIRST DAY, FRIDAY, THERE WAS NOBODY IN THE THEATER . . .
SONNY TIL
BOBBY SCHIFFMAN
. . . EXCEPT FOR A NUCLEUS OF PEOPLE WE USED TO HAVE WHO CAME TO THE FIRST SHOW EVERY FRIDAY.
THEY WOULD REVIEW THE SHOW FOR THE STREET.
DEPENDING UPON WHAT THEY SAID, WE DID BUSINESS OR DIDN'T DO BUSINESS.
HARLEM'S HIGH SPOT
APOLLO
EXTRA ADDED ATTRACTION
THE ORIOLES
ORIOLES, ORIOLES, ORIOLES . . .
ORIOLES, ORIOLES . . .
ORIOLES . . .

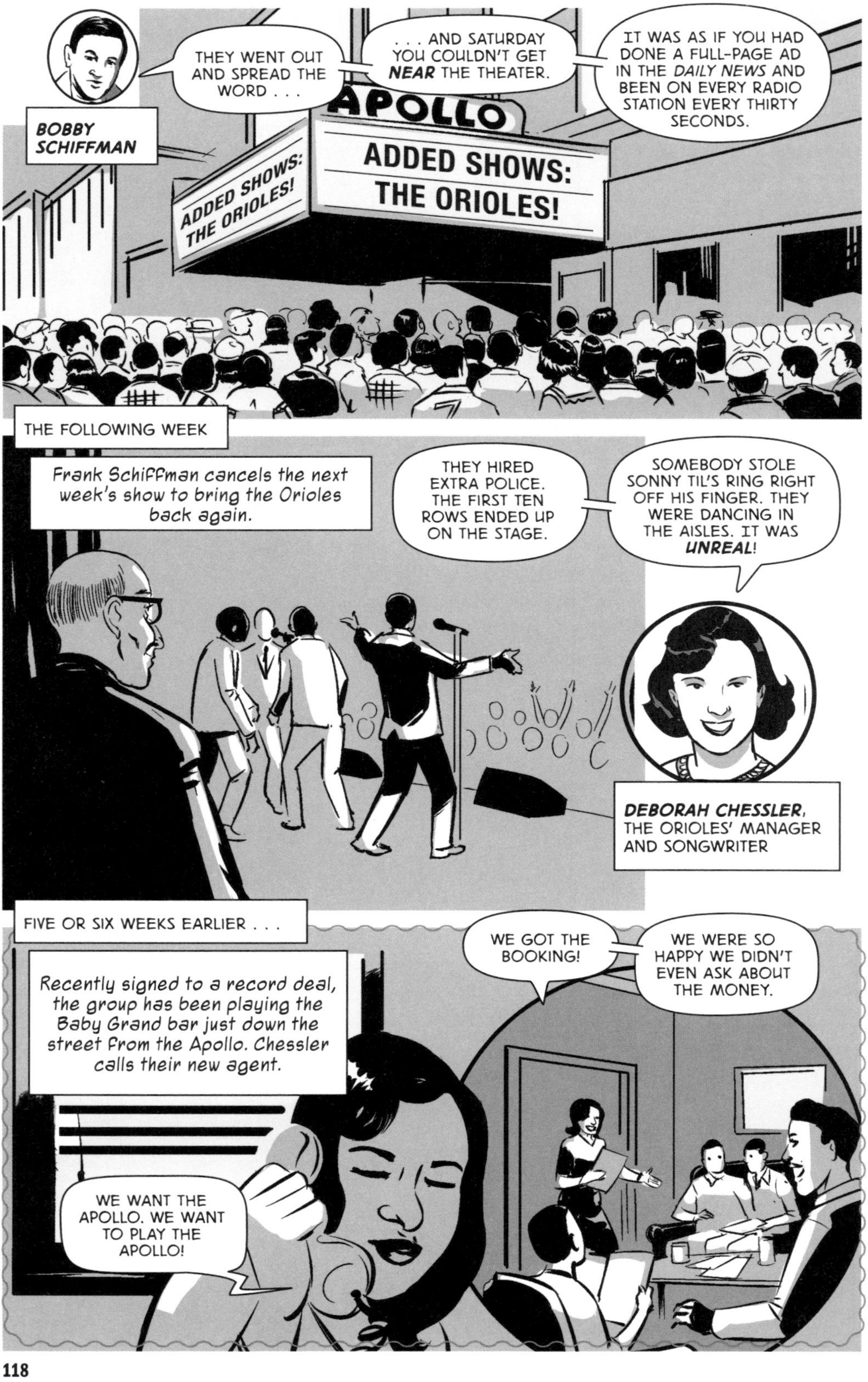
BOBBY SCHIFFMAN
THEY WENT OUT AND SPREAD THE WORD . . .
. . . AND SATURDAY YOU COULDN'T GET NEAR THE THEATER.
IT WAS AS IF YOU HAD DONE A FULL-PAGE AD IN THE DAILY NEWS AND BEEN ON EVERY RADIO STATION EVERY THIRTY SECONDS.
APOLLO
ADDED SHOWS: THE ORIOLES!
ADDED SHOWS: THE ORIOLES!
THE FOLLOWING WEEK
Frank Schiffman cancels the next week's show to bring the Orioles back again.
THEY HIRED EXTRA POLICE. THE FIRST TEN ROWS ENDED UP ON THE STAGE.
SOMEBODY STOLE SONNY TIL'S RING RIGHT OFF HIS FINGER. THEY WERE DANCING IN THE AISLES. IT WAS UNREAL!
DEBORAH CHESSLER, THE ORIOLES' MANAGER AND SONGWRITER
FIVE OR SIX WEEKS EARLIER . . .
Recently signed to a record deal, the group has been playing the Baby Grand bar just down the street from the Apollo. Chessler calls their new agent.
WE WANT THE APOLLO. WE WANT TO PLAY THE APOLLO!
WE GOT THE BOOKING!
WE WERE SO HAPPY WE DIDN'T EVEN ASK ABOUT THE MONEY.

THE ORIOLES KNOCK OUT THE APOLLO CROWD WITH A NEW SMALL-GROUP LOOK AND A FRESH SOUND: **RHYTHM AND BLUES**.

Cryin' in the Chaaaapel...

The group has a string of hits.

SONG PLUGGERS FREQUENTLY SEND THEM **DEMO RECORDS** OF SONGS, INCLUDING A TUNE INTENDED AS A COUNTRY-AND-WESTERN TEARJERKER.

IN BETWEEN SHOWS AT THE APOLLO, WE LISTENED IN THE DRESSING ROOM.

WE LEARNED "CRYIN' IN THE CHAPEL" IN ONE NIGHT.

THE NEXT NIGHT THEY DID IT IN THE THEATER.

THE FOLLOWING MORNING WE WERE DOWN AT THE RECORDING STUDIO.

IT HIT **OVERNIGHT**.

In the fall of 1953, "Cryin' in the Chapel" becomes the first R&B song to make the pop charts.

THE ORIOLES PROBABLY STARTED THE WHOLE RHYTHM-AND-BLUES SCENE. THEY WERE THE INNOVATORS.

ANYBODY LISTENING COULD REMEMBER THE MELODY, AND WENT AWAY SINGING ORIOLES SONGS.

Billboar

Yes, but there is more to rhythm and blues.

WE WERE WORKING UNDER ALL KINDS OF ADVERSE SITUATIONS. THERE WAS A LOT OF **HURT** THAT WENT ALONG WITH IT.

RUTH BROWN

After World War II, and the promise of the war years, disappointments and discrimination are an increasing burden for black America.

WHAT REALLY **SUSTAINED** US WAS THE MUSIC.

ALL OF THE THINGS THAT WENT WRONG DURING THE TRAVELS, OR THE HARASSMENT, YOU TOOK THAT OUT ONSTAGE.

THAT'S WHERE THE **FEELING** COMES FROM.

IT WAS A TOTAL EXPERIENCE. THE RHYTHM COVERED UP FOR THE BLUES.

THAT'S WHAT RHYTHM AND BLUES WAS.

JOHNNY OTIS STARTS USING THE TERM IN 1948 AFTER HE BREAKS UP HIS BIG BAND.

A BOOGIE–WOOGIE PIANO PLAYER, A GUITAR PLAYER, A COUPLE OF HORNS, AND A DRUMMER WOULD PROBABLY PLEASE PEOPLE MORE THAN A BIG FULL-BLOWN JAZZ BAND.

I **SAW** RHYTHM AND BLUES COMING.

THE JOHNNY OTIS RHYTHM AND BLUES CARAVAN.

JOHNNY OTIS BAND

Johnny Otis is an interesting cat: He is white. Veliotes is his original surname—from his Greek immigrant parents. But in every other way, he considers himself black. He grew up in a largely black neighborhood in Berkeley, California.

I DID NOT BECOME BLACK BECAUSE I WAS ATTRACTED TO NEGRO MUSIC . . .

I BECAME WHAT I AM BECAUSE AS A CHILD, I REACTED TO THE WAY OF LIFE, THE SPECIAL VITALITY, THE ATMOSPHERE OF THE BLACK COMMUNITY. I CANNOT THINK OF MYSELF AS WHITE.

Harlemites—especially the young folks—feel the music's vitality, shake under its power, and are liberated by the emotional expressiveness of rhythm and blues.

But the music meets with open derision in some circles who see it as vulgar, primitive, or trifling.

I WAS LIKE A **TRAITOR** TO SOME OF THE BROTHERS. I FELT UNEASY AROUND SOME OF THE JAZZ ESTABLISHMENT—LIKE I WAS BREAKING A SACRED TRUST.

EARLY 50'S APOLLO HEADLINERS

MAY 5, 1950
THE ORIOLES AND **BUDDY RICH**

JANUARY 4, 1951, ELLA FITZGERALD

APRIL 27, 1951, NAT KING COLE

APRIL 25, 1952, JOHNNY OTIS

AUGUST 22, 1952, DINAH WASHINGTON

JULY 3, 1953, RUTH BROWN

AUGUST 14, 1953, DUKE ELLINGTON

ONE OF THE GREATEST-EVER R&B STARS IS PLUCKED FROM COUNT BASIE'S CLASSIC BIG BAND—IF YOU CAN PLUCK A GUY WHO IS SIX-FOOT-TWO AND 250 POUNDS.

AT ATLANTIC RECORDS, WE THOUGHT **JOE TURNER** WAS ONE OF THE GREAT BLUES SINGERS OF ALL TIME. BUT WE DIDN'T KNOW WHERE HE WAS.

AHMET ERTEGUN, ATLANTIC RECORDS CO-FOUNDER

WE HEARD HE WAS OUT IN CALIFORNIA, TEXAS, OR CHICAGO . . .

I READ THAT JIMMIE RUSHING HAD QUIT THE BASIE BAND AND THAT JOE TURNER HAD TAKEN HIS PLACE.

THE FOLLOWING WEEK I SAW THAT COUNT BASIE WAS PLAYING AT THE APOLLO.

JOE TURNER SINGS STRICTLY TRADITIONAL EIGHT- OR TWELVE-BAR BLUES. BUT THE ARRANGEMENTS FOR THE STAGE HAD BECOME MUCH MORE SOPHISTICATED.

THEY PROBABLY HADN'T HAD MANY REHEARSALS, IF ANY.

JOE CAME BACK RIGHT ON THE BEAT WHERE HE WAS **SUPPOSED** TO, BUT THE ARRANGEMENT WENT ANOTHER WAY.

HA HA!

HA HA!

SO HALFWAY INTO THE SONG THEY WERE **COMPLETELY OFF**, WHICH SENT THE CROWD INTO HYSTERICAL LAUGHTER.

I FELT VERY BAD FOR JOE TURNER. I WENT BACKSTAGE DURING THE BREAK, BUT HE'D ALREADY LEFT.

EXIT →

HEAD STAGEHAND **WILLIAM SPAYNE**

AHMET ERTEGUN

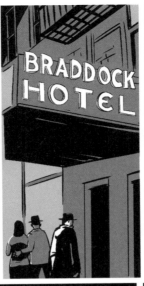

BRADDOCK HOTEL

MAN, **FORGET** ABOUT ALL THIS. I KNOW I CAN MAKE HIT RECORDS WITH YOU. WE'RE GOING TO DO A WHOLE **NEW THING**!

♪ Chains of ♪ Looooove....

I WROTE, WITH HIS HELP, A SONG CALLED "CHAINS OF LOVE," AND JESSE STONE WROTE A BEAUTIFUL ARRANGEMENT. THAT BECAME A BIG HIT!

YOU MAY HAVE HEARD OF ANOTHER SONG BIG JOE TURNER AND THIS TEAM MADE FAMOUS.

...SHAKE, RATTLE AND ROLL!

ERTEGUN IS ALSO BEHIND THE MAKING OF PERHAPS THE MOST IMPORTANT GROUP OF THE R&B ERA: *THE DRIFTERS*.

And, as so many of these tales do, the story starts at the Apollo.

APOLL

SEVENTEEN-YEAR-OLD **CLYDE MCPHATTER** WINS AMATEUR NIGHT IN 1950.

BILLY WARD HIRES CLYDE FOR HIS NEW GROUP, THE **DOMINOES**. THEY DEBUT AT THE APOLLO WITH THE ORIOLES.

OH MY GOD, THAT VOICE IS SO ANGELIC. SO MUCH GOSPEL FEELING!

AHMET ERTEGUN

A YEAR OR SO LATER, ERTEGUN HEARS THAT MCPHATTER IS NO LONGER WITH THE DOMINOES.

ARE YOU FREE?

YEAH, MAN, THEY FIRED ME!

I COULDN'T BELIEVE IT.

THAT WAS THE BEGINNING OF THE DRIFTERS.

AHMET ERTEGUN

CLYDE MCPHATTER

IT'S BEEN SAID THAT THE GROUP TAKES ITS NAME FROM THE FACT THAT THE MEMBERS HAD DRIFTED IN AND OUT OF MANY DIFFERENT GROUPS.

The Drifters hit immediately with "Money Honey," but McPhatter goes into the army in 1955, and they carry on without him.

Clyde goes solo when he gets out. The group continues until 1958, then breaks up.

HEY, MAN, WHAT ABOUT OUR GODDAMNED CONTRACT?!

BOBBY SCHIFFMAN

The group's manager had signed a multiyear contract with the Apollo. To avoid default, he asks **Ben E. King**'s group, the Five Crowns, to become the Drifters.

ATLANTIC RECORDS ASSIGNS TWO ACE SONGWRITING TEAMS TO CREATE NEW SONGS FOR THE GROUP.

Save The Last Dance For Me

This Magic Moment

There Goes My Baby

They write the biggest hits of any of the Drifters' lineups.

JERRY LEIBER AND **MIKE STOLLER,** AND **DOC POMUS** AND **MORT SHUMAN**

AFTER BEN E. KING LEAVES IN 1960, THE GROUP REORGANIZES YET AGAIN, AND CONTINUES TO PRODUCE HITS INTO THE MID-'60S.

Under The Boardwalk

Up On The Roof

On Broadway

KING AND THE DRIFTERS HAVE A RUN-IN AT THE APOLLO WITH A WILD MAN NAMED **SCREAMIN' JAY HAWKINS**, WHO HIT IN 1956 WITH "I PUT A SPELL ON YOU."

ALAN FREED TOLD ME, WITH A SONG LIKE THAT YOU NEED SOMETHING **WEIRD**.

HENRY →

Freed, the DJ who coined the term "rock and roll," helps Hawkins to devise a routine where a closed coffin is wheeled onstage . . . out of which Screamin' Jay would suddenly emerge.

Hawkins carries the coffin wherever he goes in a zebra-striped hearse. Some creeped-out stagehands *refuse* to handle it.

A matchbook would be inserted in the latch to keep the lid from locking.

SCREAMIN' JAY HAD ASKED THE DRIFTERS TO PERFORM THAT TASK FOR HIM . . .

OH DAMN!

BUT THEY NEVER DID IT.

@#$%&!!

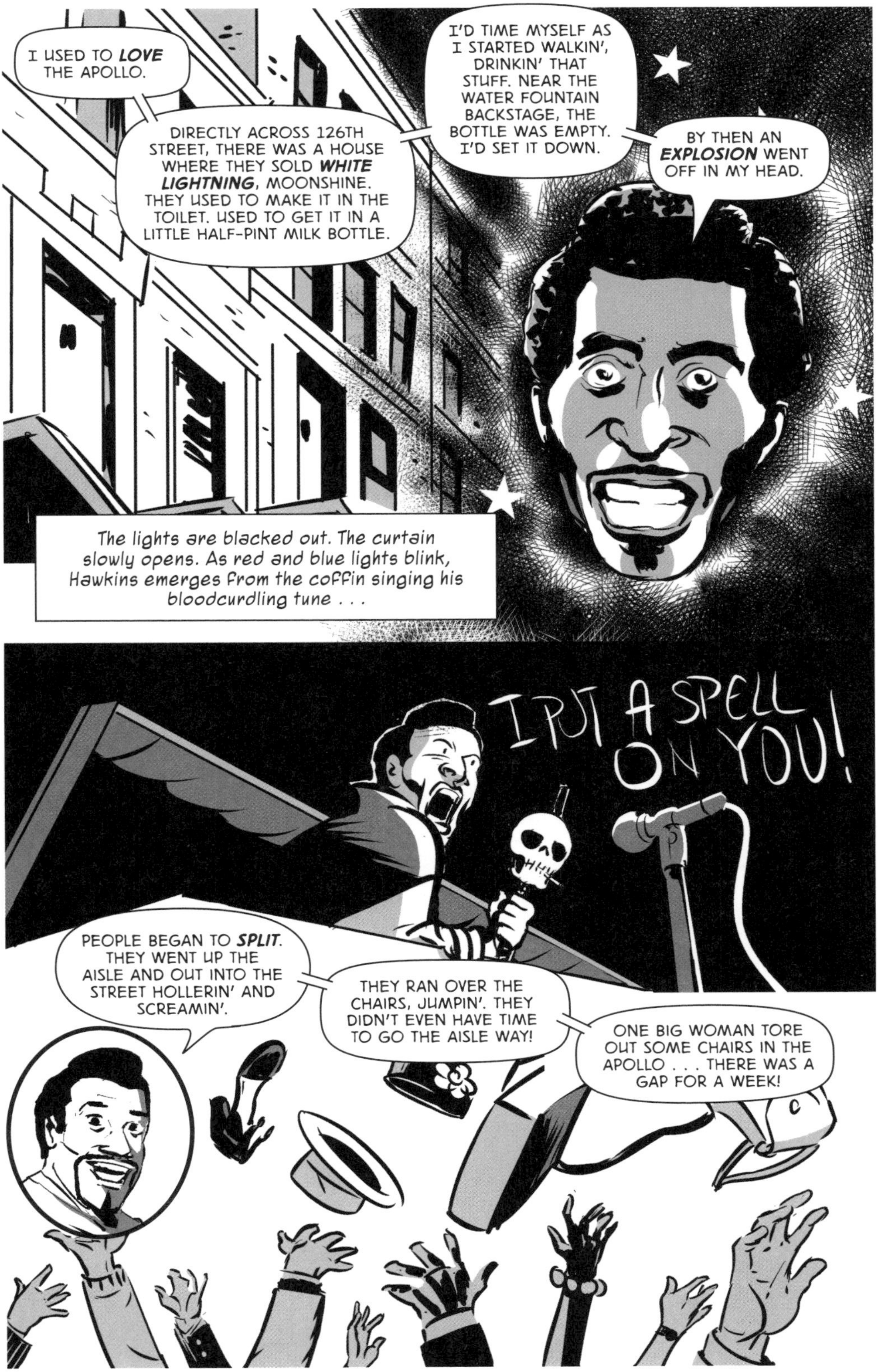
I USED TO LOVE THE APOLLO.
DIRECTLY ACROSS 126TH STREET, THERE WAS A HOUSE WHERE THEY SOLD WHITE LIGHTNING, MOONSHINE. THEY USED TO MAKE IT IN THE TOILET. USED TO GET IT IN A LITTLE HALF-PINT MILK BOTTLE.
I'D TIME MYSELF AS I STARTED WALKIN', DRINKIN' THAT STUFF. NEAR THE WATER FOUNTAIN BACKSTAGE, THE BOTTLE WAS EMPTY. I'D SET IT DOWN.
BY THEN AN EXPLOSION WENT OFF IN MY HEAD.
The lights are blacked out. The curtain slowly opens. As red and blue lights blink, Hawkins emerges from the coffin singing his bloodcurdling tune . . .
I PUT A SPELL ON YOU!
PEOPLE BEGAN TO SPLIT. THEY WENT UP THE AISLE AND OUT INTO THE STREET HOLLERIN' AND SCREAMIN'.
THEY RAN OVER THE CHAIRS, JUMPIN'. THEY DIDN'T EVEN HAVE TIME TO GO THE AISLE WAY!
ONE BIG WOMAN TORE OUT SOME CHAIRS IN THE APOLLO . . . THERE WAS A GAP FOR A WEEK!

BO DIDDLEY IS CAUSING RIOTS IN THE APOLLO, TOO, AND HE CLAIMS A **NEW** APOLLO HOUSE ATTENDANCE RECORD IN 1956.

It's a fundamental element of what will become rock and roll—as Elvis realizes on his first visit to New York when he catches Bo at the Apollo.

His self-titled first hit for Chess Records lays down a thundering beat unlike anything ever heard before.

THE FIRST TIME WE HAD BO DIDDLEY, I THOUGHT WE WERE GONNA HAVE AN UPRISING.

THE MUSIC WAS SO STIMULATING TO EVERYBODY, INCLUDING ME, THAT IT WAS WHIPPING THE CROWD INTO A **FRENZY**.

IT WAS JUST A COMPLETELY NEW, DIFFERENT STYLE.

BOBBY SCHIFFMAN

ROCK AND ROLL'S MAIN INGREDIENT WAS THE **BEAT**, AND BO DIDDLEY WAS THE LEADING EXPONENT OF THAT. TO HIM, MELODY MEANT NOTHING. LYRICS MEANT NOTHING. IT WAS THE BEAT THAT WAS INFECTIOUS.

IT WOULD DRIVE YOU **CRAZY**. HE REALLY SET THE PLACE ON FIRE.

WHEN **BUDDY HOLLY AND THE CRICKETS** DEBUT AT THE APOLLO IN 1957, CHANNELING BO DIDDLEY BAILS THEM OUT OF TROUBLE.

Cricket's guitarist *Niki Sullivan* tells Holly's biographer, John Goldrosen, about it.

THE FIRST TIME WE WENT ON WAS A WEEKDAY MATINEE.

THEY OPENED THE CURTAINS AND BUDDY STEPPED TOWARD THE MIKE.

IT'D BETTER SOUND LIKE THE RECORD!

YOU COULD HAVE HEARD A PIN DROP.

THE SAME THING ON THE EVENING SHOW, AND THE NEXT DAY—**NOTHING**.

THE THIRD DAY WE DID OUR FIRST SONG AND GOT NO RESPONSE AGAIN.

LET'S DO "BO DIDDLEY."

WE WENT INTO "BO DIDDLEY," CUTTING UP AND WORKING OUR BUNS OFF.

WHEN WE FINISHED THAT SONG, THE PEOPLE JUST WENT *BANANAS*.

FROM THEN ON, WE WERE ACCEPTED AT THE APOLLO.

Time and again the Apollo audience proves that *anyone* giving their all is cool.

BOBBY DARIN

OTHER WHITE ARTISTS ARE ALSO WARMLY WELCOMED AT THE APOLLO.

JERRY LEE LEWIS

BUDDY RICH

CHARLIE BARNET

THE FOUR SEASONS

130

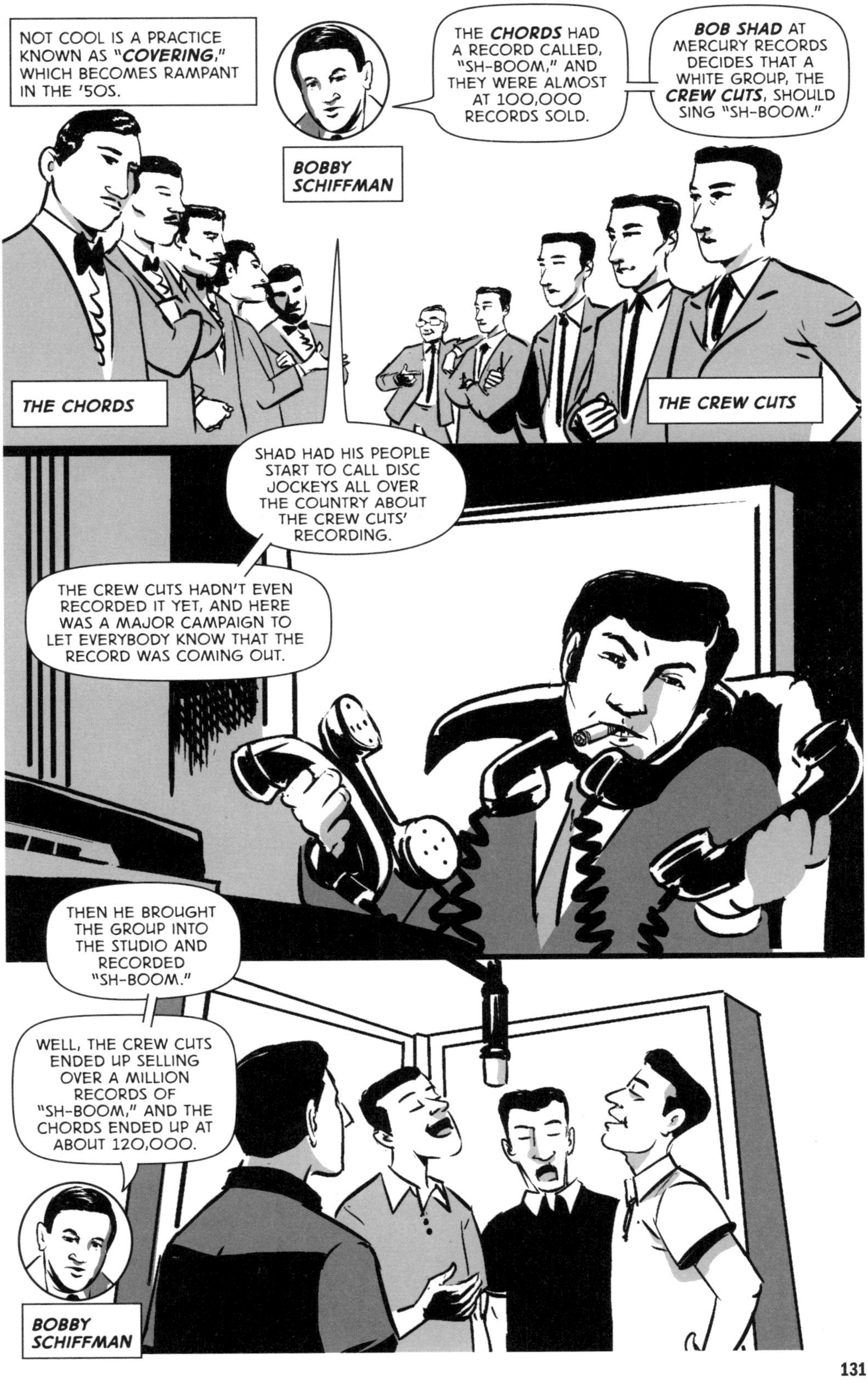
NOT COOL IS A PRACTICE KNOWN AS "*COVERING*," WHICH BECOMES RAMPANT IN THE '50S.
BOBBY SCHIFFMAN
THE *CHORDS* HAD A RECORD CALLED, "SH-BOOM," AND THEY WERE ALMOST AT 100,000 RECORDS SOLD.
BOB SHAD AT MERCURY RECORDS DECIDES THAT A WHITE GROUP, THE *CREW CUTS*, SHOULD SING "SH-BOOM."
THE CHORDS
THE CREW CUTS
SHAD HAD HIS PEOPLE START TO CALL DISC JOCKEYS ALL OVER THE COUNTRY ABOUT THE CREW CUTS' RECORDING.
THE CREW CUTS HADN'T EVEN RECORDED IT YET, AND HERE WAS A MAJOR CAMPAIGN TO LET EVERYBODY KNOW THAT THE RECORD WAS COMING OUT.
THEN HE BROUGHT THE GROUP INTO THE STUDIO AND RECORDED "SH-BOOM."
WELL, THE CREW CUTS ENDED UP SELLING OVER A MILLION RECORDS OF "SH-BOOM," AND THE CHORDS ENDED UP AT ABOUT 120,000.
BOBBY SCHIFFMAN

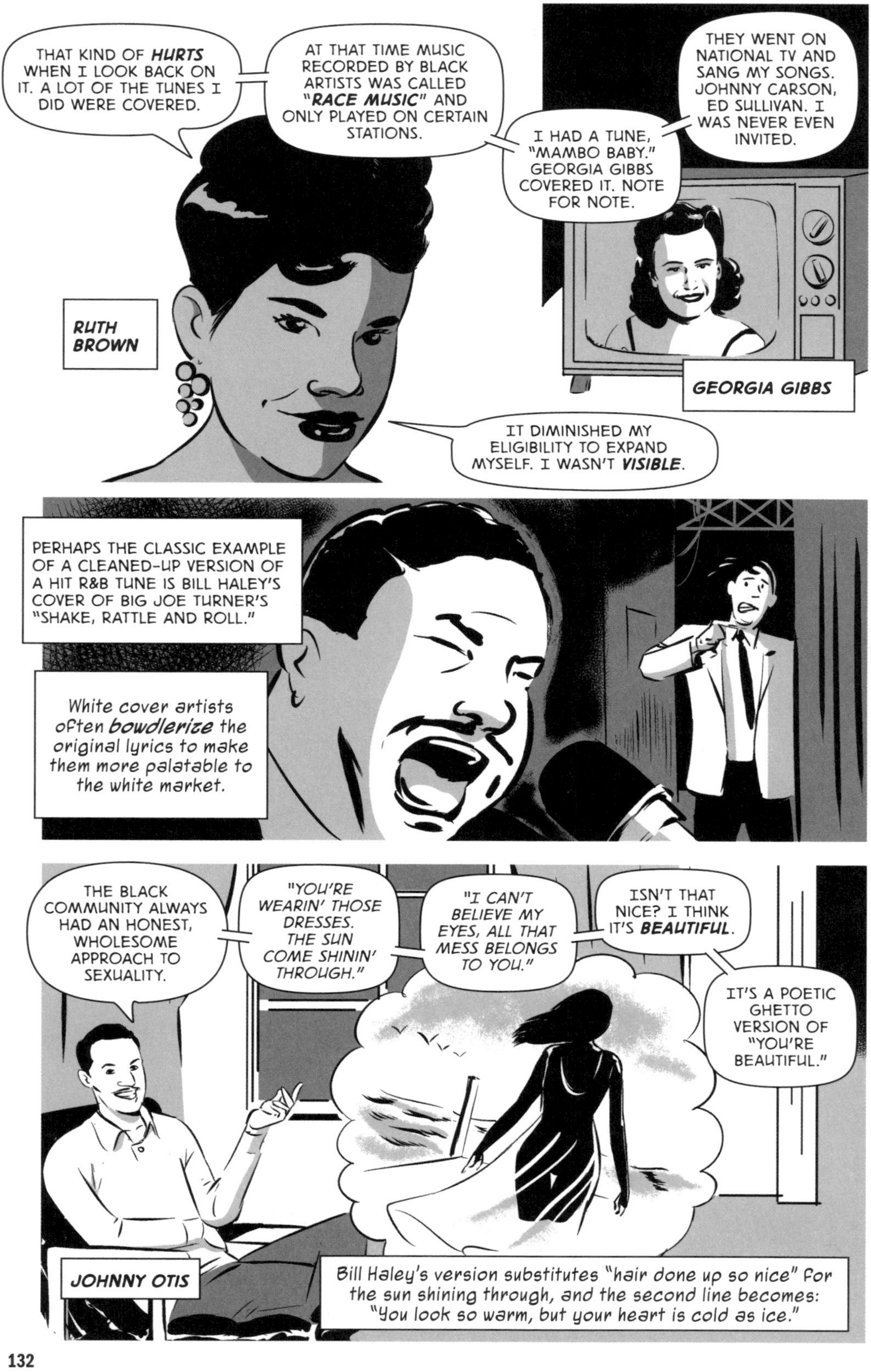
THAT KIND OF HURTS WHEN I LOOK BACK ON IT. A LOT OF THE TUNES I DID WERE COVERED.
AT THAT TIME MUSIC RECORDED BY BLACK ARTISTS WAS CALLED "RACE MUSIC" AND ONLY PLAYED ON CERTAIN STATIONS.
I HAD A TUNE, "MAMBO BABY." GEORGIA GIBBS COVERED IT. NOTE FOR NOTE.
THEY WENT ON NATIONAL TV AND SANG MY SONGS. JOHNNY CARSON, ED SULLIVAN. I WAS NEVER EVEN INVITED.
RUTH BROWN
GEORGIA GIBBS
IT DIMINISHED MY ELIGIBILITY TO EXPAND MYSELF. I WASN'T VISIBLE.
PERHAPS THE CLASSIC EXAMPLE OF A CLEANED-UP VERSION OF A HIT R&B TUNE IS BILL HALEY'S COVER OF BIG JOE TURNER'S "SHAKE, RATTLE AND ROLL."
White cover artists often bowdlerize the original lyrics to make them more palatable to the white market.
THE BLACK COMMUNITY ALWAYS HAD AN HONEST, WHOLESOME APPROACH TO SEXUALITY.
"YOU'RE WEARIN' THOSE DRESSES. THE SUN COME SHININ' THROUGH."
"I CAN'T BELIEVE MY EYES, ALL THAT MESS BELONGS TO YOU."
ISN'T THAT NICE? I THINK IT'S BEAUTIFUL.
IT'S A POETIC GHETTO VERSION OF "YOU'RE BEAUTIFUL."
JOHNNY OTIS
Bill Haley's version substitutes "hair done up so nice" for the sun shining through, and the second line becomes: "You look so warm, but your heart is cold as ice."

SOME SEE A CONNECTION BETWEEN THE WAY AFRICAN AMERICAN ARTISTS ARE ABUSED BY THE SYSTEM AND THE DRUG ABUSE THAT AFFECTS THEIR COMMUNITY.

Although the Apollo itself is relatively drug-free, there are often dealers lurking around the stage door. The temptation seems especially great for the new young stars of the rhythm-and-blues era.

THIS SYSTEM HAD PRESSURED SO MANY MARVELOUS PEOPLE, WHO DIDN'T DESERVE THAT. THEY DESERVED *REWARDS*, NOT *PUNISHMENT*.

THAT IS NOT TO SAY THAT SOME PEOPLE AREN'T JUST FOOLS. EVERYBODY ISN'T MOVED INTO A NEGATIVE LIFESTYLE BECAUSE THEY'RE BLACK. THAT'S A LOT OF CRAP.

I DON'T MEAN TO IDEALIZE PEOPLE UNNECESSARILY, BUT THAT HAS A LOT TO DO WITH IT. THAT'S WHY THERE IS MORE DOPE IN THE BLACK COMMUNITY.

THEY'RE SITTING DUCKS. THE *PRESSURE* MAKES FOR MORE *SUSCEPTIBILITY*.

133

LESLIE UGGAMS LITERALLY GROWS UP IN THE MIDDLE OF THE SCENE.

She wins Amateur Night at age seven, and the Schiffmans have Lucky Millinder create an act for her. Her first Apollo show is with Louis Armstrong.

COMING FROM THE KIND OF NEIGHBORHOOD I CAME FROM, HALF THE TIME THERE WASN'T A FATHER, OR IF THERE WAS A FATHER, THERE WERE NINE OTHER SISTERS AND BROTHERS, AND NOBODY PAID ANY ATTENTION TO YOU.

SO, WITH SOME PEOPLE IN THE BUSINESS, THEY FINALLY GOT THE ATTENTION THEY DIDN'T GET AT HOME.

NOW ALL OF A SUDDEN YOU BECOME A BIG STAR, AND PEOPLE WHO DIDN'T **RESPECT** YOU, ALL OF A SUDDEN, IT'S "WOULD YOU SIGN AN AUTOGRAPH?"

Leslie Uggams avoids the pitfalls and goes on to a successful singing and acting career.

THE POWER WAS LIKE, "OH, HEY, NOW I AM SOMEBODY! I WANT TO BE COOL . . . OH, WHAT IS THAT YOU'RE DOING? I'D LIKE TO TRY THAT."

Others are not so lucky. . .

ESTHER PHILLIPS MAKES REMARKABLE COMEBACKS FROM A TOUGH LIFE. FIRST IN THE '60S, AND THEN IN 1975, ON AN EARLY EPISODE OF *SATURDAY NIGHT LIVE*, SHE PERFORMS HER HIT DISCO REMAKE OF DINAH WASHINGTON'S "WHAT A DIFFERENCE A DAY MAKES"—A SONG THAT GOES BACK TO LITTLE ESTHER PHILLIPS'S EARLY DAYS AT THE APOLLO.

BETWEEN SHOWS I WOULD GET KIND OF *FIDGETY* BECAUSE I HAD NOBODY TO PLAY WITH. SO I'D GO DOWN AND PLAY WITH THE LIGHTS AND MESS UP THE MOVIE.

ESTHER PHILLIPS

I WAS KIND OF A LITTLE BRAT, I GUESS, BUT I WAS *BORED*.

Johnny Otis discovers the irrepressible thirteen-year-old in L.A. and records "Double Crossing Blues" with her. It becomes one of the biggest rhythm-and-blues hits of 1950, and she goes on the road with Otis.

"ARE YOU OUT OF YOUR @#$%&! MIND . . ."

LESLIE UGGAMS

DINAH WASHINGTON COULD CUSS BETTER THAN *ANYBODY* I EVER HEARD IN MY LIFE, BUT SHE HAD A HEART OF GOLD.

WE HAD HER DRESSED LIKE A LITTLE SOUTHERN GIRL. THAT'S WHAT ESTHER WAS.

SOME PEOPLE CRITICIZED US FOR THAT.

#$%#
@$%#

JOHNNY OTIS

DINAH WASHINGTON

SHE'D TELL MY MOTHER, "OK, JUANITA, TAKE BABY INTO THE DRESSING ROOM. I GOT SOME STRONG CUSS WORDS I GOTTA USE HERE."

SO DINAH WASHINGTON BRINGS LITTLE ESTHER BACK WITH HER HAIR DONE, HIGH-HEEL SHOES ON, NYLON STOCKINGS, AND A FORM-FITTING DRESS. SHE LOOKED LIKE SHE WAS THIRTY.

THAT'S *DISGRACEFUL*, HAVING HER LOOK LIKE SHE'S IN THE COTTON FIELDS!

BUT DINAH'S VOICE CARRIED *EVERYWHERE*, IT WASN'T LIKE YOU COULDN'T HEAR IT.

I COULDN'T TELL ESTHER ANYTHING, BECAUSE ESTHER WAS A VERY PRECOCIOUS CHILD, LIKE A WOMAN AT THIRTEEN, AND SHE LIKED IT.

Soon after she leaves Otis in 1952, Little Esther is a fifteen-year-old heroin addict.

ESTHER PHILLIPS

Despite her comebacks, she *succumbs* to the long-term effects of her drug abuse. She dies in 1984 at the age of forty-eight.

HER MALE COUNTERPART IS, PERHAPS, *LITTLE WILLIE JOHN*.

He was active in promoting the nascent career of his friend James Brown, who used to open for Willie John at the Apollo in the early days.

IF HE WANTED TO DO SOMETHING, HE DID IT WITHOUT EVEN A MOMENT'S HESITATION. *CAREFREE.*

LITTLE WILLIE JOHN

JAMES BROWN

ST. CLAIR PINCKNEY— JB'S MUSICAL DIRECTOR.

Another Johnny Otis discovery, the seventeen-year-old Little Willie John hits in 1955 with "All Around the World." His biggest success is "Fever" in 1956—later rearranged and covered by *Peggy Lee.*

DANNY RAY— JB'S EMCEE

HE WAS A CONSTANT RIOT ALL DAY LONG.

PEGGY LEE FEVER

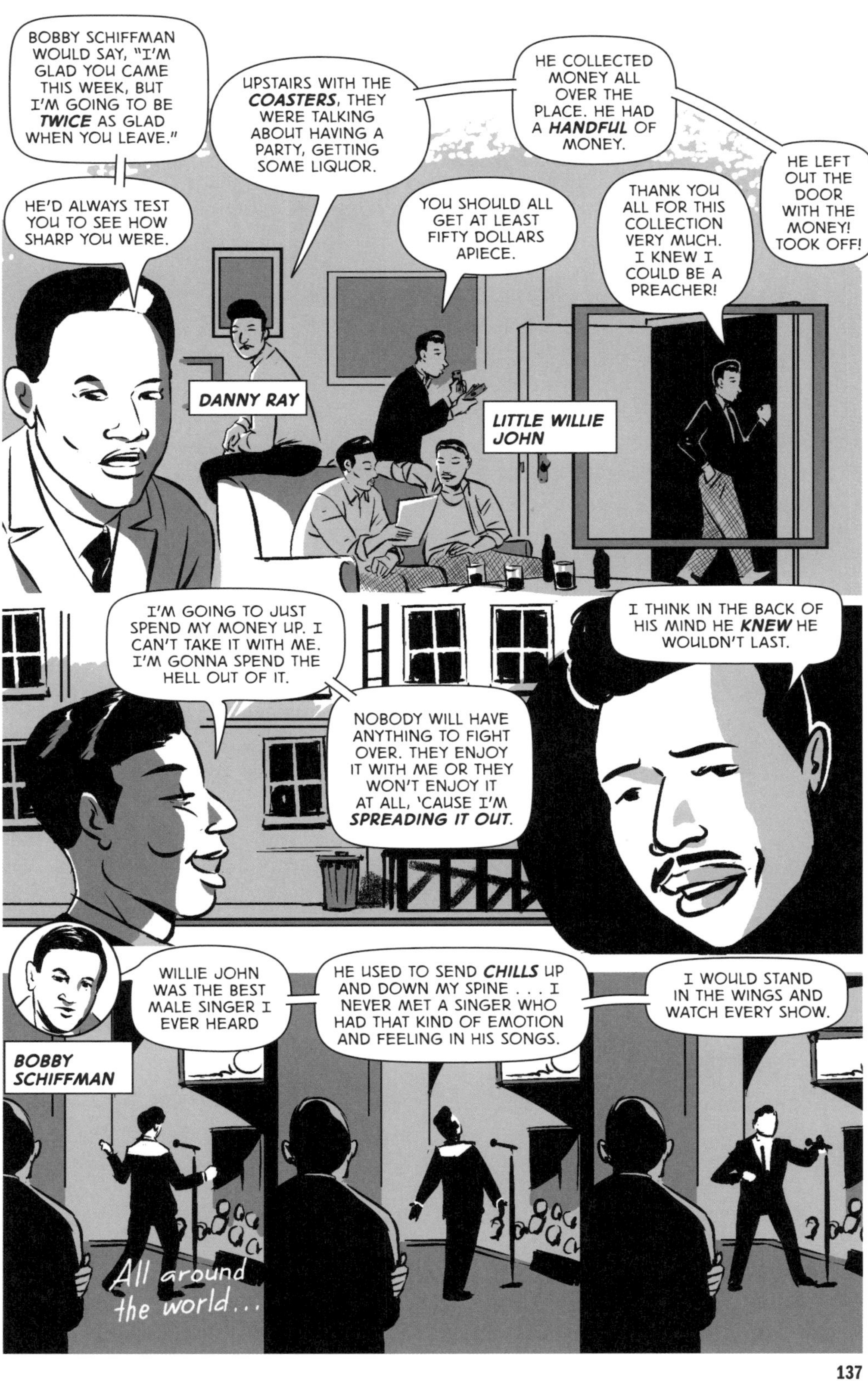
BOBBY SCHIFFMAN WOULD SAY, "I'M GLAD YOU CAME THIS WEEK, BUT I'M GOING TO BE TWICE AS GLAD WHEN YOU LEAVE."
HE'D ALWAYS TEST YOU TO SEE HOW SHARP YOU WERE.
UPSTAIRS WITH THE COASTERS, THEY WERE TALKING ABOUT HAVING A PARTY, GETTING SOME LIQUOR.
HE COLLECTED MONEY ALL OVER THE PLACE. HE HAD A HANDFUL OF MONEY.
YOU SHOULD ALL GET AT LEAST FIFTY DOLLARS APIECE.
THANK YOU ALL FOR THIS COLLECTION VERY MUCH. I KNEW I COULD BE A PREACHER!
HE LEFT OUT THE DOOR WITH THE MONEY! TOOK OFF!
DANNY RAY
LITTLE WILLIE JOHN
I'M GOING TO JUST SPEND MY MONEY UP. I CAN'T TAKE IT WITH ME. I'M GONNA SPEND THE HELL OUT OF IT.
NOBODY WILL HAVE ANYTHING TO FIGHT OVER. THEY ENJOY IT WITH ME OR THEY WON'T ENJOY IT AT ALL, 'CAUSE I'M SPREADING IT OUT.
I THINK IN THE BACK OF HIS MIND HE KNEW HE WOULDN'T LAST.
WILLIE JOHN WAS THE BEST MALE SINGER I EVER HEARD
HE USED TO SEND CHILLS UP AND DOWN MY SPINE . . . I NEVER MET A SINGER WHO HAD THAT KIND OF EMOTION AND FEELING IN HIS SONGS.
I WOULD STAND IN THE WINGS AND WATCH EVERY SHOW.
BOBBY SCHIFFMAN
All around the world...

Willie John's substance of choice is booze. His reckless lifestyle causes his career to falter.

He kills a man in a bar fight, and is sent to the Washington State Penitentiary for manslaughter in 1966.

James Brown and Bobby Schiffman spearhead an unsuccessful effort to gain his release.

I DON'T THINK I'M GOING TO GET OUT OF HERE.

DON'T *EVER* LET IT WORRY YOU. IF I GET OUT, I GET OUT. IF I STAY, I STAY . . . STILL GONNA BE THE SAME MAN IN OR OUT OF HERE.

In 1968, Little Willie John dies in prison of pneumonia. He is thirty years old.

LITTLE WILLIE JOHN

HUSBAND—DAD—BROTHER
WILLIAM E. JOHN
NOV. 15, 1937 – MAY 26, 1968
ALWAYS IN OUR MEMORY

FRANKIE LYMON HAS TO DEAL WITH THE PITFALLS OF STARDOM AT AN EVEN EARLIER AGE.

Discovered at the Apollo, Frankie and his group, the Teenagers, hit it big with their first record, "Why Do Fools Fall in Love?" a song written by the precocious thirteen-year-old.

FRANKIE LYMON TAKES ANOTHER TEENAGED STAR UNDER HIS WING.

HE WAS *YOUNGER*, BUT HE WAS *SMARTER* THAN I WAS. HE WAS A MAN. I WAS A KID.

FRANKIE WAS A *TRAGEDY*.

LITTLE ANTHONY

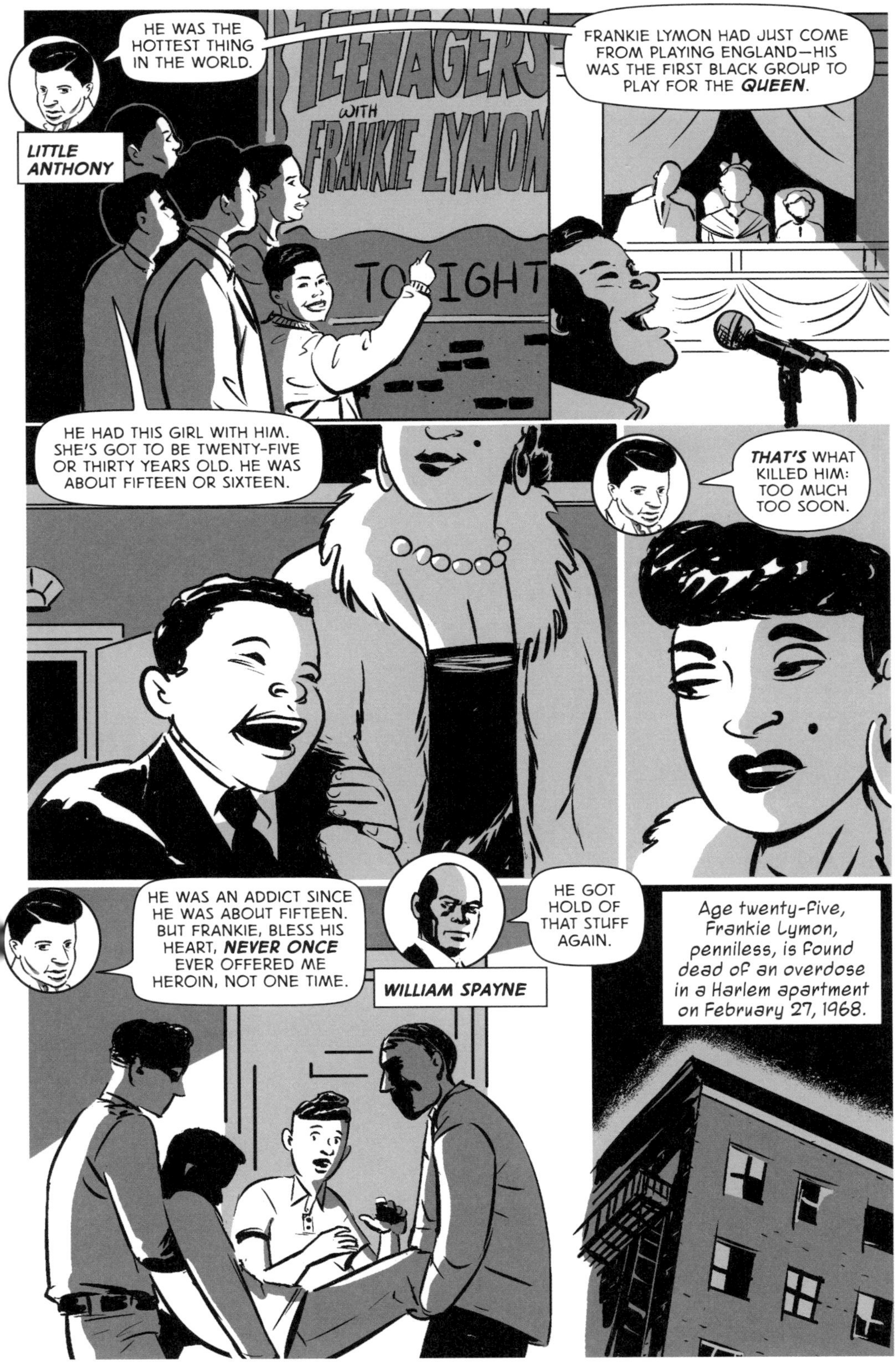

HE WAS THE HOTTEST THING IN THE WORLD.
LITTLE ANTHONY
TEENAGERS WITH FRANKIE LYMON
TO IGHT
FRANKIE LYMON HAD JUST COME FROM PLAYING ENGLAND—HIS WAS THE FIRST BLACK GROUP TO PLAY FOR THE **QUEEN**.
HE HAD THIS GIRL WITH HIM. SHE'S GOT TO BE TWENTY-FIVE OR THIRTY YEARS OLD. HE WAS ABOUT FIFTEEN OR SIXTEEN.
THAT'S WHAT KILLED HIM: TOO MUCH TOO SOON.
HE WAS AN ADDICT SINCE HE WAS ABOUT FIFTEEN. BUT FRANKIE, BLESS HIS HEART, **NEVER ONCE** EVER OFFERED ME HEROIN, NOT ONE TIME.
WILLIAM SPAYNE
HE GOT HOLD OF THAT STUFF AGAIN.
Age twenty-five, Frankie Lymon, penniless, is found dead of an overdose in a Harlem apartment on February 27, 1968.

ALL THIS SUCCESS, ALL THIS MONEY, ALL THIS ADULATION IS COMING FROM RECORD SALES AND THE VAST, UNENDING RADIO POUNDING OF HIT SONGS CREATED BY NEW YOUNG ARTISTS IN THE '50S.

Before the war, record companies *resist* the playing of their discs on the air. They think airplay will dissipate retail sales. Some companies even *ban* radio play outright.

At first, jukeboxes are the way the recording industry merchandises and publicizes its product.

After World War II, however, a *synergy* develops among . . .

1) the record companies that multiply throughout the R&B era

2) the artists and groups who are suddenly in great demand

3) the *disc jockeys* who purvey the sound to eager youngsters around the country.

THE RISE OF THE DISC JOCKEY MAY BE ONE OF THE FEW TIMES IN THE HISTORY OF INDUSTRY WHERE **MEN** REPLACE **MACHINES**.

?

Frank Schiffman has temporarily *broken stride* with the black community, which always led him to new sounds and styles.

THE APOLLO PRESENTS THE PIONEERS OF RHYTHM AND BLUES, BUT THEY ARE STILL PROGRAMMED INTO THE OLD-STYLE VARIETY SHOWS.

It isn't really working anymore. The Apollo is going through hard times.

BOBBY SCHIFFMAN, WHO IS ASSUMING MORE AND MORE **CONTROL** OVER THE APOLLO, REALIZES THAT NOT ONLY HAS A NEW SOUND ARRIVED, BUT WITH IT A WHOLE **NEW WAY** OF LISTENING TO MUSIC.

A DISC JOCKEY ON WWRL NAMED **DR. JIVE**—TOMMY SMALLS— AND I FIGURED OUT THAT PEOPLE WEREN'T COMING TO SEE THE TAP DANCER AND THE OTHER ACTS.

THEY WERE COMING TO SEE THE VOCAL ACT THAT HAD THE HIT RECORD BEING PLAYED ON THE RADIO.

WE SPAWNED THE IDEA OF **ELIMINATING** THE OTHER ACTS AND PUTTING IN THOSE ACTS THAT HAD HIT RECORDS. THAT BECAME KNOWN AS THE **R&B REVUE**.

HARLEM'S HIGH SPOT

APOLLO

ONE WEEK ONLY BEG. FRI. MAR. 30th 1956

DR. JIVE'S

NEWEST AND GREATEST

RHYTHM AND BLUES

REVUE

BO DIDDLEY — THE MOONGLOWS
TEEN QUEENS — THE SOLITAIRES
CHARLIE and RAY — DEAN BARLOW
FI-TONES · SUGAR & SPICE · CLAUDIA SWANN
Brooks Benton · Schoolboys · Buddy Griffin

BOBBY SCHIFFMAN

DR. JIVE (A.K.A. TOMMY SMALLS)

THE APOLLO WAS THE PIONEER IN THAT TYPE OF PRESENTATION.

THE GUYS THAT FOLLOWED US INTO THE WHITE MARKETPLACE, LIKE ALAN FREED WITH HIS *ROCK AND ROLL REVUE*, TOOK HIS IDEA RIGHT FROM THE APOLLO THEATER.

By the mid-'50s, these revues, featuring as many as a dozen singing acts, become the dominant form of entertainment at the theater.

BOBBY SCHIFFMAN

The R&B revues capitalize on the popularity of the DJs. *They*, not the performers, are the headliners.

DR. JIVE BRINGS HIS FIRST RHYTHM-AND-BLUES REVUE TO THE APOLLO IN 1955. MANY OTHER DJS SOON JOIN HIM.

ONE OF THE TOP DJS IS **DOUGLAS "JOCKO" HENDERSON**, WHOSE "1280 ROCKET" SHOW ON WOV IS LAUNCHED BY SPACE COMMANDER JOCKO AS HIS THEME MUSIC BLASTS OVER THE AIRWAVES.

WELL ALL ROOTHER!

GREAT GUGGA MUGGA SHOOGA BOOGA!

FROM WAY UP HERE IN THE STRATOSPHERE, WE GOTTA HOLLER MIGHTY LOUD AND CLEAR, "EE-TIDDY-O AND A HO," AND I'M BACK ON THE SCENE WITH THE RECORD MACHINE, SAYING, "OO-PAP-DOO," AND HOW DO YOU DO!

BOBBY ROBINSON HAS A VERY POPULAR RECORD STORE ON 125TH STREET.

MAN, YOU GOT TO DIG THIS GUY JOCKO. EVERYONE'S INTO HIS RADIO SHOW.

I SELL **TONNAGE** OF WHATEVER HE'S PLAYING!

WHO?

Bobby's RECORDS TAPE CENTER

BOBBY SCHIFFMAN

I HAD PUT A SHOW TOGETHER WITH **FATS DOMINO**— WHO WAS ALREADY A MAJOR STAR.

WE HAD EIGHT ACTS, AND ABOUT FIVE OF THEM HAD RECORDS IN THE TOP TEN.

AT THE LAST MINUTE, WE DECIDED TO ADD JOCKO.

WHEN JOCKO CAME IN THE FIRST DAY, HE WAS SO SCARED, HE DIDN'T KNOW WHAT TO DO.

DO I HAVE TO CLEAN MY DRESSING ROOM? CAN I COME OUT AND SELL TICKETS? WHAT DO YOU WANT ME TO DO? I'LL DO **WHATEVER** YOU WANT.

THE END OF THE WEEK, JOCKO WENT OUT LIKE A **LION**. THE THEATER WAS JAMMED ALL WEEK, AND HE, OF COURSE, THOUGHT IT WAS *HE* WHO DID THE BUSINESS!

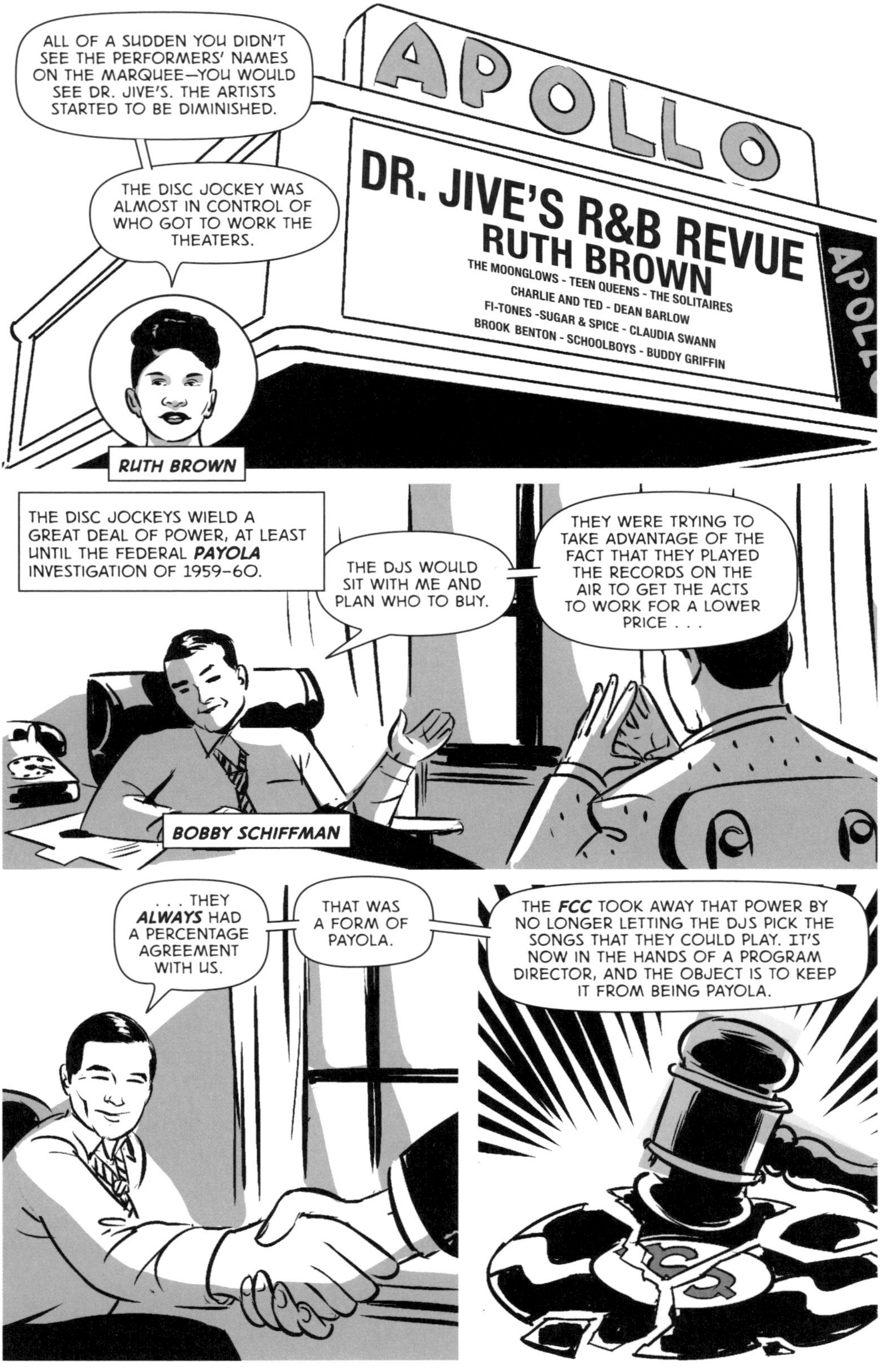
ALL OF A SUDDEN YOU DIDN'T SEE THE PERFORMERS' NAMES ON THE MARQUEE—YOU WOULD SEE DR. JIVE'S. THE ARTISTS STARTED TO BE DIMINISHED.
THE DISC JOCKEY WAS ALMOST IN CONTROL OF WHO GOT TO WORK THE THEATERS.
APOLLO
DR. JIVE'S R&B REVUE
RUTH BROWN
THE MOONGLOWS - TEEN QUEENS - THE SOLITAIRES
CHARLIE AND TED - DEAN BARLOW
FI-TONES -SUGAR & SPICE - CLAUDIA SWANN
BROOK BENTON - SCHOOLBOYS - BUDDY GRIFFIN
APOLLO
RUTH BROWN
THE DISC JOCKEYS WIELD A GREAT DEAL OF POWER, AT LEAST UNTIL THE FEDERAL PAYOLA INVESTIGATION OF 1959–60.
THE DJS WOULD SIT WITH ME AND PLAN WHO TO BUY.
THEY WERE TRYING TO TAKE ADVANTAGE OF THE FACT THAT THEY PLAYED THE RECORDS ON THE AIR TO GET THE ACTS TO WORK FOR A LOWER PRICE . . .
BOBBY SCHIFFMAN
. . . THEY ALWAYS HAD A PERCENTAGE AGREEMENT WITH US.
THAT WAS A FORM OF PAYOLA.
THE FCC TOOK AWAY THAT POWER BY NO LONGER LETTING THE DJS PICK THE SONGS THAT THEY COULD PLAY. IT'S NOW IN THE HANDS OF A PROGRAM DIRECTOR, AND THE OBJECT IS TO KEEP IT FROM BEING PAYOLA.

WE HAD DONE SHOWS WITH VARIETY ENTERTAINMENT, AND WHEN YOU COME UP WITH A FORMAT OF ALL THESE SINGING ACTS IN A ROW YOU SAY, "WHAT THE HELL IS *THIS*?"

I GOT SICK OF THIS BECAUSE I HAD NOTHING TO DO. ALL I HAD TO DO WAS GO DOWNSTAIRS, SEE THE BAND REHEARSE, AND SAY, "YOU GO FIRST, YOU GO SECOND, YOU THIRD, YOU FOURTH."

APOLLO MANAGER LEONARD REED

WHEN FRANK SCHIFFMAN SAW HIS FIRST R&B REVUE, HE COULDN'T *BELIEVE* IT.

MR. SCHIFFMAN, WHEN ARE WE GONNA GO BACK TO A *GOOD* SHOW?

I WANT TO SHOW YOU SOMETHING.

LEONARD REED

WHAT DO YOU CALL A GOOD SHOW? ONE THAT DOESN'T DO US ANY BUSINESS?

I DON'T LIKE IT EITHER, LEONARD, BUT YOU MUST LEARN THAT *MONEY* COMING THROUGH THAT GATE *IS* OUR BUSINESS.

145

WHEN A *"MAMBO CRAZE"* HITS IN THE '50S, THE SCHIFFMANS SEE ANOTHER POTENTIAL MONEYMAKER.

Latin music has *always* flowed at the Apollo. Dizzy Gillespie brought Cuban greats like *Chano Pozo* to the theater starting in the late '40s.

MIGUELITO VALDÉS

JOE LOCO

MERCEDITA VALDÉS

TITO PUENTE

LUCY FABERY

GILBERTO VALDÉS

MONGO SANTAMARÍA

 Legendary Jazz DJ **Symphony Sid Torin** has been promoting shows at the Apollo since the late '40s. He tries a Mambo Rhumba Festival of all Latin acts at the Apollo in 1954.

MAMBO ACE ANIBAL VÁZQUEZ.

Although critically popular, the Latin shows underperform at the box office.

STILL, TOP LATIN ARTISTS SUCH AS *TITO PUENTE* AND *MACHITO* CONTINUE TO HEADLINE APOLLO SHOWS, APPEALING TO *SPANISH HARLEM* AND LATIN MUSIC BUFFS FROM ALL OVER TOWN.

BUT IT IS THE RHYTHM–AND–BLUES REVUES THAT TURN THE THEATER AROUND FINANCIALLY.

BOBBY SCHIFFMAN

DURING THAT ERA, THE THEATER WAS OPERATING AT CAPACITY MORE THAN ANYTIME ELSE.

THERE WERE SITUATIONS WHERE WE WERE DOING AS MANY AS *SEVEN* SHOWS A DAY. THAT'S UNHEARD OF.

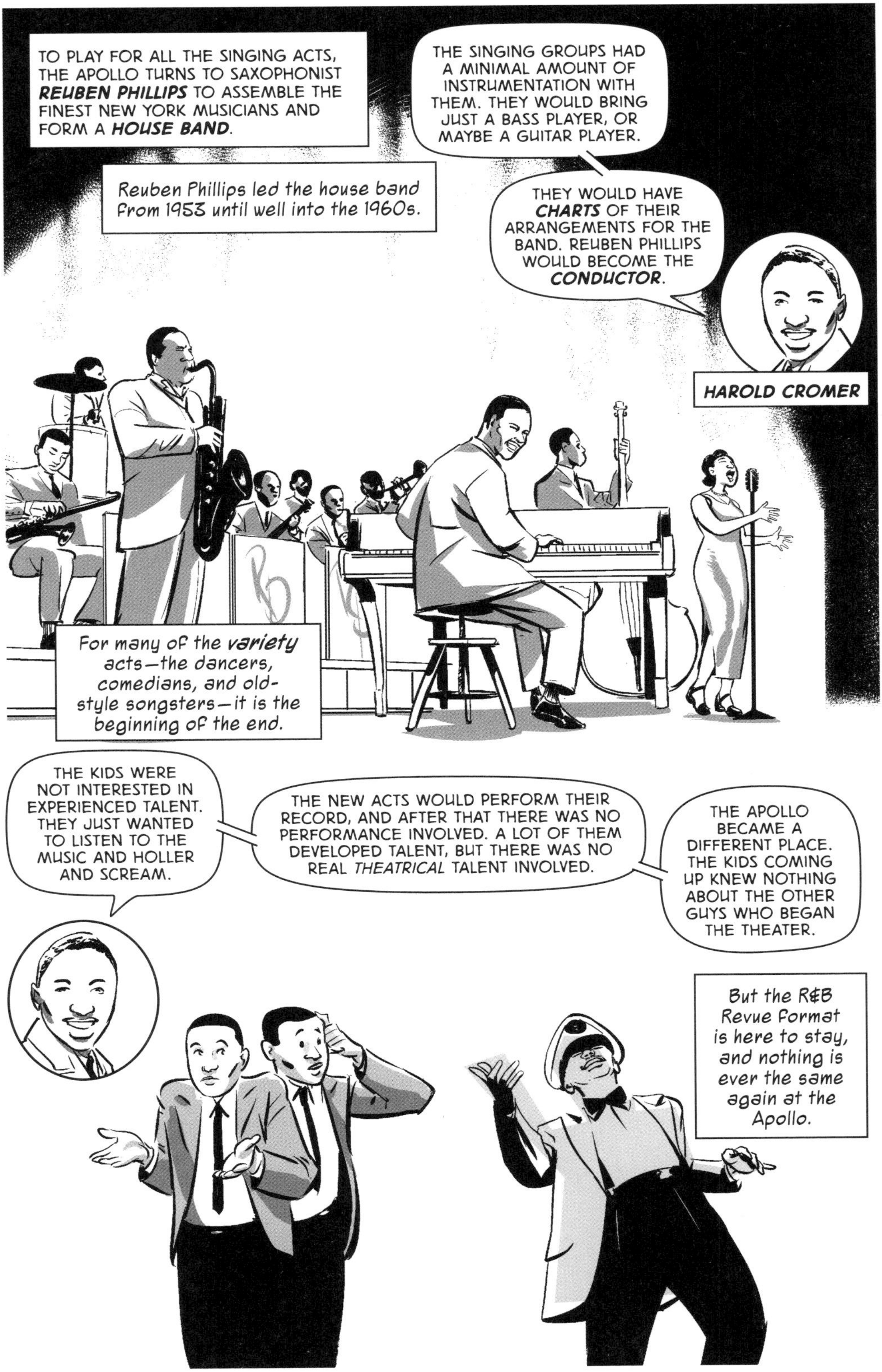
TO PLAY FOR ALL THE SINGING ACTS, THE APOLLO TURNS TO SAXOPHONIST **REUBEN PHILLIPS** TO ASSEMBLE THE FINEST NEW YORK MUSICIANS AND FORM A **HOUSE BAND**.
Reuben Phillips led the house band from 1953 until well into the 1960s.
THE SINGING GROUPS HAD A MINIMAL AMOUNT OF INSTRUMENTATION WITH THEM. THEY WOULD BRING JUST A BASS PLAYER, OR MAYBE A GUITAR PLAYER.
THEY WOULD HAVE **CHARTS** OF THEIR ARRANGEMENTS FOR THE BAND. REUBEN PHILLIPS WOULD BECOME THE **CONDUCTOR**.
HAROLD CROMER
For many of the *variety* acts—the dancers, comedians, and old-style songsters—it is the beginning of the end.
THE KIDS WERE NOT INTERESTED IN EXPERIENCED TALENT. THEY JUST WANTED TO LISTEN TO THE MUSIC AND HOLLER AND SCREAM.
THE NEW ACTS WOULD PERFORM THEIR RECORD, AND AFTER THAT THERE WAS NO PERFORMANCE INVOLVED. A LOT OF THEM DEVELOPED TALENT, BUT THERE WAS NO REAL *THEATRICAL* TALENT INVOLVED.
THE APOLLO BECAME A DIFFERENT PLACE. THE KIDS COMING UP KNEW NOTHING ABOUT THE OTHER GUYS WHO BEGAN THE THEATER.
But the R&B Revue format is here to stay, and nothing is ever the same again at the Apollo.

CHAPTER 7

Roots: Blues and Gospel at the Apollo

BOBBY SCHIFFMAN HOLDS A MEETING IN HIS OFFICE WITH EVERYONE ON AN IMPRESSIVE BLUES BILL.

WE'RE PLAYING COLLEGES ALL OVER THE COUNTRY AND THOSE KIDS ARE DIGGING IT. FOLKS UP HERE DON'T SEEM TO IDENTIFY WITH THE MUSIC.

ALL THEM **ROCK AND ROLLERS** GETTING RICH OFF THE BLUES.

BOBBY, WITH ALL THE CRAP THAT'S HAPPENING ON THE STREETS UP HERE, PEOPLE DON'T WANT TO HEAR ABOUT NO BLUES.

MAN, THESE **BLUES NIGHTS** WE'VE BEEN DOING AIN'T WORKING. WHAT'S UP?

BOBBY "BLUE" BLAND

JIMMY WITHERSPOON

T-BONE WALKER

B. B. KING

ODETTA

SONNY TERRY AND BROWNIE MCGHEE

I'LL TELL YOU WHY THAT SHOW DID POORLY, ACCORDING TO THAT DISCUSSION. BLUES REPRESENTED, AT THAT TIME, **MISERY**. AND BLACK FOLKS FROM THE STREET DIDN'T WANT TO HEAR THAT STUFF.

BOBBY SCHIFFMAN

Blues and *gospel* run through all forms of African American music.

LATE 1930S

The heart of many swing standards is pure blues. Substitute the word "baby" for "lord" in the lyrics of practically any gospel number, and it can become a *soul* tune.

Neither blues artists nor gospel artists were trained show people in the traditional sense. But the basic reason for the failure of blues and the success of gospel at the Apollo is a matter of *show business* style.

FRANK, THE BLUES ARE TERRIBLY IMPORTANT.

YOU SHOULD PLAY PEOPLE LIKE **BIG BILL BROONZY**.

NO JOHN, IT DOESN'T WORK. THIS IS THE **CITY**, AND BLUES IS THE **COUNTRY**.

JOHN HAMMOND

FRANK SCHIFFMAN

SCHIFFMAN TRIES TO MAKE IT WORK, IN HIS WAY. HE FIRST PRESENTS BLUES LEGEND *LEAD BELLY* IN A SKIT AT THE LAFAYETTE IN 1934.

OH GOVERNOR, SIR, I JUST WANTS TO SING FOR THE PEOPLE.

His interest in Lead Belly (a.k.a. Huddie William Ledbetter) derives from Lead Belly's notorious reputation as a killer.

YOUR SONGS HAVE MOVED ME TO TEARS. AS GOVERNOR OF THE GREAT STATE OF LOUISIANA, I HEREBY PARDON YOU.

The "governor" "pardons" Lead Belly thirty-one times a week. People love it.

A RETURN ENGAGEMENT TWO YEARS LATER, WITHOUT THE PRISON SHTICK OR HYPE, IS A FLOP.

The Midnight Speeeecial...

IN THE LATE '40S, A NEW BREED OF BLUES *SHOUTERS* AND GUTSY SINGERS GAINS PROMINENCE.

WYNONIE HARRIS

EDDIE "CLEANHEAD" VINSON

DINAH WASHINGTON "QUEEN OF THE BLUES"

Not blues performers in the traditional sense, their rougher, bluesy style—often backed by rockin' saxes and guitars—was a key *link* to rhythm and blues.

JOHNNY OTIS RUNS INTO RESISTANCE WHEN HE WANTS TO BRING HIS LATEST DISCOVERY, *WILLIE MAE "BIG MAMA" THORNTON,* INTO THE APOLLO.

I JUST FOUND HER IN TEXAS. SHE KNOCKED ME OUT!

YOU CAN USE HER IN THE SOUTH, BUT A BIG ROUGH CHICK—THE AUDIENCE IS NOT GOING TO DIG THAT.

BOBBY SCHIFFMAN

FRANK SCHIFFMAN

SHE CAN'T GET UP THERE WITH THOSE COWBOY TEXAS OUTFITS. GET HER SOME *GOWNS*.

WILLIE MAE, YOU WANNA WEAR SOME GOWNS?

I DON'T CARE. IF YOU WANT ME TO, I WILL.

HOOOUUUND DOG!

Elvis Presley turns her 1953 hit, penned by *Leiber and Stoller*, into his best-selling song.

JOHNNY OTIS

I HAD A WOMAN MAKE HER A SHEATH WITH A LACE MATERIAL OVER IT. THEY WERE NOT FORM-FITTING, BUT THEY LOOKED NICE.

SHE HAD THEM BIG OLE RUGGED BOOTS UNDER HER LACE GOWN!

SHE WAS REALLY SOMETHING ELSE. THEY LOVED HER AT THE APOLLO.

THE MOST SUCCESSFUL BLUESMEN AT THE APOLLO ARE THE CONSUMMATE SHOWMEN, SUCH AS *T-BONE WALKER*, WHO INSPIRES JIMI HENDRIX.

THE GREAT *B. B. KING*—AND HIS GUITAR, *"LUCILLE"*—BRINGS THE BLUES TO A NEW GENERATION OF BLACK SCHOOLCHILDREN WITH A SPECIAL APOLLO CONCERT IN 1974.

HAVE YOU EVER BEEN *HUNGRY*?

When electric guitars are added to the mix in the '40s and '50s, *country blues* morphs into *city blues*—with an edge.

150

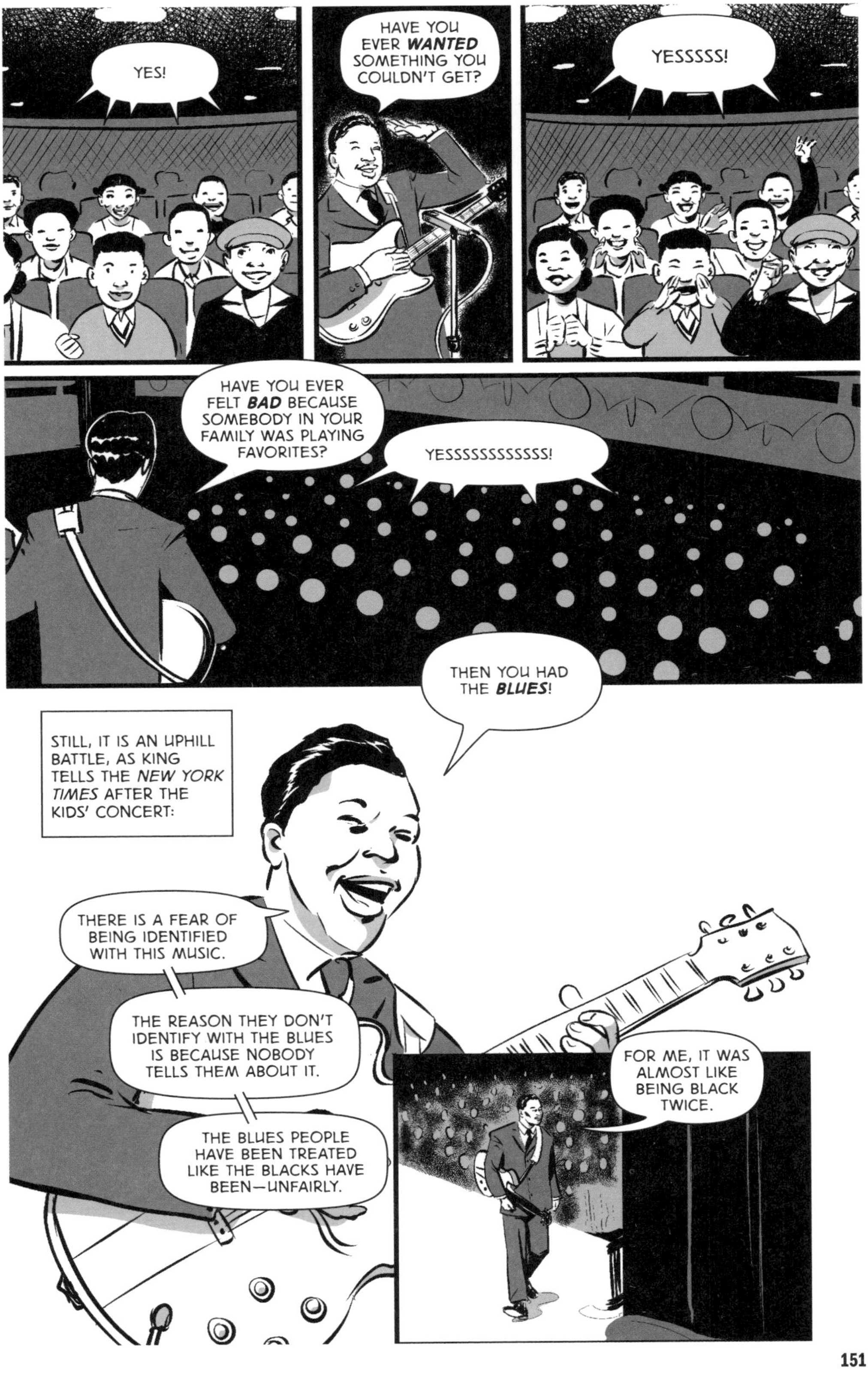
YES!
HAVE YOU EVER ***WANTED*** SOMETHING YOU COULDN'T GET?
YESSSSS!
HAVE YOU EVER FELT ***BAD*** BECAUSE SOMEBODY IN YOUR FAMILY WAS PLAYING FAVORITES?
YESSSSSSSSSSSS!
THEN YOU HAD THE ***BLUES***!
STILL, IT IS AN UPHILL BATTLE, AS KING TELLS THE *NEW YORK TIMES* AFTER THE KIDS' CONCERT:
THERE IS A FEAR OF BEING IDENTIFIED WITH THIS MUSIC.
THE REASON THEY DON'T IDENTIFY WITH THE BLUES IS BECAUSE NOBODY TELLS THEM ABOUT IT.
THE BLUES PEOPLE HAVE BEEN TREATED LIKE THE BLACKS HAVE BEEN—UNFAIRLY.
FOR ME, IT WAS ALMOST LIKE BEING BLACK TWICE.

MAXINE BROWN, WHO HAD A NUMBER OF SOUL HITS IN THE '60S, IS FIRST A *GOSPEL* SINGER.

Unlike traditional blues, gospel is a powerful attraction at the Apollo.

Religious folks, though, consider the Apollo the "*devil's house*."

MY MOTHER HAD PASSED AWAY BY THE TIME I SANG AT THE APOLLO. SHE WOULD NEVER HAVE COME TO SEE ME THERE.

I THOUGHT I WAS COMMITTING A *SIN*.

SISTER ROSETTA THARPE IS AN ARTIST EQUALLY COMFORTABLE WITH RELIGIOUS AND SECULAR MUSIC.

Down by the riverside . . .

She is virtually the only gospel singer to play the Apollo in the '30s and '40s.

The first big gospel recording star, Tharpe influences later rockers from *Little Richard* to *Jerry Lee Lewis*.

Music that begins as an amateur church endeavor turns professional, as gospel recordings become successful and gospel performers tour large churches and religious conventions.

THURMAN RUTH IS LEADER OF THE **SELAH JUBILEE SINGERS** AND A GOSPEL DJ ON WOV.

WE WERE BROADCAST ON ALL FOUR RADIO STATIONS IN BROOKLYN.

WHEN WE'D SING, THE CHURCH WOULD BE *JAMMED*.

THURMAN RUTH

IN THE '50S, GOSPEL MUSIC IS BECOMING MORE POPULAR THAN PREACHERS.

WE STARTED SINGING IN CHURCHES EVERY SUNDAY NIGHT BEFORE OUR MINISTERS WOULD PREACH.

AFTER WE'D SING, MOST OF THE FOLKS WOULD GET UP AND GO OUT BEFORE THE PREACHING.

It is inevitable that someone will think of *combining* the power and popularity of gospel with the successful rhythm-and-blues revue format.

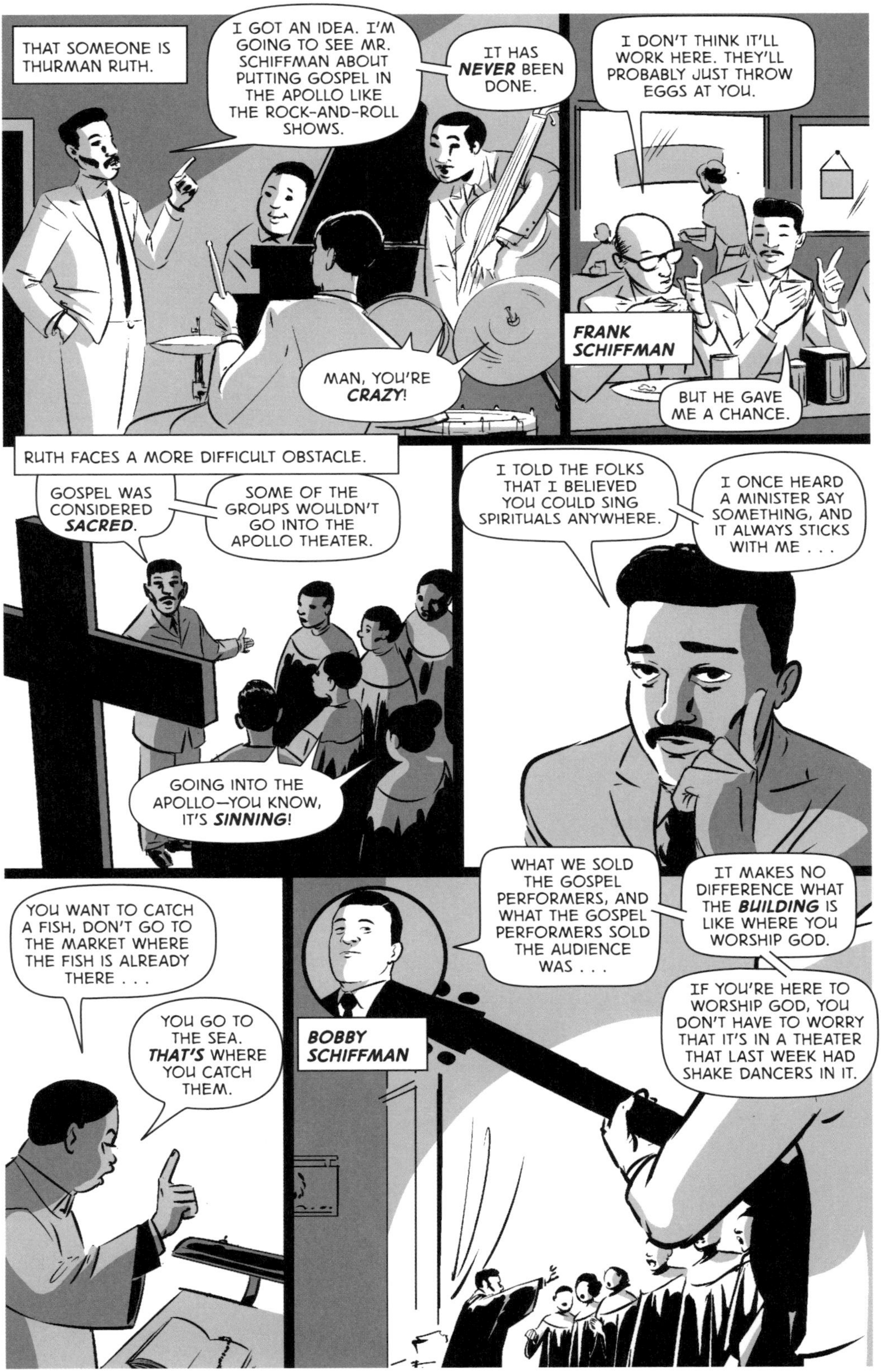

THAT SOMEONE IS THURMAN RUTH.
I GOT AN IDEA. I'M GOING TO SEE MR. SCHIFFMAN ABOUT PUTTING GOSPEL IN THE APOLLO LIKE THE ROCK-AND-ROLL SHOWS.
IT HAS NEVER BEEN DONE.
MAN, YOU'RE CRAZY!
I DON'T THINK IT'LL WORK HERE. THEY'LL PROBABLY JUST THROW EGGS AT YOU.
FRANK SCHIFFMAN
BUT HE GAVE ME A CHANCE.
RUTH FACES A MORE DIFFICULT OBSTACLE.
GOSPEL WAS CONSIDERED SACRED.
SOME OF THE GROUPS WOULDN'T GO INTO THE APOLLO THEATER.
GOING INTO THE APOLLO—YOU KNOW, IT'S SINNING!
I TOLD THE FOLKS THAT I BELIEVED YOU COULD SING SPIRITUALS ANYWHERE.
I ONCE HEARD A MINISTER SAY SOMETHING, AND IT ALWAYS STICKS WITH ME . . .
YOU WANT TO CATCH A FISH, DON'T GO TO THE MARKET WHERE THE FISH IS ALREADY THERE . . .
YOU GO TO THE SEA. THAT'S WHERE YOU CATCH THEM.
WHAT WE SOLD THE GOSPEL PERFORMERS, AND WHAT THE GOSPEL PERFORMERS SOLD THE AUDIENCE WAS . . .
BOBBY SCHIFFMAN
IT MAKES NO DIFFERENCE WHAT THE BUILDING IS LIKE WHERE YOU WORSHIP GOD.
IF YOU'RE HERE TO WORSHIP GOD, YOU DON'T HAVE TO WORRY THAT IT'S IN A THEATER THAT LAST WEEK HAD SHAKE DANCERS IN IT.

I TOLD THEM THAT THIS WOULD BE THE FIRST TIME THEY WOULD EVER BE PRESENTED IN A GREAT WAY.

BEAUTIFUL STAGE, GREAT LIGHTING, AND ACOUSTICS.

ABOVE ALL, THIS WAS THE FIRST TIME THEY WERE GUARANTEED TO HAVE *MONEY* . . .

AND THEY WERE GOING TO GET IT WHETHER THE SHOW WAS A FLOP OR NOT.

IF YOU PLAYED A CHURCH OR AUDITORIUM AND THE PEOPLE WERE NOT THERE, YOU DIDN'T GET THE MONEY.

MR. SCHIFFMAN *GUARANTEED* THE MONEY.

ONE GROUP IN THOSE DAYS COULD MAKE $3,000 FOR A WEEK'S ENGAGEMENT.

THURMAN RUTH'S GOSPEL CARAVAN DEBUTS AT THE APOLLO ON DECEMBER 15, 1955.

SINCE i LAID MY BURDEN DOWN...

Ruth maintains a *joyous* churchlike atmosphere for the Apollo gospel shows.

To insure the broadest appeal to different denominations, he features all types of religious singing . . .

THURMAN RUTH

JUBILEE SINGING IS JUST THAT: JUBILATION THAT'S FAST, A JOYOUS MEDIUM.

GOSPEL IS KIND OF SLOW WITH LOTS OF PREACHING. THEY ALMOST TALK IT MORE THAN SING IT.

SPIRITUALS IS THE OLD TRADITIONAL SONGS THAT STARTED OFF EVERYTHING: "SWING LOW, SWEET CHARIOT."

WITNESSES **TESTIFY** THE GOSPEL SHOWS ARE THE MOST STIMULATING AND EXCITING EVER SEEN AT THE APOLLO.

PEOPLE WOULD GET **OVERWHELMED**.

IT JUST FELT LIKE THE CEILING WAS GONNA BURST OPEN. PEOPLE WOULD **FAINT**.

THEY'D FALL OUT OF THE BALCONIES. IT'S TRUE.

YOU'D GET OVEREXCITED, HAPPY, AND SHOUT.

IT'S NOT LIKE A ROCK SHOW. THIS GOES A STEP FURTHER BECAUSE YOU'RE EMOTIONALLY INVOLVED IN THE SPIRIT OF GOD.

THE GOSPEL ACTS SANG FROM THE BOTTOM OF THEIR TOES OR SOMETHING.

IT WAS VERY, VERY **MOVING**.

YOUNG DIONNE WARWICK

BEVERLY LEE OF THE SHIRELLES

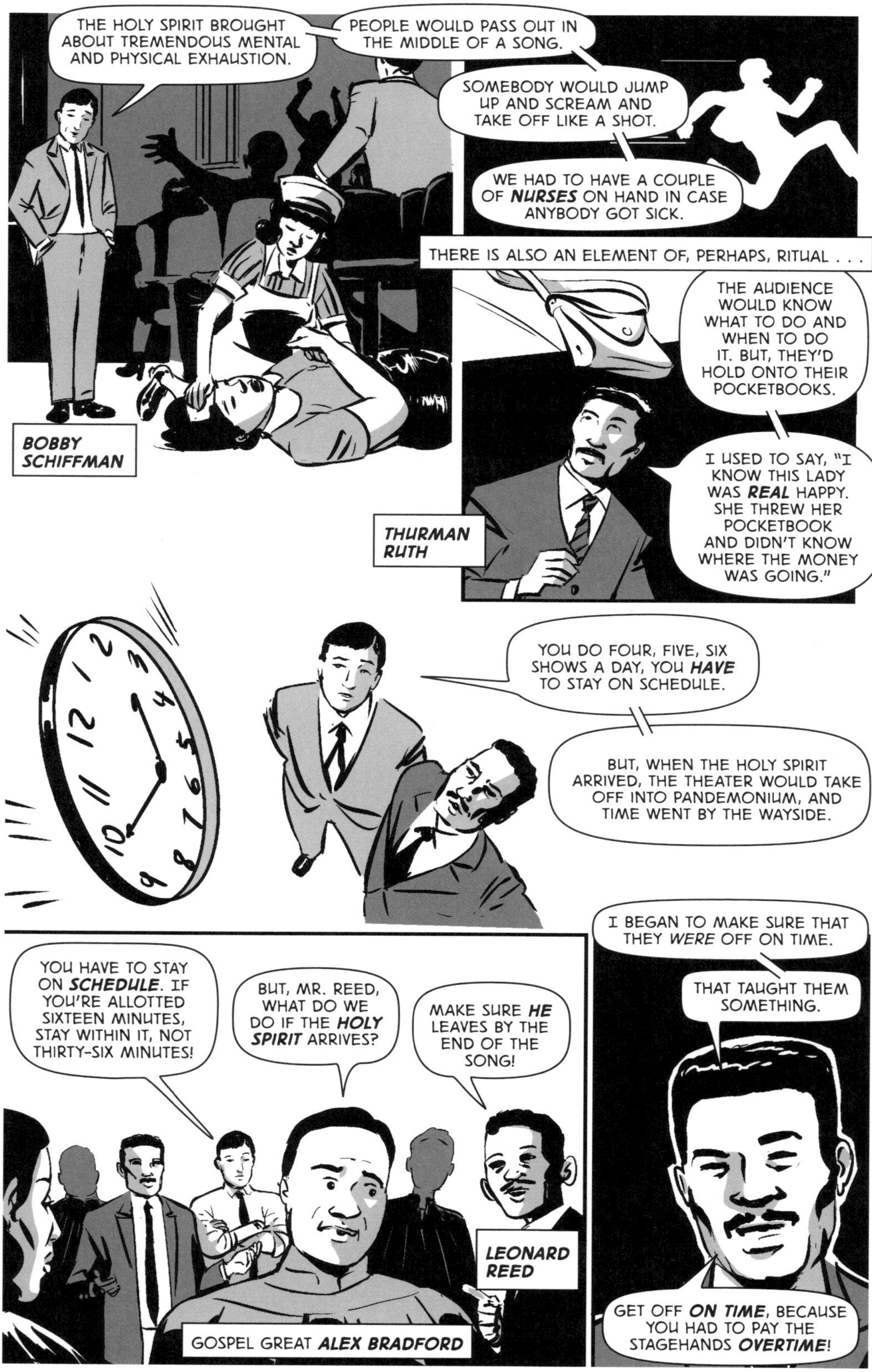
THE HOLY SPIRIT BROUGHT ABOUT TREMENDOUS MENTAL AND PHYSICAL EXHAUSTION.
PEOPLE WOULD PASS OUT IN THE MIDDLE OF A SONG.
SOMEBODY WOULD JUMP UP AND SCREAM AND TAKE OFF LIKE A SHOT.
WE HAD TO HAVE A COUPLE OF NURSES ON HAND IN CASE ANYBODY GOT SICK.
BOBBY SCHIFFMAN
THERE IS ALSO AN ELEMENT OF, PERHAPS, RITUAL . . .
THE AUDIENCE WOULD KNOW WHAT TO DO AND WHEN TO DO IT. BUT, THEY'D HOLD ONTO THEIR POCKETBOOKS.
I USED TO SAY, "I KNOW THIS LADY WAS REAL HAPPY. SHE THREW HER POCKETBOOK AND DIDN'T KNOW WHERE THE MONEY WAS GOING."
THURMAN RUTH
YOU DO FOUR, FIVE, SIX SHOWS A DAY, YOU HAVE TO STAY ON SCHEDULE.
BUT, WHEN THE HOLY SPIRIT ARRIVED, THE THEATER WOULD TAKE OFF INTO PANDEMONIUM, AND TIME WENT BY THE WAYSIDE.
YOU HAVE TO STAY ON SCHEDULE. IF YOU'RE ALLOTTED SIXTEEN MINUTES, STAY WITHIN IT, NOT THIRTY-SIX MINUTES!
BUT, MR. REED, WHAT DO WE DO IF THE HOLY SPIRIT ARRIVES?
MAKE SURE HE LEAVES BY THE END OF THE SONG!
LEONARD REED
GOSPEL GREAT ALEX BRADFORD
I BEGAN TO MAKE SURE THAT THEY WERE OFF ON TIME.
THAT TAUGHT THEM SOMETHING.
GET OFF ON TIME, BECAUSE YOU HAD TO PAY THE STAGEHANDS OVERTIME!

Nearly *everybody* who is *anybody* in the world of gospel plays the Apollo gospel shows.

ALEX BRADFORD BECOMES A GREAT INFLUENCE ON SINGERS FROM LITTLE RICHARD TO RAY CHARLES.

Too close to heaven...

BRADFORD WAS ALWAYS A WINNER: A **SHOWMAN**.

HE WENT OVER VERY BIG AT OUR FIRST SHOW.

THE **GREATEST** SINGING GROUP THAT I HAD AT THE APOLLO.

I HAD ANOTHER BIG-NAME GROUP CLOSING ONCE . . .

THE SWANEE QUINTET

. . . BUT THE SWANEE QUINTET WAS SO TOUGH THAT I HAD TO LET THEM CLOSE THE SHOW.

THE OTHER GROUP WAS COMPLAINING ALL THE TIME.

CLARA WARD AND THE WARD SINGERS

THE FOLKS USED TO COME OUT TO THE APOLLO TO SEE THE WARD SINGERS DRESS.

ALBERTINA WALKER AND THE CARAVANS

THEY WERE **REAL** BIG.

SO MANY FINE LADIES CAME OUT OF HER GROUP: **SHIRLEY CAESAR, INEZ ANDREWS, DOROTHY NORWOOD, CASSIETTA GEORGE** . . .

THEY WERE GREAT SINGERS, AND THEIR HAIRPIECES WERE SO NICE.

A GROUP MIGHT OUT-SING THEM, BUT THEY COULDN'T **OUT-DRESS** THEM.

THE DIXIE HUMMINGBIRDS

IRA TUCKER WAS ONE OF THE GREATEST LEAD SINGERS. THEY WERE MY **FAVORITE** SINGERS.

THE SWAN SILVERTONES

THE **SWAN SILVERTONES**, WITH **REVEREND CLAUDE JETER**, DID SOMETHING AT THE APOLLO THAT I'VE NEVER SEEN ANY OTHER GROUP DO.

TO ME, THEY WEREN'T REAL GOSPEL OR PURE GOSPEL.

THEY DID THAT THING WITH **PAUL SIMON**, "LOVE ME LIKE A ROCK."

THAT GROUP ALWAYS WANTED TO DO ROCK AND ROLL.

THEY HAD SO MANY FOLKS SHOUTING AND GETTING HAPPY THAT THE CARAVANS COULDN'T EVEN GO ON. CURTAIN TIME CUT THE LAST ACT OFF.

THE CARAVANS WERE OUT THERE WITH THE SWAN SILVERTONES, SHOUTING AND HAPPY THEMSELVES.

157

THURMAN RUTH INTRODUCES THE **STAPLE SINGERS** TO NEW YORK AT THE APOLLO.

WHEN I WAS A DJ IN NEW YORK, I WOULDN'T EVEN PLAY THEIR SONGS BECAUSE THEY SOUNDED SO COUNTRYLIKE, SO **DOWN HOME**.

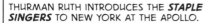

I BOOKED THEM AS A HEADLINE ACT SIX OR EIGHT WEEKS LATER.

APO

THE STAPLE SINGERS

THAT'S WHEN THEY REALLY GOT STARTED.

I WAS ON VACATION IN CHICAGO AND I WENT DOWN TO SOME CHURCH WITH IRA TUCKER AND HEARD **MAVIS STAPLES**.

MAN, I NEVER HEARD **ANYTHING** LIKE THAT IN MY LIFE. SHE TORE THE CHURCH UP.

BUT BEFORE I GOT A CHANCE, SHE LEFT GOSPEL AND GOT ON TO OTHER THINGS. NEVER PLAYED THE APOLLO FOR ME.

BROTHER RUTH, *PLEASE* LET ME PLAY YOUR APOLLO CARAVAN.

I BROUGHT **ARETHA FRANKLIN** TO NEW YORK FOR THE FIRST TIME—SHE AND HER FATHER, **REVEREND C. L. FRANKLIN**—FROM DETROIT.

HE WAS ONE OF OUR GREATEST BAPTIST PREACHERS, ONE OF THE GREATEST **REVIVAL** MINISTERS.

HIS RECORDS WERE MORE SUCCESSFUL THAN ANYONE ELSE.

ARETHA FRANKLIN

A CHANGE IS COMING—THE **SOUL STIRRERS** WITH **SAM COOKE**.

Touch the hem of his garment...

The handsome nineteen-year-old has a dramatic impact on gospel and, ultimately, pop and soul music.

By the time of the Apollo gospel shows, the Soul Stirrers has lost its founder, *R. H. Harris*, and Sam Cooke takes over.

IN 1956, AGAINST THE WISHES OF THE OTHER SOUL STIRRERS, SAM COOKE RECORDS A POP SONG, "LOVEABLE."

SAM, *LISTEN* TO ME, WE'VE BEEN FRIENDS A LONG TIME.

YOU COULD MAKE SO MUCH MORE MONEY IF YOU SING FOR THE POP MARKET.

BOBBY SCHIFFMAN

THE APOLLO IS A **CATALYST** IN THE CROSSOVER FROM GOSPEL TO SOUL MUSIC.

BROTHERS AND SISTERS, WE HAVE A VERY SPECIAL GUEST WHO'D LIKE TO SING A SONG FOR YOU TONIGHT: **MR. JAMES BROWN!**

The Apollo is virtually the *only* place where gospel people and soul people meet on **common ground**.

Our Father who art in heaven...

LITTLE ANTHONY AND THE IMPERIALS

I WAS INFLUENCED BY THE GOSPEL SINGERS AT THE APOLLO.

THE IMPERIALS NEEDED SOMETHING TO MAKE THAT AUDIENCE COME UP OUT OF THEIR SEATS.

I TOLD MY GUITAR PLAYER, "GIVE ME THAT THING THAT WE DO IN CHURCH, THAT RUN THAT EVERYBODY GETS UP ON."

AT FIRST THE SONG WAS PURE GOSPEL WITH FEW SET WORDS.

THE OLD MAN LOVED IT.

I'm Alright!

I WANT YOU TO GO DOWN TO THE BASEMENT AND PRACTICE WITH SAM. HE'S GOING TO PUT SOME **WORDS** TO IT.

FRANK SCHIFFMAN

YOU CAN TAKE AN **EMOTIONAL** THING AND TURN IT FROM A **SPIRITUAL** THING TO A **SENSUAL** THING.

Sam, working with Anthony, comes up with lyrics that make "I'm Alright" a rousing, sexy love song.

LITTLE ANTHONY

WE OPENED UP A CAN OF WORMS THAT I REGRET TO THIS DAY.

Thurman Ruth soon attracts competitors, like **Doc Wheeler** and **Fred Barr** from WWRL, who bring in their own gospel packages.

I'D COME BY WHEN THEY WERE THERE, AND THEY'D COME BY WHEN I HAD MY SHOW. IT WAS A **FRIENDLY** THING.

THURMAN RUTH

DIONNE WARWICK HAS HER OWN AMATEUR GOSPEL GROUP, AND HER MOTHER SINGS GOSPEL IN THE **DRINKARD SISTERS**.

WEDNESDAY NIGHT WAS AMATEUR NIGHT, AND IT WAS NO DIFFERENT WHEN THEY HAD GOSPEL SHOWS THERE.

BUT IT WAS FOR GOSPEL SINGERS.

OUR GROUP DECIDED TO GO UP THERE. WE WON **FIRST PRIZE**.

BUT WE NEVER WENT BACK TO SING GOSPEL AGAIN.

Despite the conflict of conscience, more and more singers make the move from gospel to **commercial** soul music.

By the early '60s, the gospel shows have lost their unique allure and fade out.

Soul music takes the gospel rhythm and feeling and secularizes its message—creating a broader appeal and attracting a **far larger** audience—both black and white.

160

CHAPTER 8

The 1960s: Soulful

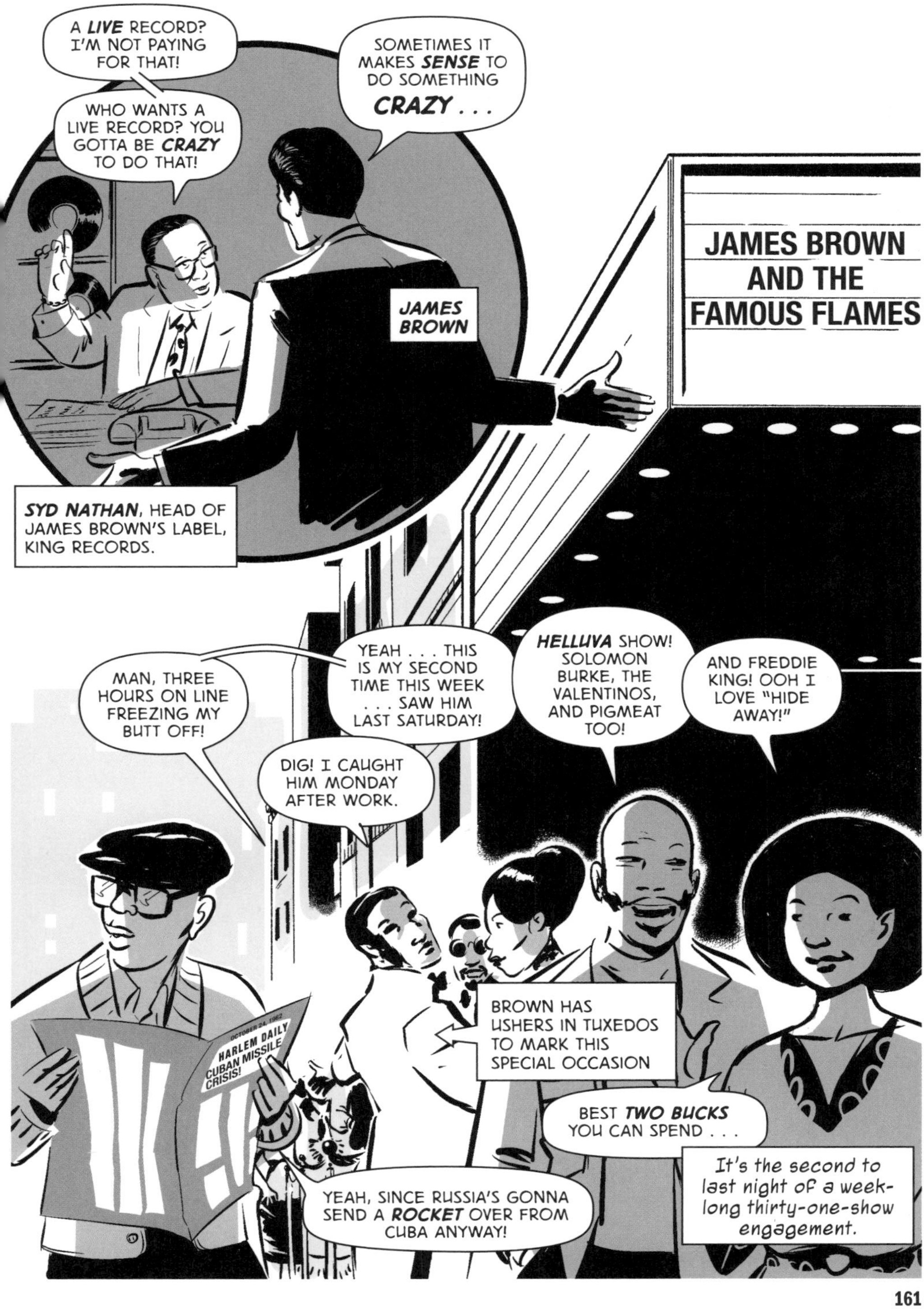
A LIVE RECORD? I'M NOT PAYING FOR THAT!
WHO WANTS A LIVE RECORD? YOU GOTTA BE CRAZY TO DO THAT!
SOMETIMES IT MAKES SENSE TO DO SOMETHING CRAZY . . .
JAMES BROWN
SYD NATHAN, HEAD OF JAMES BROWN'S LABEL, KING RECORDS.
JAMES BROWN AND THE FAMOUS FLAMES
MAN, THREE HOURS ON LINE FREEZING MY BUTT OFF!
YEAH . . . THIS IS MY SECOND TIME THIS WEEK . . . SAW HIM LAST SATURDAY!
DIG! I CAUGHT HIM MONDAY AFTER WORK.
HELLUVA SHOW! SOLOMON BURKE, THE VALENTINOS, AND PIGMEAT TOO!
AND FREDDIE KING! OOH I LOVE "HIDE AWAY!"
OCTOBER 24, 1962
HARLEM DAILY
CUBAN MISSILE CRISIS!
BROWN HAS USHERS IN TUXEDOS TO MARK THIS SPECIAL OCCASION
BEST TWO BUCKS YOU CAN SPEND . . .
YEAH, SINCE RUSSIA'S GONNA SEND A ROCKET OVER FROM CUBA ANYWAY!
It's the second to last night of a week-long thirty-one-show engagement.

MR. DYNAMITE, THE AMAZING MR. "PLEASE, PLEASE" HIMSELF—THE STAR OF THE SHOW, *JAMES BROWN AND THE FAMOUS FLAMES!*

LUCAS "FATS" GONDER

EIGHT MICS FEEDING INTO A BIG AMPEX STEREO TAPE MACHINE ARE CAPTURING EVERYTHING.

Brown puts up $5,700 of his own money to make this recording possible.

SING IT, @#$%&!

The fans are not notified in advance that the event is being recorded, so the response is *spontaneous*.

The audience response is so raw and overwhelming that the engineer actually has to minimize certain reactions for the record . . .

¡FEEL ALL RIGHT

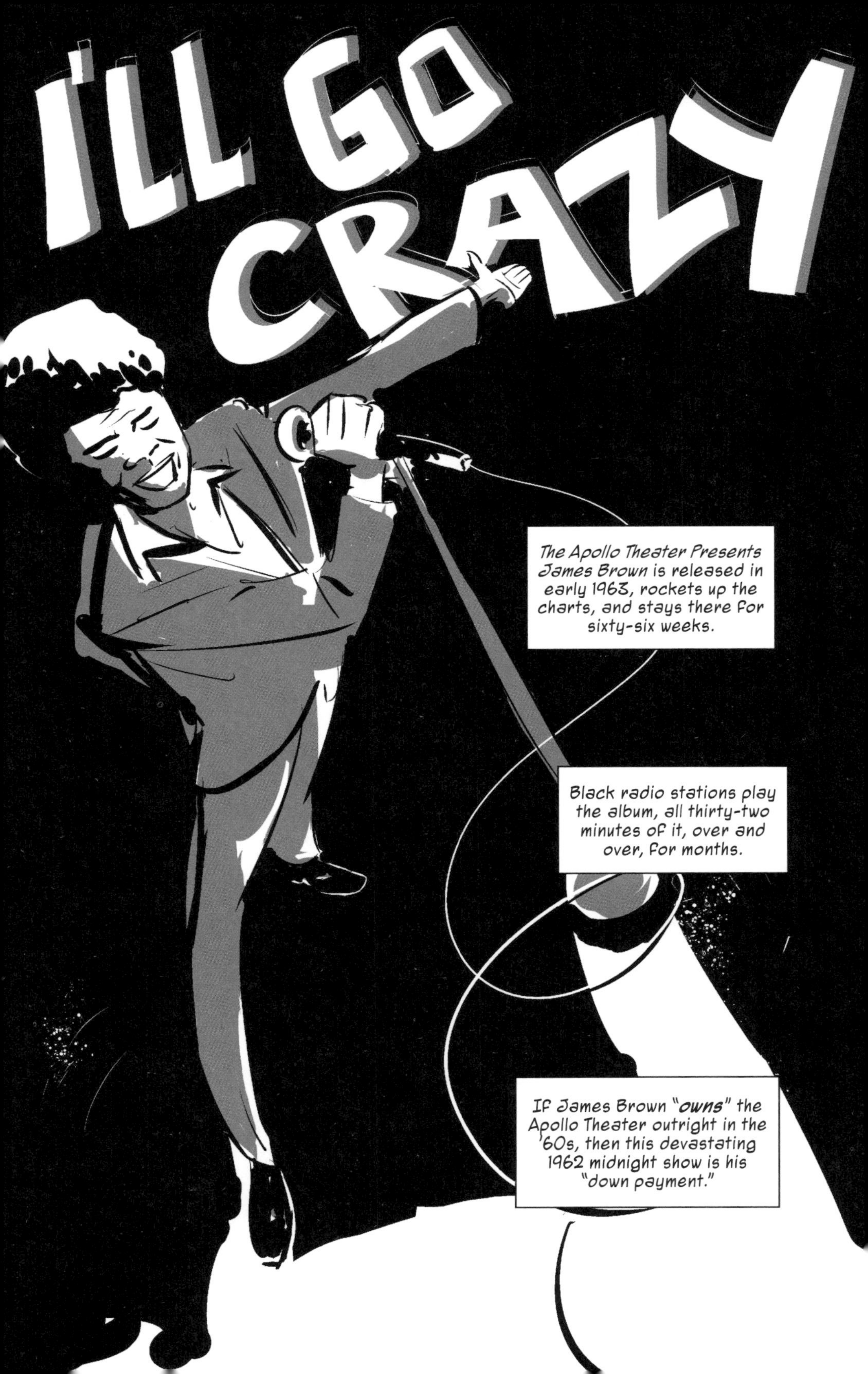
I'LL GO CRAZY
The Apollo Theater Presents James Brown is released in early 1963, rockets up the charts, and stays there for sixty-six weeks.
Black radio stations play the album, all thirty-two minutes of it, over and over, for months.
If James Brown "***owns***" the Apollo Theater outright in the '60s, then this devastating 1962 midnight show is his "down payment."

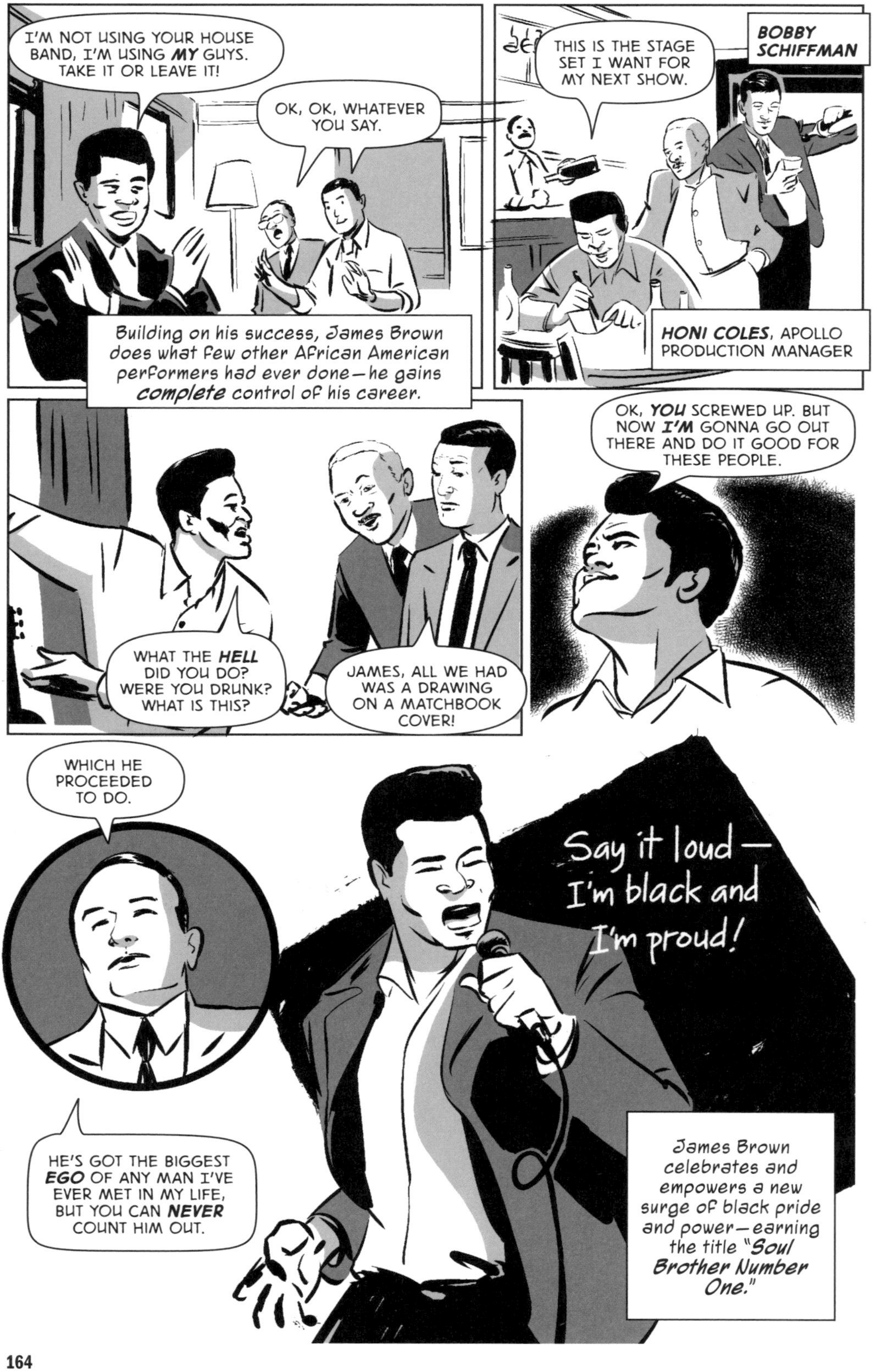
I'M NOT USING YOUR HOUSE BAND, I'M USING MY GUYS. TAKE IT OR LEAVE IT!
OK, OK, WHATEVER YOU SAY.
Building on his success, James Brown does what few other African American performers had ever done—he gains complete control of his career.
BOBBY SCHIFFMAN
THIS IS THE STAGE SET I WANT FOR MY NEXT SHOW.
HONI COLES, APOLLO PRODUCTION MANAGER
WHAT THE HELL DID YOU DO? WERE YOU DRUNK? WHAT IS THIS?
JAMES, ALL WE HAD WAS A DRAWING ON A MATCHBOOK COVER!
OK, YOU SCREWED UP. BUT NOW I'M GONNA GO OUT THERE AND DO IT GOOD FOR THESE PEOPLE.
WHICH HE PROCEEDED TO DO.
Say it loud— I'm black and I'm proud!
HE'S GOT THE BIGGEST EGO OF ANY MAN I'VE EVER MET IN MY LIFE, BUT YOU CAN NEVER COUNT HIM OUT.
James Brown celebrates and empowers a new surge of black pride and power—earning the title "Soul Brother Number One."

In the midst of historic social upheaval, its *fourth decade* as a black theater becomes the Apollo's most celebrated and successful yet.

STOP THE WAR!

Civil Rights Now!

The Apollo is selling 800,000 to one million tickets a year. A so-so week might draw 16,000 customers. An especially hot attraction can *triple* that number.

THINGS ARE CHANGING. ONLY 15 PERCENT OF OUR WEEKDAY AND 25 PERCENT OF OUR WEEKEND AUDIENCE IS WHITE NOW.

WHITES AREN'T THAT COMFORTABLE COMING UP HERE ANYMORE.

FRANK SCHIFFMAN

BOBBY SCHIFFMAN

THIS SOMEWHAT WISTFUL MOTTO APPEARS DURING A ONE-MONTH PERIOD EARLY IN 1964, WHEN FOUR WHITE PEOPLE ARE MURDERED IN HARLEM.

AIR CONDI...
★ WORLD-FAMOUS ★
APOLLO
IN THE HEART OF FRIENDLY HARLEM!
AMERICA'S GREATEST STAGE SHOWS
125th ST. near 8th Ave. · Tele. UNiversity 4–4470

. . . EVEN WHEN THE REST OF THE CITY WON'T.

HARLEM NEEDS THE APOLLO.

WE WILL ALWAYS REACH OUT TO THE PEOPLE OF HARLEM WHO LOVE THIS PLACE.

HONI COLES

165

PERCY SUTTON, THE MANHATTAN BOROUGH PRESIDENT WHO WILL ONE DAY TAKE OVER THE APOLLO

THE SCHIFFMANS HAVE TRADITIONALLY INVOLVED THEMSELVES IN HARLEM COMMUNITY AFFAIRS.

IF ALL BUSINESSMEN HAD DONE AS MUCH, COMMUNITY TENSION WOULD BE CONSIDERABLY LESSENED.

A LETTER OF APPRECIATION TO FRANK SCHIFFMAN FROM MARTIN LUTHER KING, JR. PROUDLY HUNG IN THE APOLLO OFFICE. IN PART, IT READ:

WHEN THE BRIGHT DAY OF FREEDOM EMERGES, AND THE TRAGIC EXPRESSION OF MAN'S INHUMANITY TO MAN IS CAST INTO UNENDING LIMBO, YOUR NAME WILL CERTAINLY SHINE AS ONE OF THOSE INDIVIDUALS WHO HAD THE VISION, COURAGE AND DEDICATION TO WORK FOR A REIGN OF JUSTICE AND A RULE OF LOVE.

THE APOLLO BECOMES MORE ACTIVE IN THE COMMUNITY AND IN BLACK CAUSES.

SEE, WE CAN GET TV CAMERAS **HERE** WHEN WE CAN'T GET THEM ANYWHERE ELSE IN HARLEM.

The theater hosts **dozens** of fundraisers and educational programs.

Cries for **Freedom** in the streets echo the cries of freedom in the new black music.

CRIES OF A DIFFERENT SORT ARE COMING FROM WITHIN THE THEATER AS THE APOLLO, IN 1960, FIRST USES THE WORD "SOUL" TO DESCRIBE RAY CHARLES AS THE "SOUL GENIUS."

WHAT'd I SAY

Uuh Uuh ooh ooh

THE SWEET SOUNDS OF **LOVE**, MAN!

THAT'S SOUL MUSIC, BABY!

Many radio stations ban "What'd I Say" as too sexy, but it's a giant crossover hit anyway.

THE SWEET SOUNDS OF **JACKIE WILSON** MAKE HIM THE APOLLO'S **ALL-TIME** BOX OFFICE CHAMP IN MAY 1963—UNTIL JAMES BROWN SETS **ANOTHER** RECORD THE FOLLOWING YEAR.

Higher and higher!

Lonely teardrops...

JACKIE WILSON DROVE THE WOMEN CRAZY. WE WERE FRIENDS WITH HIM AND *WE* WERE **DROOLING**.

HE WAS LIKE A VERY SLINKY, POWERFUL **LEOPARD** ONSTAGE.

Earnings from Wilson's smash hit help songwriter **Berry Gordy** to start a little record company called **Motown**.

SOUL STAR **SAM COOKE** ALSO STARTS HIS OWN RECORD LABEL, **SAR**, TWO YEARS BEFORE BROWN MAKES HIS LIVE ALBUM.

BEVERLY LEE OF THE SHIRELLES

COOKE'S SLEEK GOOD LOOKS AND **SEXY** VOICE PUSH HIS GOSPEL ROOTS TO THE LIMITS OF PROPRIETY AS HE RACKS UP HIT AFTER HIT.

Twistin' the night awaaay...

Like Ray Charles and Jackie Wilson, Sam Cooke is a vital *link* between gospel and soul.

Among his artists are Bobby Womack's group, the *Valentinos*, who appear with James Brown at the Apollo the week Brown records the live album.

HOWEVER, HE STRUGGLES WITH HIS CHOICE TO "GO POP." THE SUPERSTAR EVEN TRIES A RETURN TO GOSPEL, BUT IS RUDELY REJECTED AT A SOUL STIRRERS SHOW IN CHICAGO, ACCORDING TO AUTHOR ANTHONY HEILBUT.

COOKE IS ALSO A **GROUNDBREAKER** IN THE WHITE MARKET, THANKS TO HIS CLEAN-CUT IMAGE, GOOD LOOKS, AND SMOOTH SOUND.

GET THAT NO-GOOD BLUES SINGER DOWN!

THIS IS A **CHRISTIAN** PROGRAM.

HE DIES UNDER DISPUTED CIRCUMSTANCES ON DECEMBER 10, 1964, SHOT BY THE OWNER OF THE HACIENDA MOTEL OUTSIDE HER OFFICE DOOR.

IN CHICAGO, **200,000** FANS LINE UP TO VIEW HIS BODY.

YEARS LATER, STREET VENDORS OUTSIDE THE APOLLO SELL MEMORIAL PHOTOGRAPHS OF MARTYRS MARTIN LUTHER KING JR., JOHN F. KENNEDY, ROBERT F. KENNEDY . . . AND SAM COOKE.

His posthumous anthem, "A Change Is Going to Come," becomes a *quintessential* protest song for the Civil Rights movement.

WHOLESOME AND UNTHREATENING, THE **GIRL GROUPS** OF THE LATE '50S AND EARLY '60S, LIKE THE SHIRELLES, ARE ADORED BY BLACKS AND WHITES ALIKE.

JOCKO'S ROCKET SHIP REVUE, 1958

WELL, ALL *ROOOTHER* FOLKS . . . FOR THE FIRST TIME EVER AT THE APOLLO, OR ANYWHERE—THE SHIRELLES!

MR. PHILLIPS, WE DIDN'T KNOW WE WERE SUPPOSED TO HAVE **ARRANGEMENTS**.

NEXT TIME, HONEY. WE GOT YOU COVERED NOW.

BEVERLY LEE AND THE **SHIRELLES** WITH REUBEN PHILLIPS, APOLLO HOUSE BAND LEADER

AS WE WENT BACK TO THE APOLLO THROUGH THE YEARS, WE DEVELOPED A *FOLLOWING*.

SOME YOUNG KIDS WOULD HANG BACKSTAGE, AND WE WOULD *BABYSIT* FOR THEM BETWEEN SHOWS.

THEIR FIRST GOLD RECORD, FOR "SOLDIER BOY," IS PRESENTED TO THEM AT THE APOLLO.

I ALWAYS THOUGHT OF OUR SONGS AS VERY CORNY AND LOLLIPOP-ISH.

BUT THE PEOPLE AT THE APOLLO ACCEPTED AND LIKED THEM.

BEVERLY LEE

WE *THOUGHT* THEY WOULD WANT MORE RHYTHM AND BLUES AND SOUL.

NANCY WILSON BRINGS A **SOPHISTICATED** SOUND TO THE APOLLO THAT IS HARD TO CATEGORIZE.

MOST JAZZ BUFFS WILL SAY I'M NOT A JAZZ SINGER.

MOST RHYTHM-AND-BLUES BUFFS WILL SAY I'M NOT AN R&B SINGER.

MOST POP BUFFS WILL SAY I'M NOT A POP SINGER.

Guess who I saw today...

CANNONBALL ADDERLEY, THE STAR ALTO SAX PLAYER, SEES HER AND HELPS HER GET A RECORDING CONTRACT.

AT FIRST I WAS ON THE **BOTTOM** OF THE BILL AND HAD THE DRESSING ROOM ON THE TOP FLOOR.

DRESSING Room 11

BY THE TIME I GOT TO THE APOLLO, I WAS VERY WELL SEASONED. I HAD HAD A TELEVISION SHOW AT FIFTEEN.

THE APOLLO WAS A DIFFERENT THING. MOST PEOPLE WHO WERE IN FRONT OF ME ON THE SHOW DESERVED TO BE.

I WAS NOT AFRAID OF THE APOLLO, AND IT WAS WONDERFUL TO GET THE KIND OF RECEPTION I GOT THERE.

THE NEXT TIME I WENT BACK I WAS THE *HEADLINER*. IT HAPPENED THAT FAST.

THE FIRST TIME I HAD A PERFORMANCE AT THE APOLLO, I OPENED THE SHOW. I WAS THE *BABY* IN THE BUSINESS.

DIONNE WARWICK

SHE IS A YOUNG, CLASSICALLY TRAINED MUSICIAN SINGING BACKUP FOR THE DRIFTERS WHEN SHE MEETS *BURT BACHARACH* AND *HAL DAVID*. THEY WRITE A STRING OF HITS FOR HER.

IT'S NOT THE REGULAR I–IV–V–IV CHANGES.

THIS SONG CAN'T BE PLAYED.

HERE IS THIS KID FROM NEW JERSEY WITH THIS GODDAMNED MUSIC THAT NOBODY UNDERSTANDS. WHAT IS SHE *DOING* TO US?

I WILL SIT AND PLAY IT FOR YOU, AND THEN YOUR BAND WILL PLAY IT.

REUBEN PHILLIPS

MY MUSIC WAS PROBABLY THE *HARDEST* IN THE INDUSTRY.

ANYONE WHO HAD A HEART

THEY DON'T *UNDERSTAND* YOUR MUSIC. THEY'LL BOO YOU OFF THE STAGE.

I NEVER HAD ANY PROBLEM RELATING TO THE PEOPLE AT THE APOLLO, BECAUSE THAT WAS MY *HERITAGE*.

HAL DAVID WROTE LYRICS THAT SPOKE TO YOUR *HEART*.

EVERYBODY'S GOT ONE OF *THOSE*, REGARDLESS OF HOW RICH OR POOR YOU ARE, OR THE COLOR OF YOUR SKIN.

BOBBY SCHIFFMAN

Peeeeople...

THE MAN WHO RUNS THIS THEATER TOLD ME I CAN'T SING THIS SONG HERE. I'LL SING IT *ANYWHERE*.

I'M BRINGING DOWNTOWN *UPTOWN*!

DOWNTOWN, UPTOWN, ALL OVER THE COUNTRY—RADIO WAVES ARE BREACHING RACIAL BARRIERS.

Hundreds of hits-oriented stations play soul records in *heavy rotation*, along with white rock and roll and pop.

POWERFUL *RECORD COMPANIES* USURP DJS—HOBBLED BY THE PAYOLA SCANDAL—AND ORGANIZE SHOW PACKAGES FOR THE APOLLO CONSISTING *ENTIRELY* OF THEIR OWN RECORDING ARTISTS.

APOLLO

THIS WEEK
THE ATLANTIC CARAVAN
OF STARS

TWO COMPANIES LEAD THE BLACK RECORD BUSINESS DURING THE '60S: BERRY GORDY'S **MOTOWN** AND AHMET ERTEGUN AND JERRY WEXLER'S **ATLANTIC**.

WHAT GREW OUT OF THE RHYTHM AND BLUES OF THE '40S AND '50S WERE TWO STRAINS . . .

THERE WAS AN **ATLANTIC** STYLE, WHICH WAS SAM & DAVE, WILSON PICKETT, AND OTIS REDDING.

THEN THERE WAS ANOTHER STYLE THAT CAME OUT OF DETROIT, WHICH WAS **MOTOWN**.

IT WAS MORE **ADVANCED**, MORE SOPHISTICATED, HIPPER, AND ALSO LESS REAL AND LESS AUTHENTIC. NOT AS CLOSE TO WHAT WE TEND TO THINK OF AS AUTHENTIC BLUES.

BUT THE MOTOWN STYLE WAS MORE ADVENTURESOME, MORE POP, AND MORE REPRESENTATIVE OF WHAT THE **MODERN** BLACK PERSON WANTED TO HEAR.

AT THE TIME, WE AT ATLANTIC WERE DEVELOPING A KIND OF MODERN R&B SOUND WITH A MORE **FUNKY** STYLE.

WE HAD A LOT OF WHITE SALES, AS DID MOTOWN, BUT THE KIND OF MUSIC MOTOWN PIONEERED IS REALLY THE MUSIC THAT BECAME THE POP MUSIC OF **AMERICA**.

BERRY GORDY AND HIS SISTER, ESTHER, CAME TO SEE ME IN '62.

MR. SCHIFFMAN, WE ARE HAVING **GREAT** SUCCESS IN DETROIT WITH MANY OF OUR ARTISTS.

BOBBY SCHIFFMAN

WE'D LIKE TO DO A MOTOWN PACKAGE— YOU'D GET AN AMAZING DEAL.

I'VE NEVER HEARD OF **ANY** OF THEM!

AT FIRST, I THOUGHT IT WAS *MOTORTOWN*.

AS A MATTER OF FACT, I HAD A SIGN MADE THAT SAID MOTORTOWN, AND HAD TO CHANGE IT.

WE DID THIRTY-ONE SHOWS OVER SEVEN DAYS.

SMOKEY ROBINSON AND THE MIRACLES, DIANA ROSS AND THE SUPREMES, THE TEMPTATIONS, MARTHA AND THE VANDELLAS, MARVIN GAYE, STEVIE WONDER, THE CONTOURS, AND MARV JOHNSON.

THE **PACKAGE** COST THE APOLLO $7,000 FOR THE **WEEK**, AND SOON MOST OF THOSE PEOPLE WERE GETTING $40,000 TO $50,000 A **NIGHT, EACH.**

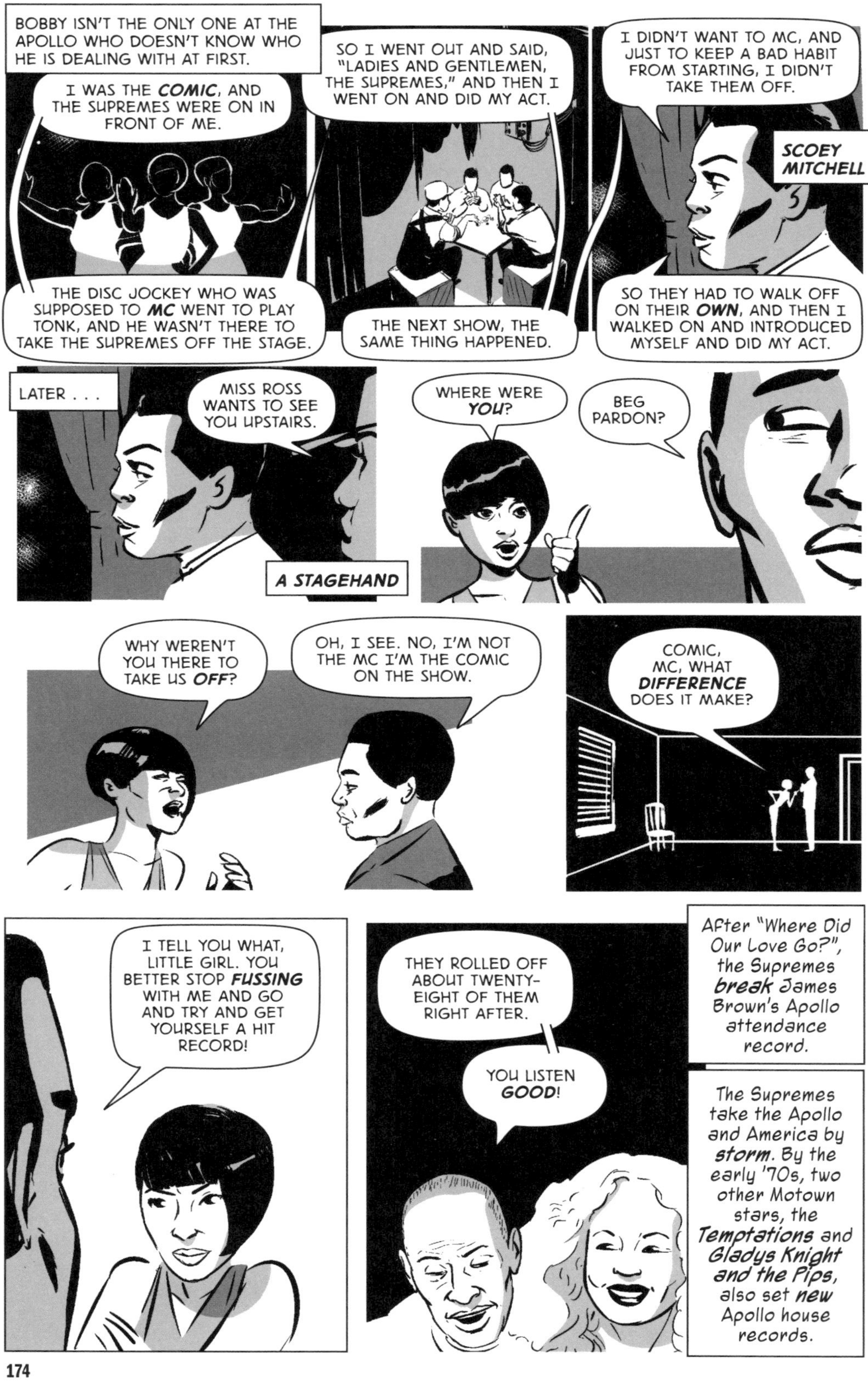
BOBBY ISN'T THE ONLY ONE AT THE APOLLO WHO DOESN'T KNOW WHO HE IS DEALING WITH AT FIRST.
I WAS THE **COMIC**, AND THE SUPREMES WERE ON IN FRONT OF ME.
THE DISC JOCKEY WHO WAS SUPPOSED TO **MC** WENT TO PLAY TONK, AND HE WASN'T THERE TO TAKE THE SUPREMES OFF THE STAGE.
SO I WENT OUT AND SAID, "LADIES AND GENTLEMEN, THE SUPREMES," AND THEN I WENT ON AND DID MY ACT.
THE NEXT SHOW, THE SAME THING HAPPENED.
I DIDN'T WANT TO MC, AND JUST TO KEEP A BAD HABIT FROM STARTING, I DIDN'T TAKE THEM OFF.
SCOEY MITCHELL
SO THEY HAD TO WALK OFF ON THEIR **OWN**, AND THEN I WALKED ON AND INTRODUCED MYSELF AND DID MY ACT.
LATER . . .
MISS ROSS WANTS TO SEE YOU UPSTAIRS.
A STAGEHAND
WHERE WERE **YOU**?
BEG PARDON?
WHY WEREN'T YOU THERE TO TAKE US **OFF**?
OH, I SEE. NO, I'M NOT THE MC I'M THE COMIC ON THE SHOW.
COMIC, MC, WHAT **DIFFERENCE** DOES IT MAKE?
I TELL YOU WHAT, LITTLE GIRL. YOU BETTER STOP **FUSSING** WITH ME AND GO AND TRY AND GET YOURSELF A HIT RECORD!
THEY ROLLED OFF ABOUT TWENTY-EIGHT OF THEM RIGHT AFTER.
YOU LISTEN **GOOD**!
After "Where Did Our Love Go?", the Supremes **break** James Brown's Apollo attendance record.
The Supremes take the Apollo and America by **storm**. By the early '70s, two other Motown stars, the **Temptations** and **Gladys Knight and the Pips**, also set **new** Apollo house records.

GORDY'S SHOP HAS SOME OF THE ASSEMBLY-LINE TRAITS OF HIS POWERFUL INDUSTRIAL NEIGHBORS IN DETROIT.

BOBBY AND FRANK SCHIFFMAN

HONI COLES

CHOLLY ATKINS

EDDIE HOLLAND

LAMONT DOZIER

BRIAN HOLLAND

BERRY GORDY

SMOKEY ROBINSON

BUT IN MANY WAYS, BERRY GORDY AND MOTOWN DO WHAT FRANK SCHIFFMAN AND THE APOLLO HAVE **ALWAYS** DONE.

GORDY AND HIS TEAM WORK CLOSELY WITH HIS ARTISTS, **NURTURING** THEM, **TRAINING** THEM, SOMETIMES **HONING** ACTS FOR MONTHS BEFORE RELEASING A RECORD OR SENDING THEM ON THE ROAD.

MARVIN GAYE

BERRY GORDY

NO AMOUNT OF COACHING OR HIT RECORDS CAN INSTILL ENOUGH CONFIDENCE IN THE PRINCE OF MOTOWN AT THE APOLLO.

MARVIN GAYE WAS VERY MUCH AFFECTED BY HIS FEELING THAT HE WAS LOUSY ONSTAGE.

IN TRUTH, THERE WAS A LOT TO BE DESIRED IN HIS OFFERING, IN THE BEGINNING.

BOBBY SCHIFFMAN

STILL, HE WAS EXTREMELY POPULAR. THE GIRLS AND GUYS ABSOLUTELY **ADORED** HIM.

STILL, HE WAS ALWAYS VERY **NERVOUS** ABOUT GOING ON THE STAGE.

HI PAL, WHAT TIME DO YOU WANT ME TO PICK YOU UP AT LA GUARDIA?

MY FLIGHT GETS IN AT ELEVEN FRIDAY MORNING.

WE HAD A TREMENDOUS ADVERTISING CAMPAIGN, AND WERE EXPECTING TO SELL OUT EVERY SHOW.

WHERE ARE YOU?

BOBBY, I COULDN'T *DO* IT.

I GOT OFF THE PLANE, AND WAS SO SCARED I GOT ON ANOTHER PLANE AND WENT *BACK* TO DETROIT.

MARVIN, WE'RE *SOLD OUT*!

I CAN'T HELP IT. I'M AFRAID.

@#$%&!

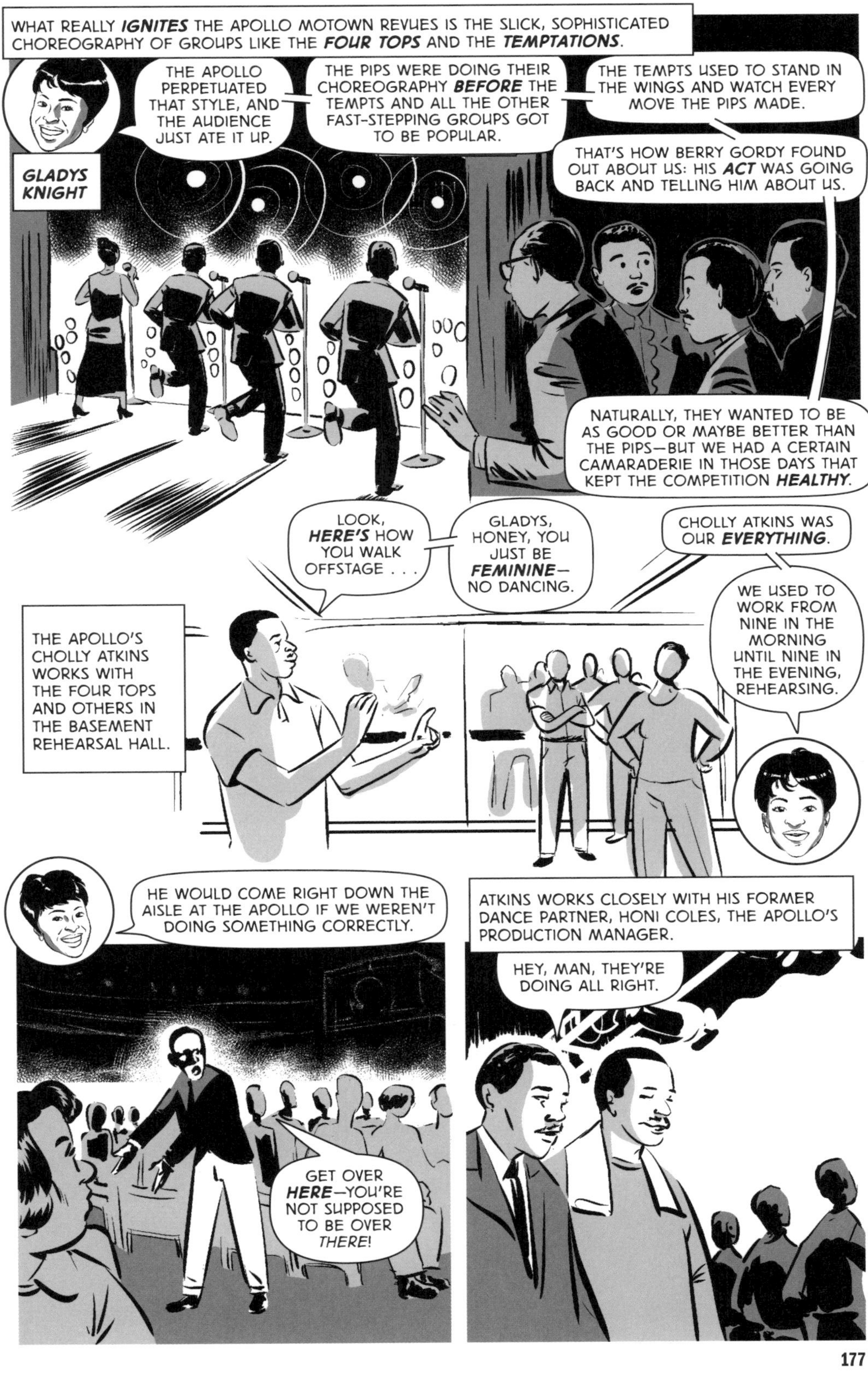

WHAT REALLY **IGNITES** THE APOLLO MOTOWN REVUES IS THE SLICK, SOPHISTICATED CHOREOGRAPHY OF GROUPS LIKE THE **FOUR TOPS** AND THE **TEMPTATIONS**.
GLADYS KNIGHT
THE APOLLO PERPETUATED THAT STYLE, AND THE AUDIENCE JUST ATE IT UP.
THE PIPS WERE DOING THEIR CHOREOGRAPHY **BEFORE** THE TEMPTS AND ALL THE OTHER FAST-STEPPING GROUPS GOT TO BE POPULAR.
THE TEMPTS USED TO STAND IN THE WINGS AND WATCH EVERY MOVE THE PIPS MADE.
THAT'S HOW BERRY GORDY FOUND OUT ABOUT US: HIS **ACT** WAS GOING BACK AND TELLING HIM ABOUT US.
NATURALLY, THEY WANTED TO BE AS GOOD OR MAYBE BETTER THAN THE PIPS—BUT WE HAD A CERTAIN CAMARADERIE IN THOSE DAYS THAT KEPT THE COMPETITION **HEALTHY**.
THE APOLLO'S CHOLLY ATKINS WORKS WITH THE FOUR TOPS AND OTHERS IN THE BASEMENT REHEARSAL HALL.
LOOK, **HERE'S** HOW YOU WALK OFFSTAGE . . .
GLADYS, HONEY, YOU JUST BE **FEMININE**—NO DANCING.
CHOLLY ATKINS WAS OUR **EVERYTHING**.
WE USED TO WORK FROM NINE IN THE MORNING UNTIL NINE IN THE EVENING, REHEARSING.
HE WOULD COME RIGHT DOWN THE AISLE AT THE APOLLO IF WE WEREN'T DOING SOMETHING CORRECTLY.
GET OVER **HERE**—YOU'RE NOT SUPPOSED TO BE OVER *THERE*!
ATKINS WORKS CLOSELY WITH HIS FORMER DANCE PARTNER, HONI COLES, THE APOLLO'S PRODUCTION MANAGER.
HEY, MAN, THEY'RE DOING ALL RIGHT.

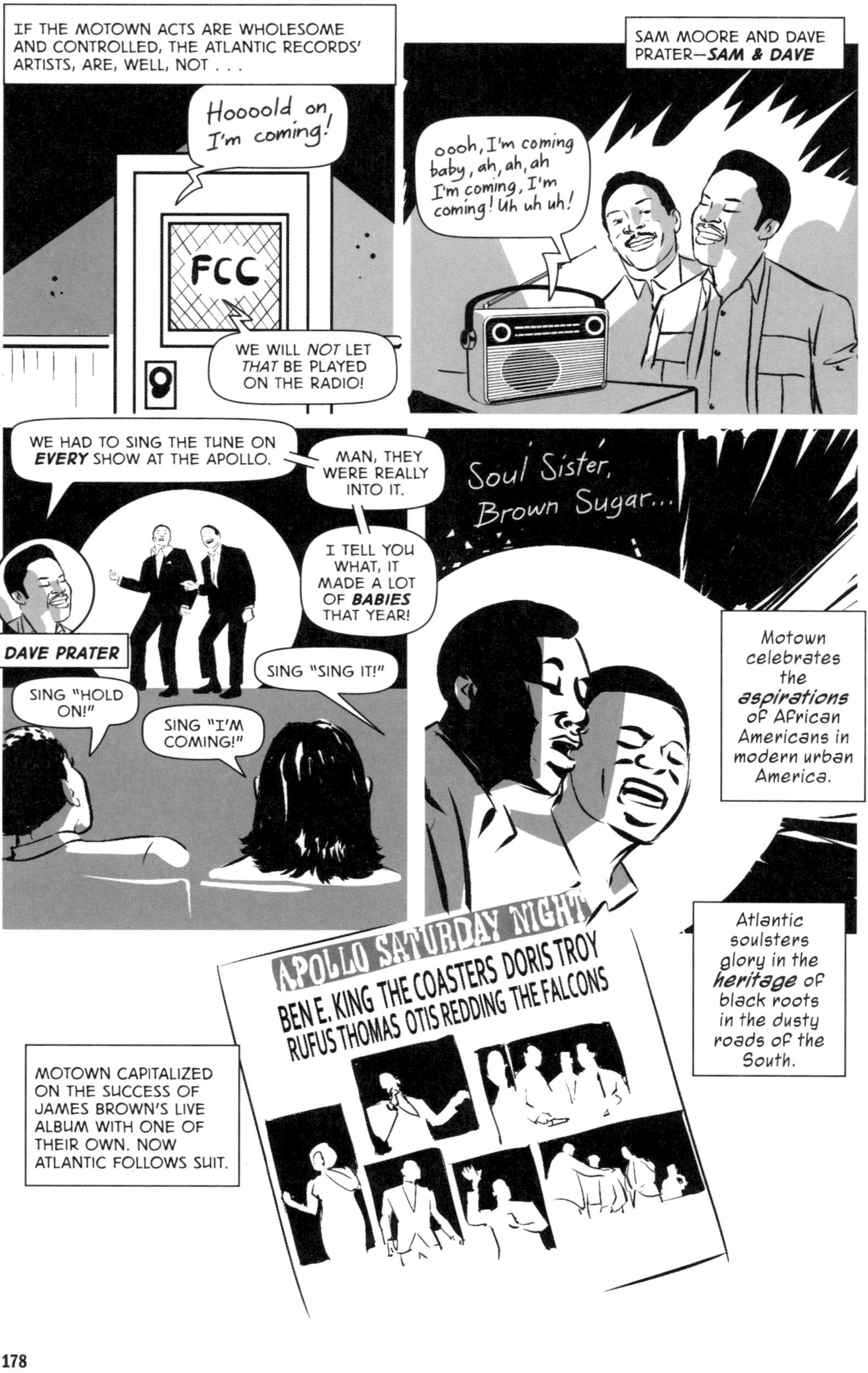

IF THE MOTOWN ACTS ARE WHOLESOME AND CONTROLLED, THE ATLANTIC RECORDS' ARTISTS, ARE, WELL, NOT . . .
Hoooold on, I'm coming!
FCC
WE WILL NOT LET THAT BE PLAYED ON THE RADIO!
SAM MOORE AND DAVE PRATER—SAM & DAVE
oooh, I'm coming baby, ah, ah, ah I'm coming, I'm coming! Uh uh uh!
WE HAD TO SING THE TUNE ON EVERY SHOW AT THE APOLLO.
MAN, THEY WERE REALLY INTO IT.
I TELL YOU WHAT, IT MADE A LOT OF BABIES THAT YEAR!
DAVE PRATER
SING "HOLD ON!"
SING "I'M COMING!"
SING "SING IT!"
Soul Sister, Brown Sugar...
Motown celebrates the aspirations of African Americans in modern urban America.
Atlantic soulsters glory in the heritage of black roots in the dusty roads of the South.
APOLLO SATURDAY NIGHT
BEN E. KING THE COASTERS DORIS TROY
RUFUS THOMAS OTIS REDDING THE FALCONS
MOTOWN CAPITALIZED ON THE SUCCESS OF JAMES BROWN'S LIVE ALBUM WITH ONE OF THEIR OWN. NOW ATLANTIC FOLLOWS SUIT.

FIDEL CASTRO MAKES A POINT OF STAYING HERE ON 125TH STREET IN 1960.

HOTEL THERESA

OTIS REDDING

MAN, I DON'T KNOW ABOUT THIS. I THINK WE'RE TOO **COUNTRY**.

YOU REALLY THINK THEY'RE GOING TO GO FOR WHAT I DO, WHAT *WE* DO DOWN HOME?

ATLANTIC CARAVAN OF STARS

OTIS REDDING

BEN E. KING

Like many other Apollo first-timers, *Otis Redding* doesn't realize he needs charts for the *King Curtis* band, who will back him.

DAMN, ONLY 400 BUCKS FOR THIS GIG, AND NOW I GOTTA PAY FOR CHARTS?!

Otis, like his Motown counterpart, Marvin Gaye, is not confident in his stage presence.

These arms of miiiiinnnnne...

HE WAS **INEPT** ONSTAGE.

ATLANTIC CO-FOUNDER JERRY WEXLER

OTIS, REMEMBER WHAT RUFUS THOMAS SAID: "FIND ONE WOMAN IN THE CROWD, AND SING TO HER."

DESPITE HIS INERTIA, THE WOMEN AT THE APOLLO **LOVED** HIM.

ATLANTIC STAR **SOLOMON BURKE** DID NOT LACK CONFIDENCE IN ANYTHING.

His gospel-imbued sound was *fundamental* to the emergence of soul music and influenced many, including Mick Jagger.

SING IT PRETTY NOW!

OOH! AHH! OOH!

GET YOUR POPCORN HERE!

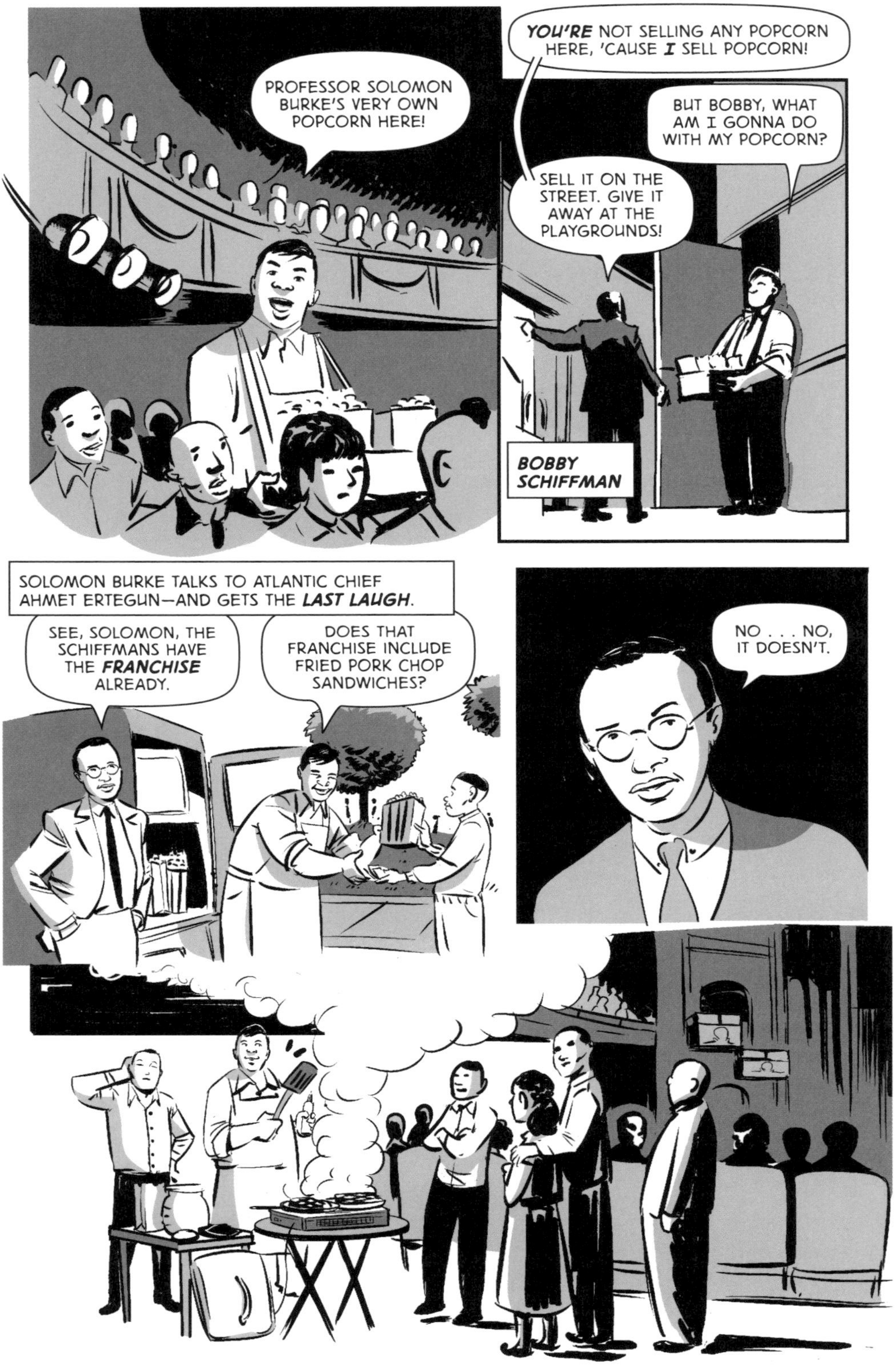
PROFESSOR SOLOMON BURKE'S VERY OWN POPCORN HERE!
YOU'RE NOT SELLING ANY POPCORN HERE, 'CAUSE I SELL POPCORN!
BUT BOBBY, WHAT AM I GONNA DO WITH MY POPCORN?
SELL IT ON THE STREET. GIVE IT AWAY AT THE PLAYGROUNDS!
BOBBY SCHIFFMAN
SOLOMON BURKE TALKS TO ATLANTIC CHIEF AHMET ERTEGUN—AND GETS THE LAST LAUGH.
SEE, SOLOMON, THE SCHIFFMANS HAVE THE FRANCHISE ALREADY.
DOES THAT FRANCHISE INCLUDE FRIED PORK CHOP SANDWICHES?
NO . . . NO, IT DOESN'T.

1961. BEFORE SHE MAKES HER CLASSICS FOR ATLANTIC RECORDS, JOHN HAMMOND RECORDS *ARETHA FRANKLIN* FOR COLUMBIA.

COME ON, FRANK, GIVE HER A SHOT. SHE'S *MARVELOUS*.

I DON'T KNOW, JOHN, SHE HAS NO TRACK RECORD SINGING POP. SHE'S A *GOSPEL* SINGER.

TRUST ME.

FRANK SCHIFFMAN

JOHN HAMMOND

I BOOK HER WITH SAM COOKE AND LITTLE ANTHONY AND SHE *NEVER* SHOWS UP!

NOW SHE COMES . . . THREE DAYS *LATE*?!

I'M HOLDING YOU PERSONALLY RESPONSIBLE!

Rock a bye your baby with a dixie melody . .

THE APOLLO HELPS TRAIN HER AND NURTURE HER IMMENSE TALENT.

1971. ARETHA FRANKLIN'S APOLLO APPEARANCE IS A NOW MAJOR *CULTURAL EVENT.*

i aint never loved a man

THE TWO OPENING-NIGHT SHOWS CANNOT ACCOMMODATE THE THRONGS.

SHE'S HOME— ARETHA FRANKLIN

LOTS OF CELEBRITIES FOR THE *QUEEN OF SOUL* TONIGHT . . .

THERE'S *REVEREND JESSE JACKSON*, AND THERE, *ZULU CHIEF MANGOSUTHU GATSHA BUTHELEZI.*

THIS IS THE MOST *OVERWHELMING* THING WE'VE EVER HAD IN THE THEATER.

PETER LONG, APOLLO'S P.R. DIRECTOR

REVIEW:

The thousands of black people who saw and heard Miss Franklin were more than an audience. They were part of a black interaction. They came not only to see and hear "Lady Soul" . . . but also to participate with her in an **exultation** of her blackness.

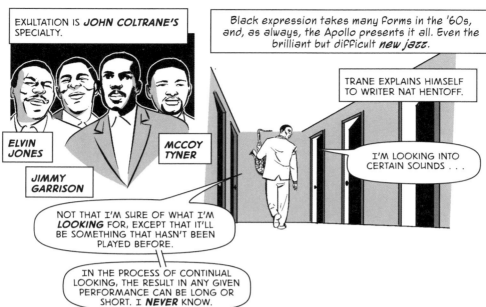

EXULTATION IS *JOHN COLTRANE'S* SPECIALTY.

ELVIN JONES

JIMMY GARRISON

MCCOY TYNER

Black expression takes many forms in the '60s, and, as always, the Apollo presents it all. Even the brilliant but difficult *new jazz*.

TRANE EXPLAINS HIMSELF TO WRITER NAT HENTOFF.

I'M LOOKING INTO CERTAIN SOUNDS . . .

NOT THAT I'M SURE OF WHAT I'M *LOOKING* FOR, EXCEPT THAT IT'LL BE SOMETHING THAT HASN'T BEEN PLAYED BEFORE.

IN THE PROCESS OF CONTINUAL LOOKING, THE RESULT IN ANY GIVEN PERFORMANCE CAN BE LONG OR SHORT. I *NEVER* KNOW.

UNFORTUNATELY, THE CROWD AT THE APOLLO ISN'T ALWAYS WILLING TO FOLLOW TRANE ON HIS JOURNEY.

HE WAS PLAYING "MY FAVORITE THINGS" FOR ABOUT HALF AN HOUR.

IT WAS THE '60S, AND THERE WAS A LOT OF *TROUBLE* IN THE AIR. RACISM. THE BLACK MAN HOLLERING FOR FREEDOM.

THE PLACE WAS *PACKED* WHEN HE WENT IN THERE. WHEN HE LEFT, THERE WASN'T BUT A *HANDFUL* OF PEOPLE.

COLTRANE WAS TAKING HIS FEELINGS OUT THAT HE HAD AGAINST THE HAPPENINGS OF THE TIME . . . TAKING IT OUT ON HIS HORN.

LIONEL HAMPTON

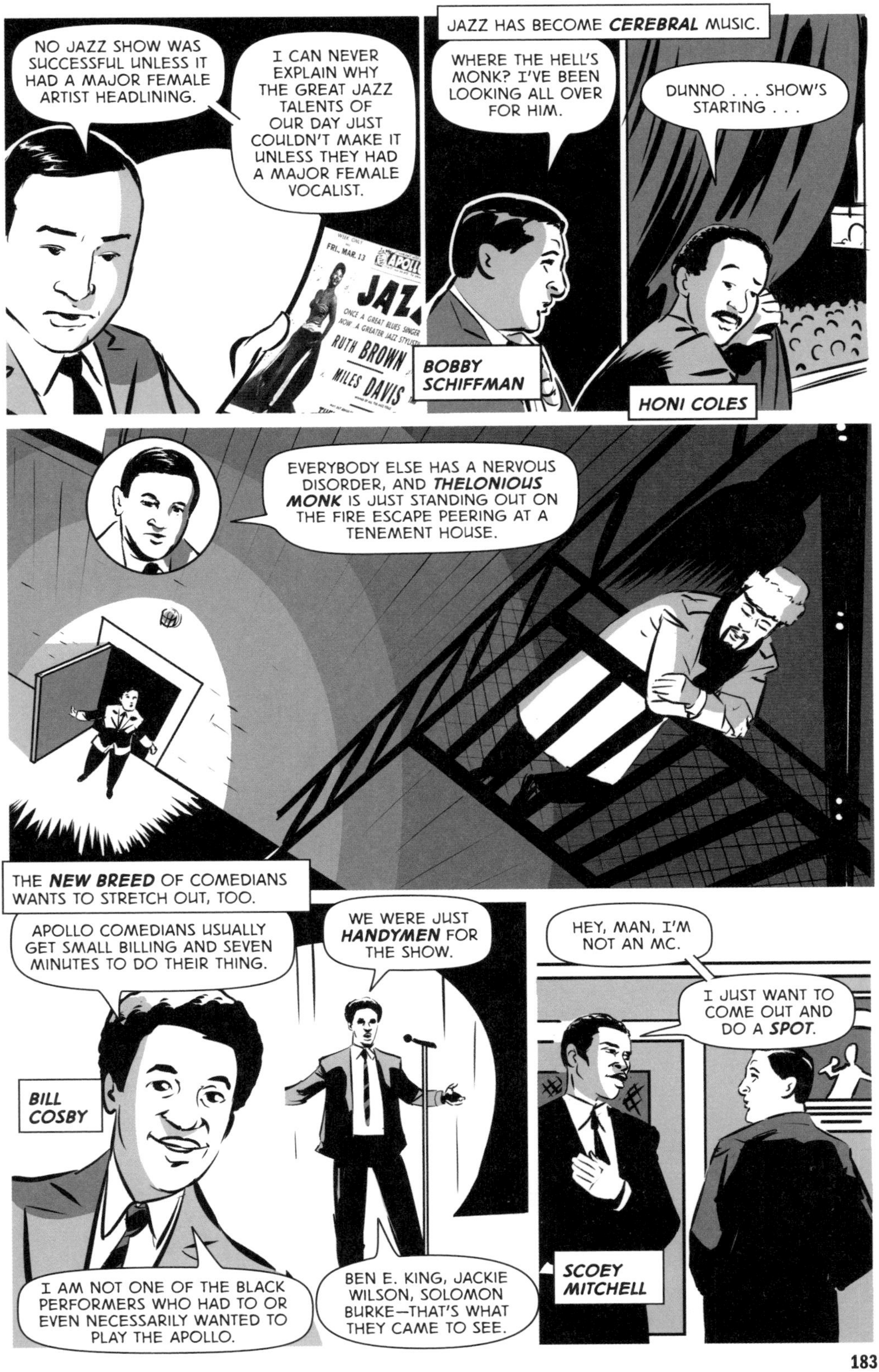

NO JAZZ SHOW WAS SUCCESSFUL UNLESS IT HAD A MAJOR FEMALE ARTIST HEADLINING.
I CAN NEVER EXPLAIN WHY THE GREAT JAZZ TALENTS OF OUR DAY JUST COULDN'T MAKE IT UNLESS THEY HAD A MAJOR FEMALE VOCALIST.
FRI. MAR. 13
APOLLO
JAZZ
ONCE A GREAT BLUES SINGER NOW A GREATER JAZZ STYLIST
RUTH BROWN
MILES DAVIS
JAZZ HAS BECOME CEREBRAL MUSIC.
WHERE THE HELL'S MONK? I'VE BEEN LOOKING ALL OVER FOR HIM.
BOBBY SCHIFFMAN
DUNNO . . . SHOW'S STARTING . . .
HONI COLES
EVERYBODY ELSE HAS A NERVOUS DISORDER, AND THELONIOUS MONK IS JUST STANDING OUT ON THE FIRE ESCAPE PEERING AT A TENEMENT HOUSE.
THE NEW BREED OF COMEDIANS WANTS TO STRETCH OUT, TOO.
APOLLO COMEDIANS USUALLY GET SMALL BILLING AND SEVEN MINUTES TO DO THEIR THING.
BILL COSBY
I AM NOT ONE OF THE BLACK PERFORMERS WHO HAD TO OR EVEN NECESSARILY WANTED TO PLAY THE APOLLO.
WE WERE JUST HANDYMEN FOR THE SHOW.
BEN E. KING, JACKIE WILSON, SOLOMON BURKE—THAT'S WHAT THEY CAME TO SEE.
HEY, MAN, I'M NOT AN MC.
I JUST WANT TO COME OUT AND DO A SPOT.
SCOEY MITCHELL

THE FIRST TIME *RICHARD PRYOR* PLAYED THE APOLLO WE PAID HIM $350 AND HE WAS OUTRAGEOUS!

YOU KNOW THE OLD ADAGE ABOUT BLACK FOLKS HAVING RHYTHM?

WELL, ON THE FINALE, EVERYTHING RICHARD DID WAS INTENTIONALLY *OUT OF SYNC*.

HE WAS IN THE WRONG KEY. HE WAS TAPPING HIS FOOT AT THE WRONG BEAT.

THE REST ONSTAGE KEPT MUGGING WITH HIM. HE WAS A BRILLIANT COMIC!

BOBBY SCHIFFMAN

COUNT BASIE, BILLY ECKSTINE, COLES AND ATKINS, AND *FREDA PAYNE*

HE WAS *DIRTY*, AND THERE WERE PEOPLE WHO WALKED.

BUT RICHIE WAS BEFORE HIS TIME. HIS COMEDY ROUTINES WERE VERY STREET-ORIENTED AND *FRESH*. THE PEOPLE JUST LOVED HIM.

OFFSTAGE, RICHIE'S A VERY SOFT-SPOKEN, EASY TO TALK TO, UNASSUMING PERSON.

AS OPPOSED TO *REDD FOXX*, WHO IS ONSTAGE ALL THE TIME. FOXX IS FOXX ALL THE TIME.

REDD FOXX AND BOBBY SCHIFFMAN ARE CLOSE FRIENDS AND *PRANKSTERS*.

Both avid hunters, they even appear together on television on *American Sportsman*.

FOXX, YOU'RE GOING TO HAVE TO TAKE OUT THE *BLUE* STUFF.

I'M NOT GONNA DO IT.

BLUE = DIRTY

PLEASE DON'T SCREW ME OVER, THIS IS A FAMILY THEATER. I CAN'T HAVE YOU JOKING ABOUT FILTHY STUFF . . .

I'M NOT GONNA TAKE IT OUT.

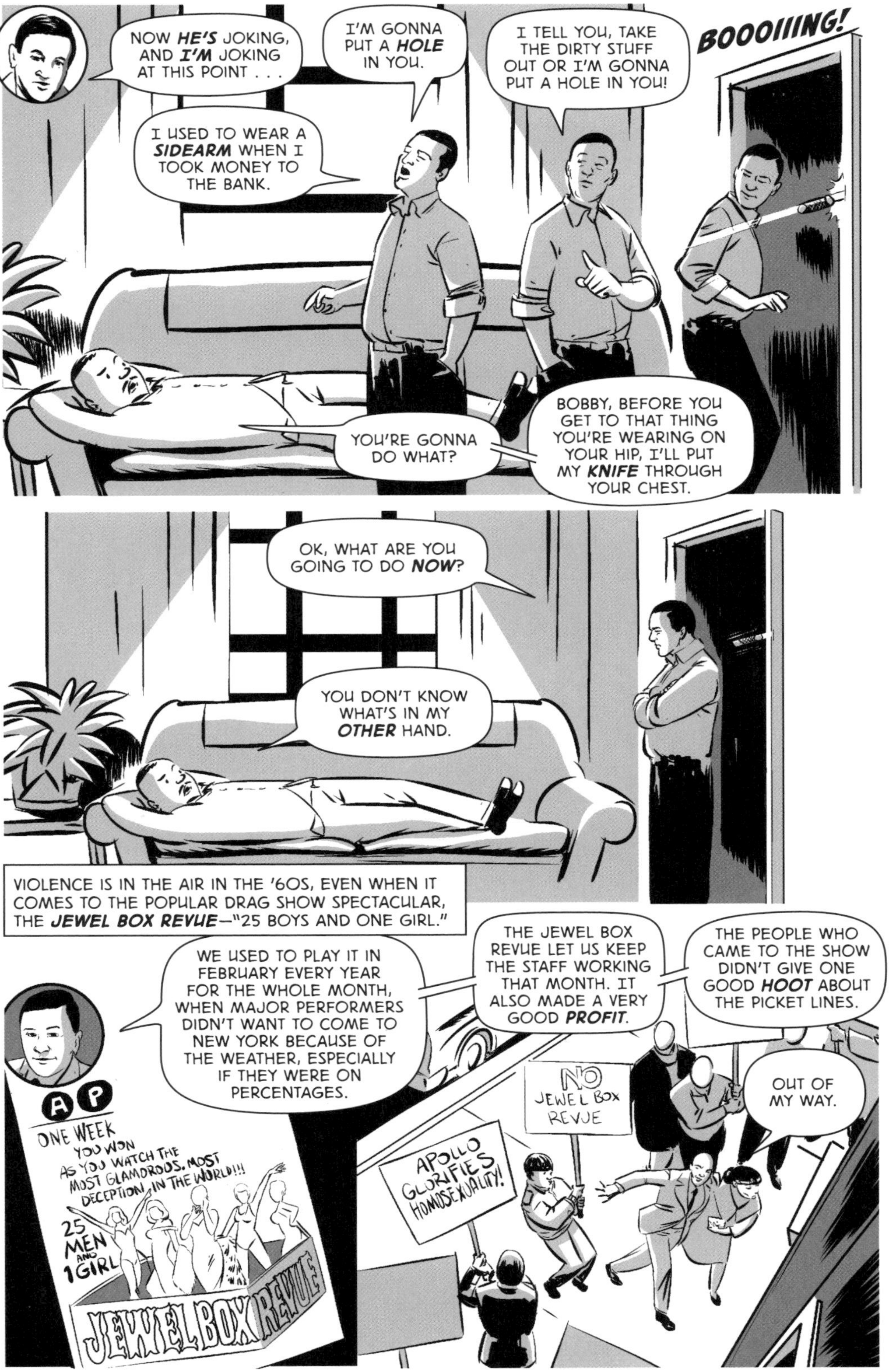

NOW HE'S JOKING, AND I'M JOKING AT THIS POINT . . .
I USED TO WEAR A SIDEARM WHEN I TOOK MONEY TO THE BANK.
I'M GONNA PUT A HOLE IN YOU.
I TELL YOU, TAKE THE DIRTY STUFF OUT OR I'M GONNA PUT A HOLE IN YOU!
BOOOIIING!
YOU'RE GONNA DO WHAT?
BOBBY, BEFORE YOU GET TO THAT THING YOU'RE WEARING ON YOUR HIP, I'LL PUT MY KNIFE THROUGH YOUR CHEST.
OK, WHAT ARE YOU GOING TO DO NOW?
YOU DON'T KNOW WHAT'S IN MY OTHER HAND.
VIOLENCE IS IN THE AIR IN THE '60S, EVEN WHEN IT COMES TO THE POPULAR DRAG SHOW SPECTACULAR, THE JEWEL BOX REVUE—"25 BOYS AND ONE GIRL."
WE USED TO PLAY IT IN FEBRUARY EVERY YEAR FOR THE WHOLE MONTH, WHEN MAJOR PERFORMERS DIDN'T WANT TO COME TO NEW YORK BECAUSE OF THE WEATHER, ESPECIALLY IF THEY WERE ON PERCENTAGES.
THE JEWEL BOX REVUE LET US KEEP THE STAFF WORKING THAT MONTH. IT ALSO MADE A VERY GOOD PROFIT.
THE PEOPLE WHO CAME TO THE SHOW DIDN'T GIVE ONE GOOD HOOT ABOUT THE PICKET LINES.
AP
ONE WEEK
25 MEN AND 1 GIRL
JEWEL BOX REVUE
NO JEWEL BOX REVUE
APOLLO GLORIFIES HOMOSEXUALITY!
OUT OF MY WAY.

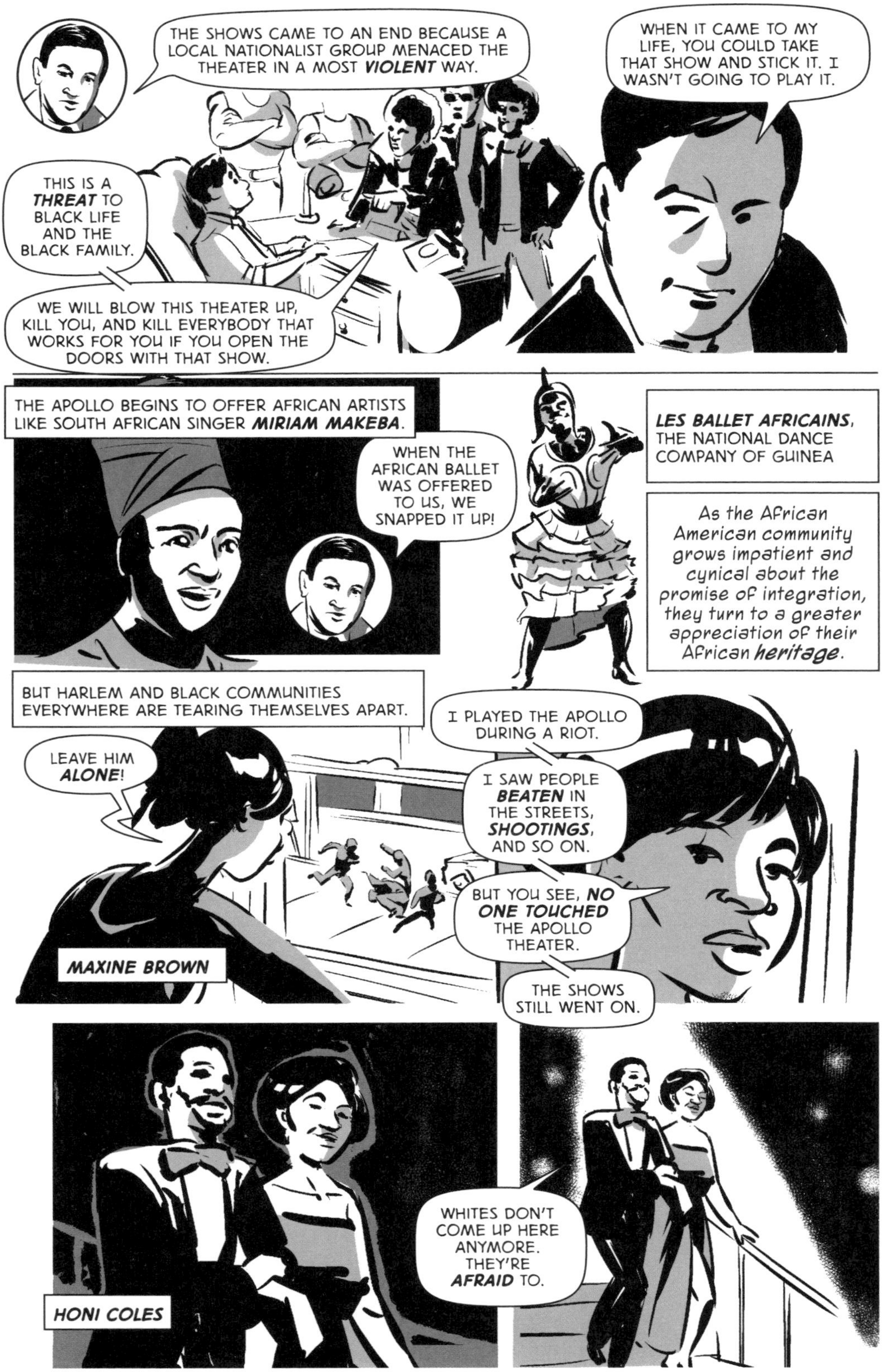
THE SHOWS CAME TO AN END BECAUSE A LOCAL NATIONALIST GROUP MENACED THE THEATER IN A MOST VIOLENT WAY.
WHEN IT CAME TO MY LIFE, YOU COULD TAKE THAT SHOW AND STICK IT. I WASN'T GOING TO PLAY IT.
THIS IS A THREAT TO BLACK LIFE AND THE BLACK FAMILY.
WE WILL BLOW THIS THEATER UP, KILL YOU, AND KILL EVERYBODY THAT WORKS FOR YOU IF YOU OPEN THE DOORS WITH THAT SHOW.
THE APOLLO BEGINS TO OFFER AFRICAN ARTISTS LIKE SOUTH AFRICAN SINGER MIRIAM MAKEBA.
WHEN THE AFRICAN BALLET WAS OFFERED TO US, WE SNAPPED IT UP!
LES BALLET AFRICAINS, THE NATIONAL DANCE COMPANY OF GUINEA
As the African American community grows impatient and cynical about the promise of integration, they turn to a greater appreciation of their African heritage.
BUT HARLEM AND BLACK COMMUNITIES EVERYWHERE ARE TEARING THEMSELVES APART.
LEAVE HIM ALONE!
I PLAYED THE APOLLO DURING A RIOT.
I SAW PEOPLE BEATEN IN THE STREETS, SHOOTINGS, AND SO ON.
BUT YOU SEE, NO ONE TOUCHED THE APOLLO THEATER.
THE SHOWS STILL WENT ON.
MAXINE BROWN
WHITES DON'T COME UP HERE ANYMORE. THEY'RE AFRAID TO.
HONI COLES

Throughout the '60s, the Apollo is *protected*, even when the rest of the community is *devastated*.

In July 1964, the worst riot in Harlem in more than two decades breaks out when an off-duty cop shoots and kills a Harlem teenager.

One dies, 140 are injured, and 500 arrested. The violence spreads to the black neighborhoods of Brooklyn.

Trouble continues in the '60s, culminating in more rioting in the aftermath of the assassination of *Martin Luther King Jr.* in Memphis on April 4, 1968.

Yet, as the Civil Rights movement alters the *consciousness* of the nation, other areas of *opportunity* become available at last to African Americans.

The system the Apollo works within and against for so many years *collapses*.

The general acceptance of black culture into American popular culture is the beginning of something *new*, but it is also the beginning of the *end* for the Apollo Theater.

Ironically, it is the Apollo itself that becomes a *casualty* of this revolution.

CHAPTER 9

The 1970s: Funky

JAN. 31, 1970

Billboard SINGLES

HOT 100

3 3 4 **I WANT YOU BACK** 12
The Jackson 5 'The Corporation' Motown 1157

The Jacksons had approached James Brown about hiring the then unknown group.

THE **JACKSON 5** WITH THEIR FATHER, JOE—A COUPLE OF YEARS EARLIER

THE FIRST PORTENT OF ONE OF THE GREATEST MUSIC SUCCESS STORIES EVER . . .

JAMES WOULDN'T DO IT.

SAM MOORE

WE COULDN'T HANDLE THEM AS AN ACT ON THE SHOW WITH US.

WE DIDN'T HAVE THE MONEY BECAUSE WE HAD JUST STARTED MAKING MONEY, AND HAD JUST BOUGHT A BIG OLE BUS.

SO THEY CAME TO TALK TO **US** AT THE APOLLO.

BUT WE TALKED TO HONI COLES, AND HE PUT THEM ON THE AMATEUR SHOW.

DAVE PRATER OF SAM & DAVE

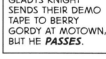

GLADYS KNIGHT SENDS THEIR DEMO TAPE TO BERRY GORDY AT MOTOWN, BUT HE **PASSES**.

PROBABLY FEBRUARY 1968—SOME SAY IT WAS AUGUST 1967, BUT THE APOLLO WAS CLOSED FOR SUMMER RENOVATIONS THEN.

THE YOUNGSTERS ARE BROUGHT BACK FOR TWO ENCORES AND THEY EASILY WIN.

THEIR FIRST PROFESSIONAL APOLLO ENGAGEMENT STARTS THE WEEK OF MAY 24, 1968.

The unknowns are mistakenly called the **Jive Five** *in the Amsterdam News preview.*

DAMN!

THE NEXT THING I HEARD, DIANA ROSS HAD THEM.

ABOUT SIX MONTHS LATER, BERRY GORDY HAD A HIT OUT WITH THEM!

DAVE PRATER

If ever one can say the rest is history, *this* is that time!

JAMES BROWN IS AS BIG AS THEY GET IN THE EARLY '70S.

– IN 1971, JAMES BROWN IS THE HIGHEST-PAID BLACK ENTERTAINER IN THE WORLD.

– BETWEEN 1969 AND 1971 HE HAS SEVENTEEN TOP-TEN HITS ON THE RHYTHM-AND-BLUES CHARTS.

– THE MEDIA CALL HIM THE "BLACK MESSIAH" AND "THE MOST POWERFUL BLACK MAN IN AMERICA."

– HE OWNS THREE OF THE ONLY FIVE BLACK-OWNED RADIO STATIONS IN THE COUNTRY.

– HIS EMPIRE IS OVERSEEN BY A STAFF OF EIGHTY-FIVE WITH AN ANNUAL PAYROLL OF A MILLION DOLLARS.

– HE FILLS YANKEE STADIUM FOR A CONCERT ON JUNE 22, 1968.

AND THE APOLLO IS THERE FOR HIM, TOO, WHEN THINGS GO SUDDENLY, WILDLY *BAD*.

YET JAMES BROWN *NEVER* FORGETS THE APOLLO, EVEN THOUGH HE MAKES MUCH MORE ELSEWHERE.

JAMES BROWN

JAMES BROWN ENDORSES NIXON IN 1972 AND IS BADLY **SHAKEN** BY WHAT HE SEES AT HIS FIRST APOLLO SHOW AFTER THE ELECTION.

ONE OF BROWN'S ENTOURAGE APPEARS ONSTAGE AT THE OPENING SHOW TO DEFEND THE SINGER.

AFTER THE NIXON THING— IT WAS LIKE A BIG **BOMB**.

BLAH BLAH BLAH

WE WAS CATCHING **HELL**.

DANNY RAY

IT **HURT**. EVERY LOCATION ON THE CIRCUIT SUDDENLY BECAME ALREADY "BOOKED," UNAVAILABLE TO US, NO OPEN DATES FOR US TO PLAY.

ST. CLAIR PINCKNEY

Yet even with all the controversy, the usual lines of James Brown fans *throng* 125th Street all week.

IF THE APOLLO IS TO KEEP GOING IN THIS NEW ERA, IT NEEDS TO BE ABLE TO BOOK THE **SUPERSTARS** WHOSE CAREERS IT HAS ALWAYS SUPPORTED AND ENCOURAGED . . .

YOU HAVE TO PLAY FOR THE PEOPLE OF **HARLEM**!

SMOKEY ROBINSON, JAMES BROWN, SAMMY DAVIS JR., DIONNE WARWICK, GLADYS KNIGHT, AND **NANCY WILSON**

. . . EVEN IF THEY CAN NOW MAKE **MUCH** MORE MONEY ELSEWHERE WITHOUT DOING AS MANY SHOWS.

BOBBY SCHIFFMAN

TOWARD THE END, IN THE '70S, AN ACT THAT WAS IN DEMAND COULD MAKE MORE MONEY IN **ONE NIGHT** IN A BIGGER AND BETTER LOCATION THAN THEY COULD MAKE AT THE APOLLO IN A **WHOLE WEEK**.

AND, IF YOU HAD AN ACT IN THE **APOLLO** FOR SIX DOLLARS, THAT ACT COULD SELL TICKETS FOR SIXTEEN DOLLARS **DOWNTOWN**, OR TWENTY DOLLARS OR FIFTY DOLLARS.

WE ASKED ACTS TO WORK AT A GREAT FINANCIAL **SACRIFICE**.

The Apollo: 1,683 seats

Carnegie Hall: 2,800

Lincoln Center: 4,500

The Felt Forum: 4,500

Madison Square Garden: 20,000

The Nassau Coliseum: 19,000

The Byrne Arena: 22,000

Many top stars are happy to come home and help keep the Apollo going.

SELLING OUT AN ENTIRE WEEK *IN ADVANCE* HAS NEVER HAPPENED BEFORE.

APOLLO

Gladys Knight and the Pips
ENTIRE WEEK—SOLD OUT!

Gladys Knight and the Pips
ENTIRE WEEK—SOLD OUT!

OUT!

Jam-packed, big star shows are very profitable.

I GET GOOSE PIMPLES THINKING ABOUT IT NOW . . .

EARLY ON, WE GAVE PERFORMERS A SHOWCASE WHERE THEY COULD NURTURE THEIR TALENT . . . AND THEY *OWED* US.

THE FIRST TIME I PLAYED GLADYS KNIGHT AND THE PIPS, I PAID THEM $800 FOR THIRTY-ONE SHOWS OVER SEVEN DAYS.

THE LAST TIME, I PAID $80,000 FOR SIXTEEN SHOWS.

That is a lot of money for the Apollo, but she can make that in one or two shows in a larger venue.

THERE WAS NO WAY, BASED ON THE LONGSTANDING PERSONAL RELATIONSHIP I HAD WITH THEM, THAT THEY COULD SAY NO TO ME IF I SAID *I NEED YOU.*

BOBBY SCHIFFMAN

DIONNE WARWICK *COMES BACK* EVERY YEAR, STARTING IN THE LATE '6OS.

I PRACTICALLY PAID MONEY TO GO IN AND DO IT THE WAY I WANTED TO DO IT.

AND THEY MADE AN AWFUL LOT OF MONEY, WHICH IS GOOD, BECAUSE IT KEPT THE DOORS OPEN.

YOU WILL *NEVER* CLOSE THE APOLLO. NOT AS LONG AS I LIVE!

THE APOLLO WANTS DIONNE TO FEEL APPRECIATED, AND THEY PULL OUT ALL THE STOPS.

IT GAVE THEM THE **LEVERAGE** THEY NEEDED TO ATTRACT OTHER PERFORMERS.

THE THEATER WAS **GORGEOUS**. THEY BUILT SCENERY FOR ME. WE DID LIGHTING.

THE SOUND HAS ALWAYS BEEN IMPECCABLE IN THAT THEATER.

AFTER THAT, LOU RAWLS WENT BACK IN, NANCY WILSON, THE TEMPTATIONS . . .

I BROUGHT **EVERYBODY** BACK TO THE APOLLO!

NANCY, IT'S GETTING REALLY **TOUGH** TO GO ON. YOU CAN PLAY ANYWHERE YOU WANT NOW.

YOU HAVE TO KEEP THE APOLLO GOING! IT'S **NEEDED**!

BOBBY SCHIFFMAN

NANCY WILSON

I PLAYED THERE BECAUSE I FELT I SHOULD.

I PLAYED THERE BECAUSE THE SCHIFFMANS WERE THE KIND OF PEOPLE YOU SHOULD GO PLACES FOR.

I PLAYED THERE BECAUSE IT MADE THEM FEEL GOOD.

AGAIN, THE APOLLO DOES EVERYTHING IT CAN TO MAKE IT **SPECIAL**.

NANCY WILSON

THE AUDIENCE AND THE PEOPLE OF THE COMMUNITY NEEDED US PERFORMERS.

I PLAYED THERE BECAUSE I KNEW THEY **WANTED** ME THERE.

EVERY PERSON WHO WORKED THE APOLLO HAD A TUX ON.

THAT WAS QUITE A NIGHT.

IT'S GREAT FOR THE APOLLO WHILE IT LASTS.

IN ALL THE YEARS THAT THE APOLLO WAS IN BUSINESS, 1970 TO 1974 WERE THE **BANNER YEARS** FINANCIALLY.

The Apollo can also thank a new crop of hit-makers for that.

If Detroit is the capital of black music in the '60s, *Philadelphia* becomes the star-making center of black America in the early '70s.

THE *PHILADELPHIA INTERNATIONAL* RECORD LABEL LAUNCHES IN 1971.

KENNY GAMBLE, LEON HUFF, AND *THOM BELL*

THE NEW PHILLY STARS KEEP THE APOLLO BUSY.

THE DELFONICS

THE SOUND OF PHILADELPHIA
TSOP

THE THREE DEGREES

THE O'JAYS

SOME, LIKE THE SPINNERS, WHO WERE APOLLO OPENERS FOR YEARS, COME BACK AS BIG STARS IN THE '70S.

THE STYLISTICS

Hey Mister Big Man, you're killing me!

PHILADELPHIA NATIVE *PATTI LABELLE* AND HER VARIOUS BLUEBELLES HAVE BEEN PLAYING THE APOLLO SINCE THEIR STRUGGLING DAYS IN THE EARLY '60S.

I REMEMBER WHEN WE WERE NOT MAKING VERY MUCH MONEY, WE'D BUY HOT DOGS AND KEEP THEM ON THE LIGHTBULBS ALL DAY!

They *treasure* the Apollo.

THE SPINNERS

If you don't know me by now...

ONE OF THE BIGGEST PHILADELPHIA INTERNATIONAL GROUPS IS *HAROLD MELVIN AND THE BLUE NOTES*, FEATURING *TEDDY PENDERGRASS.*

Even when the giant 1974 hit, "Lady Marmalade," makes Patti's Labelle the first African American group to play the *Metropolitan Opera House.*

PENDERGRASS PLAYS THE HARD-LUCK SEXPOT.

THEIR 1975 APOLLO ENGAGEMENT STARTS OUT STRONG.

BUT AFTER **ARGUING** WITH HAROLD AT THE APOLLO, TEDDY DOESN'T SHOW UP FOR THE SUNDAY SHOWS.

LADIES AND GENTLEMEN, WE REGRET TO INFORM YOU THAT TEDDY PENDERGRASS WILL **NOT** BE PERFORMING WITH THE GROUP . . .

The Apollo takes a big hit at a precarious time for the theater.

THE BUSINESS STARTED **CHANGING** A LOT.

BLACK PERFORMERS STARTED GETTING PLAYED ON WHITE STATIONS, AND THE CAREERS AND THE MONEY STARTED GROWING.

This great *breakthrough* for African American artists is *bad news* for Harlem's High Spot.

LESLIE UGGAMS

A LOT OF PEOPLE FELT, "I'M AT THE POINT WHERE I DON'T HAVE TO DO FOUR OR FIVE SHOWS A DAY."

THEY HAD SO MUCH OTHER INCOME FROM RECORD ROYALTIES, AND LATER ON TELEVISION SHOWS, AND FURTHER ON EVEN MOTION-PICTURE PRODUCTION.

WHEN THEY DECIDE TO WORK LESS AND LESS, THEY ARE **NOT** GOING TO WORK 125TH STREET.

125TH STREET TURNED INTO A **MUCH-DEPRIVED** STREET. DIRTY. CRIME.

AFTER THE RIOTING, ALL THE STOREKEEPERS ON 125TH STREET PUT IN THOSE STEEL DOORS THAT CLOSED OVER THE WINDOWS, SO THE STREET WAS UNATTRACTIVE.

IT WAS LIKE A **FORTRESS**. THAT DOES NOT LEND ITSELF TO ENCOURAGING PEOPLE TO COME.

THE CITY OF NEW YORK FELL VERY SHORT IN ITS OBLIGATIONS TO PROVIDE HARLEM WITH THE SAME SERVICES AS THE REST OF THE CITY.

GEOGRAPHICALLY, 125TH STREET IS IN A VERY FAVORABLE SITUATION. **ALL** OF THE MAJOR HIGHWAYS CROSS THERE.

YOU GOT **ALL** THE MAJOR SUBWAY LINES. ALL THE MAJOR BUS LINES.

IT SHOULD HAVE **DEVELOPED**.

BOBBY SCHIFFMAN

BUT OBVIOUSLY THE CITY FATHERS TOOK THE POSITION THAT THERE ARE JUST BLACK FOLKS UP THERE, WE'LL DO THEM **LAST**.

195

AT THE HEIGHT OF HOLLYWOOD'S BRIEF ENCHANTMENT WITH BLACK FILMS, THE APOLLO CAN ONLY BOOK CHEAP B-GRADE QUICKIES OR PLAYED-OUT MOVIES.

A story of Southern hospitality.

a WILLIAM WYLER film
THE LIBERATION OF L.B. JONES

By the mid-'70s, the Apollo is only presenting twenty-two weeks of live entertainment a year.

To fill in *empty* weeks, the theater turns to *movies* that might appeal to the African American community.

THE APOLLO FIGHTS TO GET A MAJOR BLACK MOVIE *PREMIERE*.

Nearly every *Uptown Saturday Night* star has appeared at the Apollo, even director and co-star *Sidney Poitier*.

Instead, Warner Bros. opens the film on Broadway and shuttles premiere-goers up to Harlem for an *after-party*.

You can still go uptown without getting your head beat in by going downtown to see Uptown Saturday Night.

ADDING GREAT *INSULT* TO THIS INJURY IS A HORRENDOUSLY *TONE-DEAF* AD.

THE APOLLO *FIGHTS BACK*, PROTESTS, AND EVEN FILES A RESTRAINT OF TRADE SUIT AGAINST HOLLYWOOD.

Cleopatra Jones and the *Casino of Gold*

WARNER BROS. AGREES TO OPEN ITS NEXT BIG *"BLAXPLOITATION"* FLICK SIMULTANEOUSLY AT THE APOLLO AND ON 86TH STREET.

JIM CROW LIVES! 125th IS STILL THE BACK OF THE BUS, MOVIEWISE THAT IS.

"IT'S A GREAT VICTORY FOR THE PEOPLE OF THIS COMMUNITY! MOVIE TIMES AT THE APOLLO ARE . . ."

VARIETY

New York, Wednesday, August 6, 1975

BLACKS SHUN PIC AT HARLEM SITE
"Apollo Experiment" Fails to Pull Locals

BUT IT DOESN'T WORK OUT.

Peril is knocking on the Apollo's door.

OH, COME IN . . .

OH, JESUS, **NO!**

GLADYS KNIGHT

WELL, YOU KNOW WHAT IT IS, ALL RIGHT . . .

WE GOT ROBBED TWO OR THREE TIMES AT THE APOLLO.

I WAS JUST GLAD THEY DIDN'T **KILL** US.

SMOKEY ROBINSON COMES BACK FOR AN SRO SHOW IN DECEMBER 1975.

The Apollo and the great stars who continue to make it their home are no longer _immune_ to the violence and despair in the streets.

You've really got a hold on me...

SOME FOOL LIGHTING FIRECRACKERS?

The outside world _crashes in_ on the Apollo.

AN EIGHTEEN-YEAR-OLD RECENTLY PAROLED FOR ROBBERY IS **SHOT DEAD** AND TWO OTHERS WOUNDED.

It is said the victim knows enemies are trying to get him. But he probably thinks he's _safe_ at the Apollo.

It is a place that is respected and revered; to hurt it would be to hurt oneself, to commit violence there would be to commit violence in one's own _home_.

LIKE A **PRO**, SMOKEY ROBINSON FINISHES OUT A SUCCESSFUL WEEK, BUT SAYS HE WON'T COME BACK.

The gunman obviously doesn't feel that way.

197

WITHIN A MONTH, IN JANUARY 1976, THE APOLLO THEATER **CLOSES** ITS DOORS.

THE APOLLO HAS BEEN QUIETLY UP FOR SALE SINCE THE MID-'60S.

CLOSED
Thanks for the Memories

We're CLOSED

WITH THE ADVENT OF MALCOLM X AND THE STRONG GROWTH OF NATIONALISTIC PRIDE IN THE BLACK COMMUNITY . . .

. . . WHICH WAS A VERY VALID AND WORTHWHILE FORCE . . .

IT WAS WITH THE GREATEST HEARTACHE THAT I RELINQUISHED MY INVOLVEMENT WITH THAT COMMUNITY.

BOBBY SCHIFFMAN

. . . THERE CAME THE FEELING THAT THE BLACK COMMUNITY SHOULD OWN AND OPERATE THEIR **OWN** INSTITUTIONS.

WE HAD SEVERAL OFFERS FROM WHITE BUSINESSMEN WHO WANTED TO BUY THE APOLLO, BUT WE ALWAYS TURNED THEM DOWN.

FOR YEARS, THE AIM OF MANAGEMENT OF THE APOLLO WAS TO SELL IT TO A BLACK ENTREPRENEUR.

WE WERE WAITING FOR A BLACK ORGANIZATION TO COME ALONG THAT HAD THE KNOWLEDGE, WISDOM, AND MONEY TO BUY THE APOLLO.

Ads appear in the classified sections of the *Wall Street Journal*, the *New York Times*, and the *Village Voice* in 1975.

Classifieds

For Sale; Harlem's World Famous Apollo Theater.

ASKING PRICE: TWO MILLION DOLLARS, INCLUDING AN "OFFICE BUILDING"

Since 1972, plans and deals have been floated by prominent African American figures.

Nothing works. Bobby takes a job at booking agency, *Universal Attractions*.

UNIVERSAL ATTRACTIONS
BOBBY SCHIFFMAN
BOOKING AGENT

MANHATTAN BOROUGH PRESIDENT **PERCY SUTTON** AND *AMSTERDAM NEWS* OWNER **CLARENCE JONES**

NEW YORK
Amsterdam News

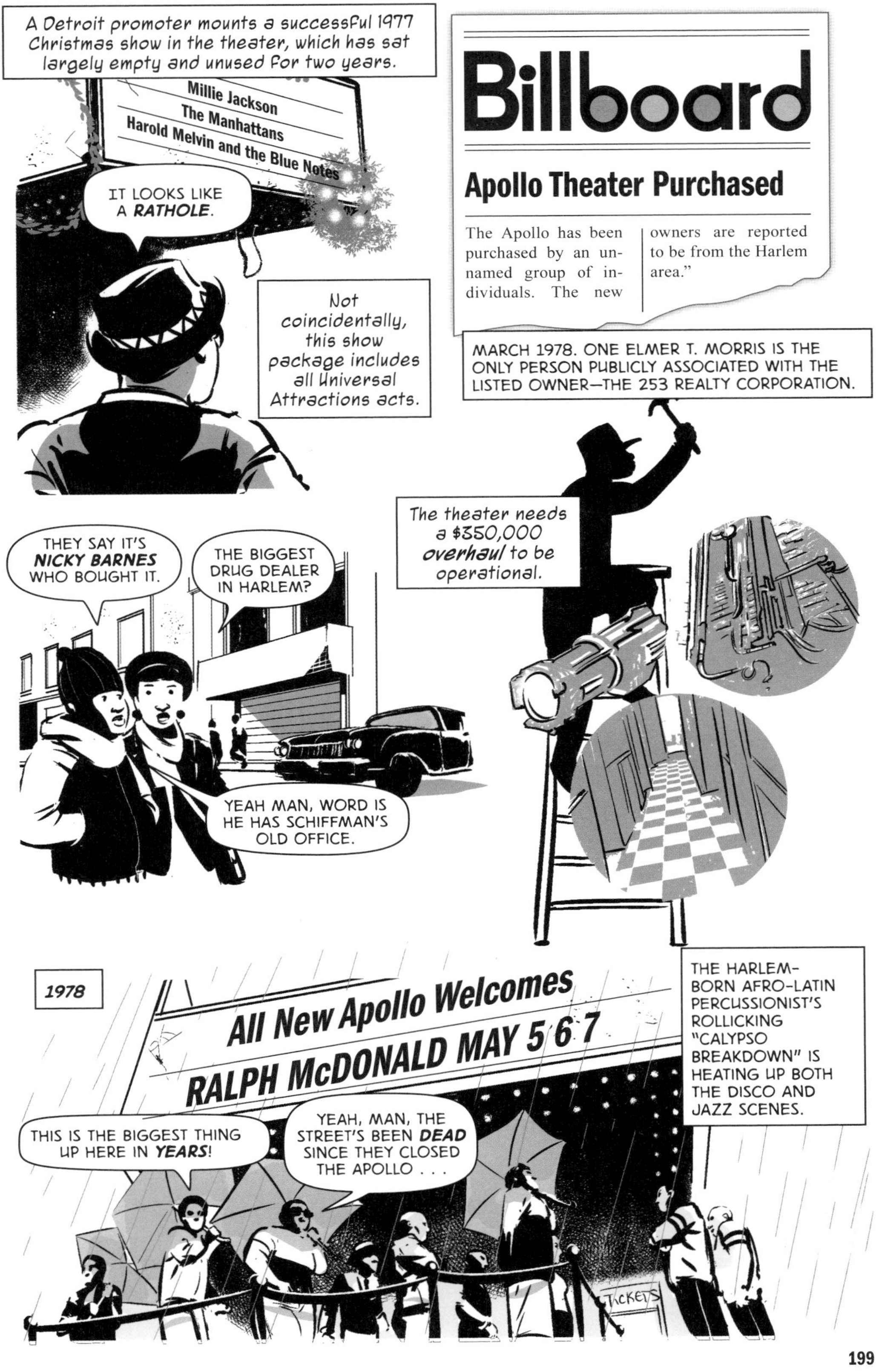

A Detroit promoter mounts a successful 1977 Christmas show in the theater, which has sat largely empty and unused for two years.
Millie Jackson
The Manhattans
Harold Melvin and the Blue Notes
IT LOOKS LIKE A *RATHOLE*.
Not coincidentally, this show package includes all Universal Attractions acts.
Billboard
Apollo Theater Purchased
The Apollo has been purchased by an unnamed group of individuals. The new owners are reported to be from the Harlem area."
MARCH 1978. ONE ELMER T. MORRIS IS THE ONLY PERSON PUBLICLY ASSOCIATED WITH THE LISTED OWNER—THE 253 REALTY CORPORATION.
THEY SAY IT'S *NICKY BARNES* WHO BOUGHT IT.
THE BIGGEST DRUG DEALER IN HARLEM?
YEAH MAN, WORD IS HE HAS SCHIFFMAN'S OLD OFFICE.
The theater needs a $350,000 *overhaul* to be operational.
1978
All New Apollo Welcomes
RALPH McDONALD MAY 5 6 7
THE HARLEM-BORN AFRO-LATIN PERCUSSIONIST'S ROLLICKING "CALYPSO BREAKDOWN" IS HEATING UP BOTH THE DISCO AND JAZZ SCENES.
THIS IS THE BIGGEST THING UP HERE IN *YEARS*!
YEAH, MAN, THE STREET'S BEEN *DEAD* SINCE THEY CLOSED THE APOLLO . . .
TICKETS

The crowd is so *happy* the Apollo is back that, after waiting through *problems* with the theater's new reserved seating system . . .

GLADYS KNIGHT, WILSON PICKETT, WILLIS REED, PAUL SIMON, HARLEM REP. **CHARLES RANGEL**

. . . they don't even mind waiting again as the show starts nearly an hour late . . .

. . . and again as two banks of speakers fail.

I USED TO LIVE EIGHT BLOCKS FROM HERE. THIS COMMUNITY GAVE ME THE **FUNDAMENTALS** I WENT OUT INTO THE WORLD WITH.

NOW I CAN BRING SOMETHING **HOME** TO THE COMMUNITY.

RALPH MCDONALD

WE ARE FAMILY!

SISTER SLEDGE

1978 is a *hopeful* year as the Apollo once again presents the latest thing— disco—

—and brings back old *favorites*.

I'D RATHER PLAY FOR MY FOLKS HERE THAN AT THE WHITE HOUSE!

JAMES BROWN

IT IS HARD TO REGULARLY BOOK TALENT, THOUGH, AS MARTIN TELLS THE *AMSTERDAM NEWS* . . .

WE'RE OFFERING THEM **TOP DOLLAR** FOR A HOUSE OUR SIZE FOR THEM TO PLAY HERE FROM THREE TO FIVE DAYS.

THE **O'JAYS** COLDLY REJECTED OUR $40,000 OFFER.

APOLLO TALENT COORDINATOR **SPARKY MARTIN**

I DON'T KNOW WHO THESE NEW OWNERS ARE, AND I'M NOT TAKING ANY **CHANCES**.

AND, I HEAR THEY OWE BACK TAXES, TOO.

The O'Jays

APOLLO

Bob Marley and the Wailers

Now only the **toughest** aren't afraid to play the Apollo . . . to still make it home.

THURSDAY, OCTOBER 25, 1979, THE BEGINNING OF A FOUR-NIGHT STAND

Unsatisfied with being the darling of white hipsters, Bob Marley wants to **reach out** more directly to African Americans . . . and he knows where to do it.

It's Marley's first time back in the city since surviving an assassination attempt in Jamaica.

RITA MARLEY AND **JUDY MOWATT** AS THE **I-TWOS.**

BOB MARLEY & THE WAILERS

SURVIVAL

I SHOT THE SHERIFF

IT IS A **PROPHETIC** TITLE FOR THE THEATER, TOO.

The Wailers become the first **reggae** band to play the Apollo as Marley proclaims a pan-African message with a militant new album.

201

THE IRS MAKES ITS MOVE THE VERY NEXT MONTH AND **SHUTS** THE APOLLO FOR FAILURE TO TURN OVER PAYROLL TAXES.

The New York Times

'MISTER UNTOUCHABLE'

This Is Nicky Barnes. The Police Say He May Be Harlem's Biggest Drug Deal...

NEVER DID TRUST THOSE NEW OWNERS.

OLE NICKY BARNES GOT LIFE AND THEN **RATS** THEM ALL OUT TRYING TO GET A PRESIDENTIAL PARDON! BUNCH OF THEM GUYS GOT ARRESTED.

DOLL THOMAS, MARCH 1, 1980

HE SAID THAT ELMER MORRIS USED TO BE A COP AND TAUGHT NICKY'S BOYS HOW TO SHOOT!

DECLARED **BANKRUPTCY** OF COURSE. SAW THAT COMING . . .

BUT MAN, THE APOLLO AIN'T DONE YET.

IT'S **NEVER** GONNA BE DONE!

GEORGE CLINTON AND "P-FUNK" ARE HEROES IN HARLEM--FUNK ROYALTY.

Their shows, over the weekend of March 1, 1980, are the *last* live Apollo shows of the original era . . . spectacles of abandon perfectly in keeping with the theater's grand tradition.

Clinton, leader of *Parliament Funkadelic*, bypasses *Madison Square Garden* to help keep the Apollo going.

P-Funk!

GEORGE CLINTON . . .

I KNEW HIM BACK IN THE '50S WITH THE PARLIAMENTS. JERSEY BOY, STARTED SINGING IN HIS BARBERSHOP . . .

TAKES . . . ME . . . *BACK* . . .

THE P-FUNK SIGN STANDS FOR CLINTON'S MOTTO: "ONE NATION UNDER A GROOVE."

HEY, WE GONNA SEE FUNKADELIC!

DAMN, WHAT WOULD MR. SCHIFFMAN THINK OF ALL THIS *REEFER* SMOKING?

DOLL THOMAS

NOT MANY *WHITE* PEOPLE . . . WHEN I FIRST GOT HERE WEREN'T HARDLY NO *BLACK* PEOPLE!

LET'S HEAR IT FOR THE *BRIDES OF FUNKENSTEIN!*

A NEW GOLD CURTAIN.

203

SOME THINGS *NEVER* CHANGE . . .

There isn't a kid in the house who doesn't envy this guy. He's a star. He's the *show*.

He is *home*.

It's Saturday night at the Apollo!

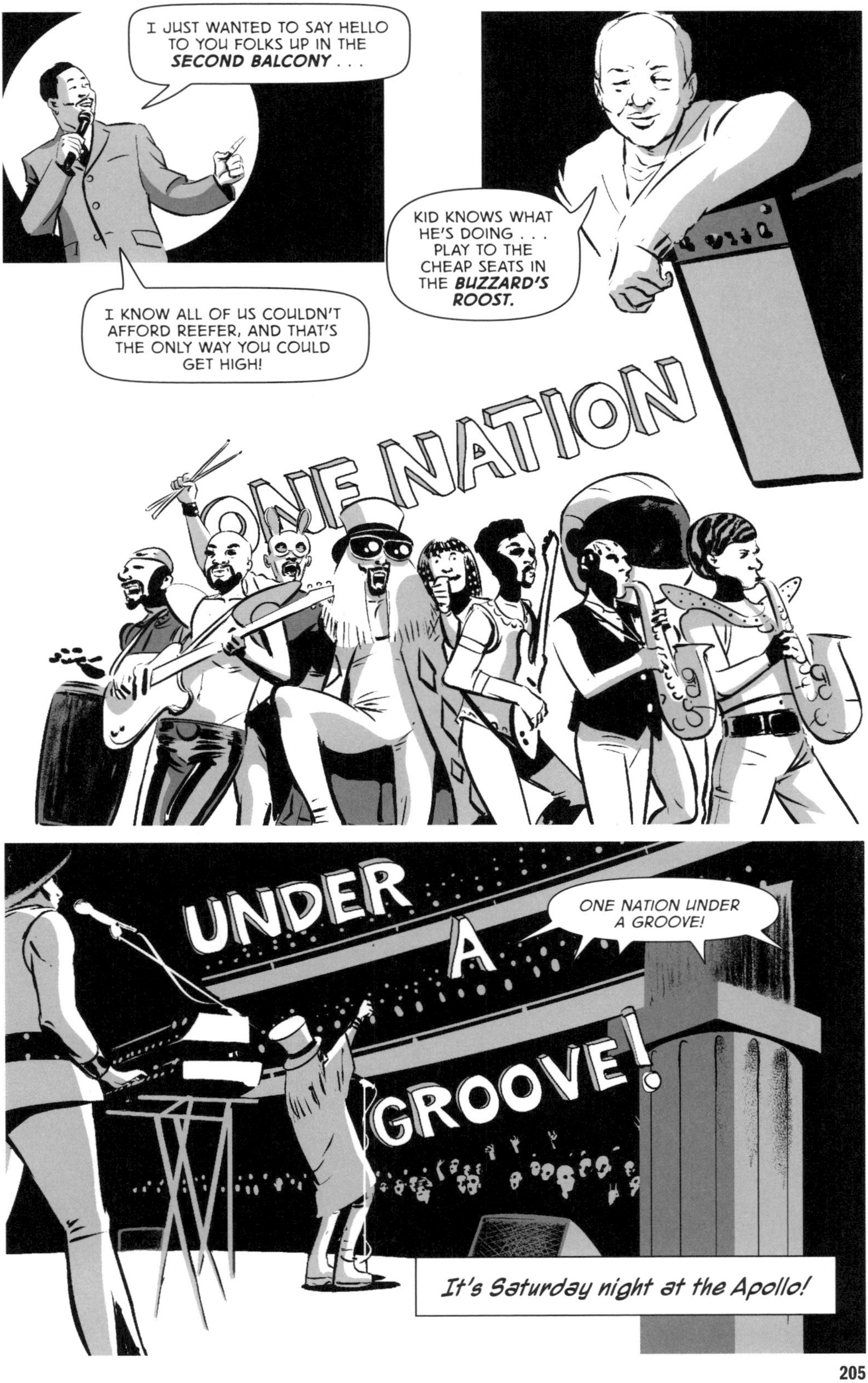
I JUST WANTED TO SAY HELLO TO YOU FOLKS UP IN THE ***SECOND BALCONY*** . . .
I KNOW ALL OF US COULDN'T AFFORD REEFER, AND THAT'S THE ONLY WAY YOU COULD GET HIGH!
KID KNOWS WHAT HE'S DOING . . . PLAY TO THE CHEAP SEATS IN THE ***BUZZARD'S ROOST.***
ONE NATION
UNDER A GROOVE!
ONE NATION UNDER A GROOVE!
It's Saturday night at the Apollo!

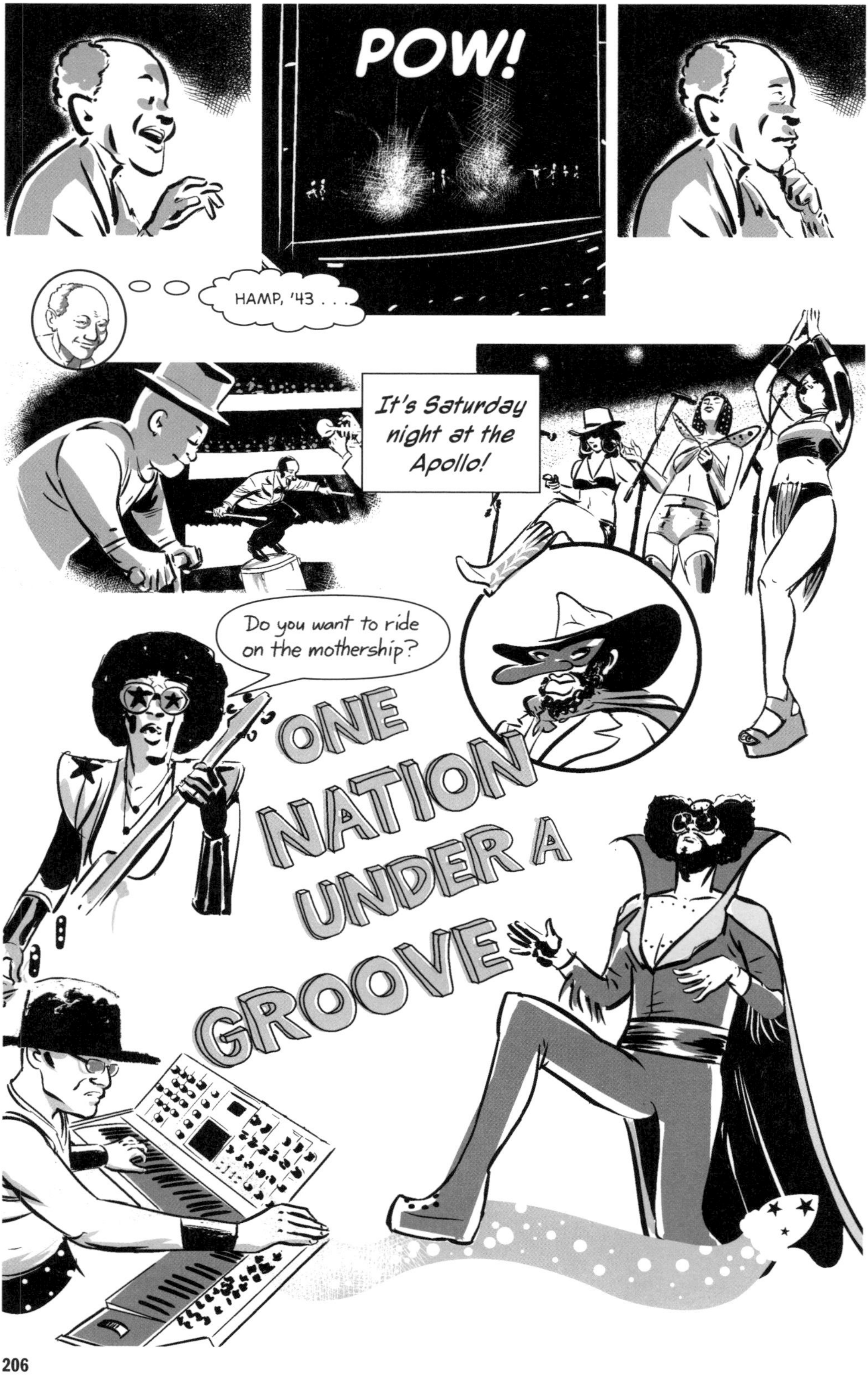
POW!
HAMP, '43 . . .
It's Saturday night at the Apollo!
Do you want to ride on the mothership?
ONE NATION UNDER A GROOVE

It's Saturday night at the Apollo!

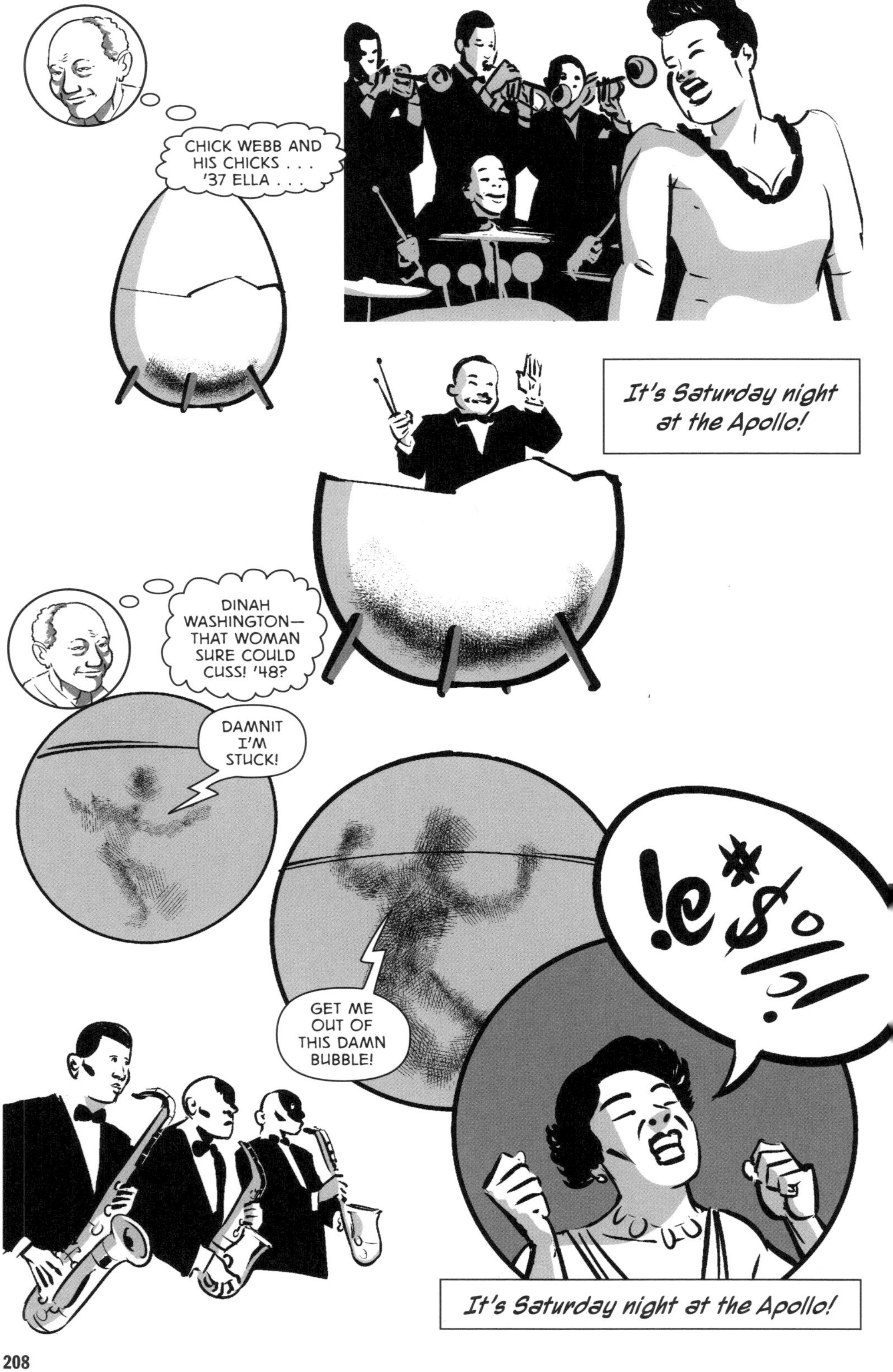
CHICK WEBB AND HIS CHICKS . . . '37 ELLA . . .
It's Saturday night at the Apollo!
DINAH WASHINGTON— THAT WOMAN SURE COULD CUSS! '48?
DAMNIT I'M STUCK!
GET ME OUT OF THIS DAMN BUBBLE!
!@*$%!
It's Saturday night at the Apollo!

WELL ALL ROOTHER . . .

It's Saturday night at the Apollo!

JOCKO'S ROCKET SHIP, '61. . . NOW *THAT* WAS A MOTHERSHIP!

ONE NATION UNDER A GROOVE

THAT'S KIND OF CATCHY!

ONE
NATION
UNDER A
GROOVE

As the Apollo will
always be . . .

How the Apollo Got Its Groove Back

(The End—and a New Beginning)

A LONGTIME FRIEND OF THE APOLLO STEPS IN TO TRY TO GET THE THEATER'S GROOVE BACK AFTER 253 REALTY'S BANKRUPTCY.

Percy Sutton's Inner City Broadcasting Corporation takes over in 1981.

MAY 1983, WORK BEGINS ON A *TOTAL OVERHAUL* THAT WILL ULTIMATELY COST SIXTEEN MILLION DOLLARS.

On June 29, 1983, the Apollo is designated a *cultural landmark*.

BILLY MITCHELL IS A NEWLY HIRED USHER IN 1984 AS SUTTON SEEKS TO BREATHE **NEW LIFE** INTO THE APOLLO.

It takes some effort to *win back* the people of Harlem.

THE APOLLO'S OPENING BACK UP!

YEAH, RIGHT, HEARD *THAT* BEFORE.

THEY AIN'T GONNA MAKE IT.

IT WAS SO **DISHEARTENING.**

WE COULDN'T GET PEOPLE TO GO THROUGH THE DOORS THE FIRST FEW MONTHS.

THE THEATER HAD BEEN CLOSED FOR QUITE AWHILE.

THE ECONOMY WAS SCREWED UP.

THE MUSIC HAD CHANGED AND DIDN'T APPEAL TO OLDER FOLKS.

BEFORE YOU KNEW IT, THIS WAS THE PLACE TO *BE* AGAIN.

IT WAS A REAL PARTY!

THEN PEOPLE STARTED *TRICKLING* IN.

IT WAS SOMETHING *NEW* TO A NEW GENERATION.

Billy Mitchell becomes the Apollo's tour director, and over the years inherits the name "*Mr. Apollo*" from Doll Thomas.

BEFORE RENOVATIONS ARE EVEN FINISHED, THE APOLLO *REOPENS* WITH A CHRISTMAS EVE AMATEUR NIGHT SHOW IN 1983.

An active Apollo becomes a good thing for 125th Street once again.

AMATEUR NIGHT

ON A BEAUTIFUL MAY NIGHT IN 1985, THE RENOVATED APOLLO *SPARKLES*.

It boasts new purple carpet, crystal chandeliers, and red-and-gold trimmed box seats.

DOWNTOWN, A SPECIAL RECEPTION FOR 500 GUESTS IN THE SUBWAY STATION AT 57TH STREET AND SIXTH AVENUE IS IN FULL SWING.

57 Street

AT 7 PM THE GUESTS BOARD A *1948-ERA A TRAIN* FOR THE RIDE TO THE 125TH STREET STATION.

SIR BOB GELDOF

ANDY WARHOL

DICK CAVETT

REV. JESSE JACKSON

CORETTA SCOTT KING

TONIGHT
Motown Returns to the Apollo

BILL COSBY HOSTS THE LIVE TAPING OF NBC'S *THREE-HOUR SPECIAL*.

ENTERTAINMENT WAS WHAT THE APOLLO WAS ALWAYS ABOUT AND WHAT IT IS STILL ABOUT.

SPEAK OUT IF SOMETHING MOVES YOU . . .

Stevie Wonder revives twelve-year-old Little Stevie playing "Fingertips."

AL GREEN, PATTI LABELLE, LITTLE RICHARD, AND MAVIS STAPLES, BACKED BY A NEW JERSEY GOSPEL CHOIR

LITTLE RICHARD, WILSON PICKETT, AND CHUCK JACKSON

Didn't it rain...

SIXTY ARTISTS, FROM SARAH VAUGHAN TO GEORGE MICHAEL, PERFORM.

You'll never walk alone...

THE SHOW IS A SMASH, AND THE TELEVISION SPECIAL GARNERS TEN EMMY NOMINATIONS AND WINS FOR OUTSTANDING VARIETY, MUSIC OR COMEDY PROGRAM.

SUTTON POURS MILLIONS INTO MAKING THE APOLLO A STATE-OF-THE-ART VIDEO AND AUDIO PRODUCTION FACILITY.

BARBRA STREISAND SHOOTS HER MUSIC VIDEO, "SOMEWHERE," AT THE APOLLO IN 1985.

Soooomewhere...

Dozens of music videos for acts such as Stevie Wonder, Whitney Houston, and U2 are shot there.

PATTI LABELLE AND B. B. KING RECORD *LIVE ALBUMS*.

LL COOL J HOSTS THE FIRST EPISODE OF THE *IT'S SHOWTIME AT THE APOLLO* TV SHOW IN SEPTEMBER 1987.

The show is the theater's greatest broadcasting success, syndicated nationally.

The theater continues to respond to the new music of the streets.

It runs for nearly 1,100 episodes over twenty-one years in various iterations . . . so far.

RUN-DMC

DOUG E. FRESH

ICE CUBE

PUBLIC ENEMY

MANY OF THE GREATS OF **RAP** PERFORM AT THE APOLLO AND MAKE IT HOME.

Rapmania
The Roots of Rap

THE DEBUT PERFORMANCE OF THE *JUICE CREW ALL-STARS* WORLD TOUR, NOVEMBER 18, 1988

Leave the crack alone!

The Juice Crew All-Stars, a Queens, New York, collective of hip-hop musicians, features Big Daddy Kane, Roxanne Shanté, Marley Marl, Kool G. Rap, and Biz Markie

TWO SOLD-OUT NIGHTS IN 1987

Sutton runs into many of the same problems the theater experiences in the 1970s, as well as new *challenges*.

REAGAN CUTS ARTS FUNDING!
RECESSION HITS NEW YORK!

AUDIO AND VIDEO OUTFITS ALL OVER THE CITY GO OUT OF BUSINESS.

The Apollo still finds it difficult to compete for established talent.

The Apollo's production business *dries up*.

IN JUNE 1991, PERCY SUTTON, UNABLE TO CONTINUE BY HIMSELF, ASKS THE STATE TO **STEP IN**.

"WORKING WITH CONGRESSMAN CHARLES RANGEL, SUTTON TODAY ESTABLISHED THE NONPROFIT APOLLO THEATER FOUNDATION WITH RANGEL AS CHAIRMAN."

THE ANNUAL SHORTFALL, MADE UP BY SUTTON AND HIS COMPANY, IS SAID TO REACH TWO MILLION DOLLARS.

NONPROFIT, HAH!

YEAH, NEVER-WAS-PROFIT.

Ralph Cooper Sr.
We Love and Miss You

RALPH COOPER'S FUNERAL AND WAKE ON AUGUST 10 AND 11, 1992, IS AN EMOTIONAL AND SYMBOLIC **BREAK** WITH THE APOLLO'S PAST.

In April 1998, the *Daily News* initiates a series of hard-hitting articles and editorials criticizing the Apollo's financial dealings and decrying the dilapidated condition of the theater.

DAILY NEWS

SHOWDOWN AT THE APOLLO

BY THE LATE '90S PROBLEMS **MOUNT**, AND FINGER-POINTING BECOMES NEARLY AS COMMON AS FOOT-TAPPING AT THE APOLLO.

217

THE NEWSPAPER WINS A **PULITZER PRIZE** FOR ITS COVERAGE.

IT'S NOT AN AWARD MANY IN THE COMMUNITY ARE PROUD OF, OR HAPPY ABOUT.

CHARLIE RANGEL CARES MORE ABOUT HARLEM THAN ANY OF THEM!

EVERY TIME A BLACK MAN TRIES TO SUCCEED THEY TEAR HIM DOWN.

AND PERCY SUTTON SPENT HIS OWN DOUGH TO SAVE THE APOLLO.

Sutton settles a state lawsuit, pays the foundation one million dollars—with Time Warner kicking in half—and Congressman Rangel resigns as chairman of the Apollo Board.

IN 1997, SUTTON AND RANGEL HAD REACHED OUT TO **RICHARD D. PARSONS**, TIME WARNER'S PRESIDENT, THE CORPORATE ANGEL WHO WOULD ULTIMATELY BECOME THE APOLLO'S SAVIOR.

CORPORATE PATRONAGE AND LARGESSE— ENJOYED BY OTHER CULTURAL INSTITUTIONS LIKE CARNEGIE HALL AND LINCOLN CENTER FOR YEARS—HELPS TURN THE APOLLO AROUND.

Parsons, who later becomes CEO of AOL Time Warner, is not only one of the most **powerful** African American executives in the world, he is also chairman of the Upper Manhattan Empowerment Zone.

BEVERLY SILLS, OPERA STAR AND FORMER CHAIRWOMAN OF LINCOLN CENTER, BOARD MEMBER UNTIL 2002. **PHARRELL WILLIAMS**, SUPERSTAR, BOARD MEMBER STARTING IN 2014.

THE NEW MILLENNIUM STARTS WITH A GORGEOUS NEW FAÇADE AND MARQUEE.

Begun in 1999, another restoration project is unveiled in December 2005.

The marquee and sign look as much as possible like the original . . . only now powered by thousands of programmable LEDs.

Happy!

Ah, reidi ancora qual eri allora quando il cor ti diedi allora, ah, reidi a me,

Parsons begins the tradition of attracting a wide array of **heavy-hitters** from the highest levels of culture and business to the Apollo Foundation board.

Final **price tag** for the outside renovation is said to be 17.9 million dollars.

Total new renovation costs for the theater at this point: 65 million?

AT TODAY'S APOLLO, A LOT OF ATTENTION GOES TO THE BIG STARS AND CELEBRITIES WHO WANT TO EXPERIENCE THE APOLLO *MYSTIQUE* AND PAY TRIBUTE TO ITS HISTORY.

PRESIDENT OBAMA

PRESIDENT CLINTON

BUT THERE IS A REAL EFFORT TO REACH OUT TO ALL.

These are mostly exclusive, invitation-only affairs.

METALLICA

JAY-Z

Chris Rock does a special low-price show for the community while at the theater taping his 1999 HBO special.

WHO AND WHAT THE COMMUNITY IS IS *EVOLVING*.

ACTUALLY, THE APOLLO IS JUST DOING WHAT IT'S ALWAYS DONE . . .

. . . FIGURING OUT WAYS TO KEEP THE DOORS OPEN!

Gentrification is pricing out some longtime Harlem residents, while bringing welcome new amenities and life to the neighborhood for others.

DOLL THOMAS

APOLLO THEATER WALK OF FAME

KIDS, THIS IS *OUR* THEATER, *OUR* CULTURE.

BILLIE HOLIDAY

APOLLO PRESIDENT AND CEO *JONELLE PROCOPE* AND *CASSANDRA WILSON*

WE HONOR OUR PAST, BUT ALWAYS THINK ABOUT WHERE THE APOLLO IS GOING IN THE FUTURE . . .

JONELLE PROCOPE

The Apollo stays at the forefront with series like "Africa Now!", celebrating contemporary African music.

It also presents a robust education program.

BUT THE HEART OF THE APOLLO PERHAPS BEATS STRONGEST ON WEDNESDAY NIGHTS.

COMMON

ANGELA BASSETT

BLACK THOUGHT

AMATEUR NIGHT

BOO!!

BOO!!

IN APRIL 2018, A STELLAR CAST STAGES *TA-NEHISI COATES*'S BRILLIANT BOOK *BETWEEN THE WORLD AND ME*, DIRECTED BY THE APOLLO'S *KAMILAH FORBES*.

Amateur Night is where locals *still* rule, even as gaggles of Wall Streeters and tourists help pack the place weekly.

PULL BACK THE CURTAIN AND IT IS *STILL* THE APOLLO.

IT'S *HARLEM'S HIGH SPOT*.

THE APOLLO WILL *ALWAYS* BE THAT.

A NOTE ON SOURCES AND METHODS

I've been describing the scenes and telling the stories in *Showtime at the Apollo: The Epic Tale of Harlem's Legendary Theater* for decades. To see them depicted so beautifully in the vibrant art that pops off these pages is a thrill for me. It has also been a wonderful opportunity to revisit this great and complex story—to distill it into a narrative that carries readers along from the earliest days of Harlem to the present.

Work on my book, *Showtime at the Apollo: The Story of Harlem's World Famous Theater*—originally published by Holt, Rinehart and Winston in 1983—began in 1980 when I was twenty-five. Over the years there have been a number of editions, including a revised version that I published with my own Mill Road Enterprises in co-operation with the Apollo Theater Foundation, timed for the Apollo's 70th anniversary in 2004. It is currently available as an e-book, updated in 2014.

It may be puzzling for younger readers to realize how different times were for writers and researchers when the original work on this book took place. I wrote the manuscript on my father's hand-me-down, tanklike, gray metal Underwood Five manual typewriter. "Cut and paste" meant just that: cutting pages apart with scissors and pasting edited, rearranged sections together with library paste—or in my case, tape—over and over again. Changes were made by hand in pencil. New versions had to be retyped.

Before the Internet and the computer age, there was no instant and widely sourced information available with a few quick clicks. I spent many months over a couple of years in the New York Public Library's main branch; at their Library for the Performing Arts at Lincoln Center; and at the NYPL's Schomburg Center for Research in Black Culture in Harlem, digging into clip files—manila folders filled with photocopies or actual "clips" cut from the pages of newspapers and magazines.

The core of my early research—and absolutely essential to understanding the true course of history of the Apollo—something that had not been fully or veritably written at the time—was the immersive year I spent in Columbia University's Butler Library, poring through roll after roll of microfilm of the old Harlem newspaper the *New York Age*.

People's memories are not always the most reliable sources of actual dates, and their recollections, while wonderful for telling the story and providing context, cannot always be relied on for specifics. Furthermore, I knew that the only way for me to truly understand the Apollo's history would be to create an accurate time line, since one didn't exist. The Apollo did not have records of who played there and when. I did not then know about the Schiffman family's performer booking note cards and business logs, which at any rate were far from complete nor completely chronological, and did not emerge until nearly twenty years after my book was initially published.

As I looked through the *New York Age* microfilm, I realized that the Apollo ran detailed advertisements listing each week's lineup of performers in every issue. From these ads I transcribed—by hand, in script, on yellow lined pads—every show (with very few gaps) and most performers for each week of the Apollo's history, from its inception in 1934 until the early 1970s. This 300-plus-page document formed the indispensable, original Rosetta stone of the Apollo's history. Just transcribing and reading it, week by week and year by year, was an incomparable way to understand the Apollo's development and to imprint the theater's history in my mind.

Armed with that essential knowledge, I reached out to interview the people who lived that history. It is their stories and experiences that matter most and are invaluable in telling the story of the Apollo.

In addition to the countless hours spent with former owner Bobby Schiffman, who had never before been so thoroughly and relentlessly interviewed, I spoke with Estrellita Brooks-Morse, Maxine Brown, Ruth Brown, Benny Carter, Carol Carter, Deborah Chessler, Harold "Stumpy" Cromer, Jimmy Cross, Sammy Davis Jr., Billy Eckstine, Ahmet Ertegun, "Little Anthony" Gourdine, John Hammond, Lionel Hampton, Screamin' Jay Hawkins, Andy Kirk, Gladys Knight, Beverly Lee, David McCarthy, Herbie Mills, Billy Mitchell, Scoey Mitchell, Johnny Otis, Esther Phillips, St. Clair Pinckney, Dave Prater, Jonelle Procope, Danny Ray, Leonard Reed, Timmie Rogers, Thurman Ruth, Sandman Sims, John "Bubbles" Sublett, Percy Sutton, Francis "Doll" Thomas, Big Joe Turner, Leslie Uggams, Eddie "Cleanhead" Vinson, Dionne Warwick, Tom Whaley, and Nancy Wilson. Harold Cromer and Sandman Sims were also very helpful personal guides for me.

I taped most interviews on my trusty Sony Walkman Professional and transcribed them myself using a cassette transcriber with a foot pedal, allowing me to reverse and fast-forward. It also had a nifty speed adjustment knob to slow down difficult-to-understand passages—state of the art for the early 1980s!

To organize my research, I created index cards with important pieces of information, each with a subject head. This collection grew to a couple of thousand cards. After sorting them by subject, I spread them out in piles on the carpet of my living room in the upstate Owego, New York, apartment where I wrote the book. I arranged and rearranged the piles of cards into chapters and then arranged the cards within each chapter to lay out the plan of the book. After that, all I had to do was write it.

A number of books proved invaluable in my research, especially *Blues People* by LeRoi Jones (Amiri Baraka), *Honkers and Shouters* by Arnold Shaw, *The Gospel Sound* by Anthony Heilbut, *The Sound of Soul* by Phyl Garland, *Jazz Dance* by Marshall and Jean Stearns, *This Was Harlem* by Jervis Anderson, and *Uptown: The Story of Harlem's Apollo Theater* by Jack Schiffman. Newer books published after mine include Schiffman's *Harlem Heyday* (1984) and *Amateur Night at the Apollo* (1990) by Ralph Cooper. I contributed two essays and the time line for *Ain't Nothing Like the Real Thing: How the Apollo Theater Shaped American Entertainment* (2010), the companion publication to the exhibition of the same name produced by the National Museum of African American History and Culture in collaboration with the Apollo Theater Foundation.

The Frank Schiffman Apollo Theatre Collection, 1935–1973, Archives Center, National Museum of American History at the Smithsonian, is a fascinating treasure trove comprised of material donated by Bobby and Jack Schiffman in 1996 and processed in 2002. There are boxes filled with letters and telegrams, financial ledgers, phone books, accounting documents, Frank's booking cards with notes on hundreds of performers, print media, pamphlets, scrapbooks, flyers, promotional broadcasts, publicity shots, and more.

The Apollo's indispensable tour director and in-house historian, Billy Mitchell, generously gave me and James a thorough and informative backstage and all-around tour of the theater in October 2017, which helped James more accurately picture the place he was about to illustrate.

Today, thanks to the wonders of the Internet, I have been able to further check, double-check, and just surf endlessly through information and images that have helped corroborate *Showtime at the Apollo: The Epic Tale of Harlem's Legendary Theater.*

Ted Fox

INDEX